Human Behavior
and Life Insurance

PRENTICE-HALL INTERNATIONAL, INC., *London*
PRENTICE-HALL OF AUSTRALIA, PTY., LTD., *Sydney*
PRENTICE-HALL OF CANADA, LTD., *Toronto*
PRENTICE-HALL FRANCE, S.A.R.L., *Paris*
PRENTICE-HALL OF JAPAN, INC., *Tokyo*
PRENTICE-HALL DE MEXICO, S.A., *Mexico City*

G. HUGH RUSSELL, Ph.D.
G. Hugh Russell and Associates
Psychologists to Management

KENNETH BLACK, JR., Ph.D., C.L.U.
The Regents' Professor of Insurance
School of Business Administration
Georgia State College

Human Behavior
and Life Insurance

PRENTICE-HALL, INC., Englewood Cliffs, New Jersey

Current printing (last digit):

13   12

© 1963 BY PRENTICE-HALL, INC.
ENGLEWOOD CLIFFS, N.J.

LIBRARY OF CONGRESS CATALOG CARD NO.: 63-13273

PRINTED IN THE UNITED STATES OF AMERICA

C

To Our Families

Preface

This volume is written specifically to help the life underwriter become aware of a vast sea of obvious and hidden forces which influence his own behavior and that of his client. It is intended to make a little more clear the delicate, shifting balance between human fulfillment and failure which always exists within us and between us.

This volume contains general ideas, principles, and even techniques useful in finding satisfactory solutions to the problems we face in our daily interpersonal relationships. Throughout this volume we shall stress two important ideas concerning these general principles of behavior. The first is that the human being is incredibly complex in the way he thinks and interacts with others. The second is that while we isolate one idea or influence or motive for purposes of discussion, we must recognize that in actual life situations these influences intermingle and affect each other. The more we learn about human behavior, the more we will realize just how complicated and many-sided man is.

In our attempts to deal with another human being, we will find that it is virtually impossible for us to keep in mind at one time all of the ideas and concepts which will be presented in this

vii

volume. Nevertheless, an understanding of these insights from the fields of psychology, sociology, and general semantics will provide us guidance and increase the probability of success in our efforts to motivate behavior change. Achieving a better understanding of human behavior can help us find new insights and new perspectives and approaches to life problems. Unfortunately, no book can be written which can tell us exactly how to apply a principle in a specific real life situation. Despite the illustrations and examples offered in connection with the material presented, the reader must always be the bridge between the generalizations and the application of them to a specific situation.

The overall plan of this volume is first to discuss some general concepts which help explain how we develop into the kind of person we are and second to examine how this information can be put to good use in our work with people. In Part One, Man in Development, we discuss the growth and development of the individual to show how he becomes a personality unlike anyone else anywhere. Chapter 1 traces the emergence of the dependent infant to the mature adult through a series of learning experiences. Chapter 2 reveals the often hidden but very powerful influence of the family and larger social groups as they mold the individual into a conforming, adjusting citizen. The life underwriter will begin to relive some of his own personal selling experiences and see in a new light the various pressures which motivate his prospects to buy or not to buy life insurance.

Part Two, Man in Communication, deals with the complexities and perplexities of that human skill we all take for granted, language. The life underwriter depends heavily on words to convey a message to the prospect and to move the prospect to take some action. In Chapter 3 we put our language under a microscope to see what words really are and how they influence the very way we think. Chapter 4 discusses some major obstacles to clear communication, but then continues to show how we can overcome these obstacles and become better interviewers and better listeners.

With the material in Part One and Two as background, Part Three, Man in Motivation, applies these concepts to the field of human motivation. The life underwriter will acquire greater skill in motivating people the more he understands what motivation is and how it works. Chapter 5 shows how motivation is tied in not only with our early development from childhood but also with the social surroundings we have as adults. Chapter 6 translates these general ideas into specific techniques which can be used to change attitudes and hence change behavior.

This volume would not be complete without looking at human behavior in perspective to see how man decides on which course of action to take when he is faced with many conflicting alternatives. Part Four, Man in Balance, throws light on the process of maintaining a proper balance between our needs and wants and obligations. Man makes value judgments; he is concerned about the rightness and wrongness of what he does. Chapter 7 raises a question about the role ethics plays in human behavior in general and in the selling interview in particular.

It should be noted that this volume has brought together some important concepts from the fields of psychology, sociology, anthropology, general semantics, and cybernetics as they help explain the behavior of the human being. There has been a particular effort to avoid the used of technical terminology in order to present the material in a form which is easily read. There are many valid and significant concepts in these fields of knowledge which have been omitted in view of the specific purposes for which the material was prepared.

It is hoped, however, that this exposure to the interrelationships which exist in these fields and the recognition of their significance to the professional life underwriter will stimulate additional study and reading, leading to an increasing understanding of the complex activity known as human behavior. To this end, a bibliography of significant readings has been included.

The authors would like to express their appreciation to the many persons who have given their help in the preparation of this volume. Special thanks go to Dr. Earl C. Brown, Professor of Psychology, University of Alabama, Tuscaloosa, and to Dr. Michael Mescon, Professor of Human Relations, Georgia State College, Atlanta, and to Dr. Robert E. Garren, Head of Department of Sociology, Georgia State College, Atlanta, all of whom read the entire manuscript and made many helpful suggestions.

The material in this volume was originally written at the specific request of the American College of Life Underwriters for use in the national CLU Program. Special appreciation is expressed to The American College of Life Underwriters at Bryn Mawr, Pennsylvania for its counsel and financial assistance in developing the original material. Also, Mr. G. Victor Hallman, C.L.U., of the American College staff gave generously of his time and attention to the project. Needless to say, any remaining errors or oversights in the manuscript are the sole responsibility of the authors.

Atlanta, Georgia   G.H.R.

                                                                K.B., Jr.

Contents

015380

xi

5   The Fundamentals of Motivation (*Cont.*)

*tives · Emotions are intensely motivating ·
Emotions are both useful and harmful · Emotions
regulate behavior · How emotions become motives · Emotions can become generalized · The
role of emotions is often overlooked · Generalized
emotions help explain complex behavior · Empathy and understanding*

6   Motivation and Behavior Change   211

Human Behavior
and Life Insurance

Introduction

Most of us live, work, and play in the company of other people. From the trauma of birth to that of death, our lives are filled with human contacts, some of which are satisfying and some disappointing. Whether we rise to our highest achievements or sink to our lowest depths depends largely upon the skill with which we deal with other human beings.

Into this lifetime of human meandering we come as rank amateurs, possessing little or no ability to defend ourselves or even to provide for ourselves. But we lose our amateur standing as we hurt and get hurt, as we love and get loved, and as we are taught and as we teach. Learning to be human is a casual thing. It is an important thing. It is a vital life-giving and life-saving thing. But *learning* to be human is exactly what takes place. It is a *learning* activity. Man is the only animal that records a history. He is unique in his language abilities, in his ability to help his fellow creatures, and his descendants profit from his individual and collective mistakes and successes.

Ask most men what they want from life and somewhere in the answer will be the concept of a search for security. Security is

1

freedom from fear. It is, of course, many things more. But it is, surely, the relative absence of paralyzing, disruptive, agonizing fear. And this fear is so often a fear of the unknown. Perhaps man's greatest uniqueness among animals is his ability to rise above his environmental limitations through the use of knowledge or an awareness of the heretofore unknown. Man conquers fear through knowledge. He transcends the limits of space, gravity, climate, and disease through knowledge. He becomes a more effective per‑ son through knowledge. He becomes human through knowledge.

Man strives to understand himself

About twenty-four centuries ago the philosopher Socrates said: "Know thyself." Socrates was not the first to speculate about the nature of the material and measurable world, but he was one of the first to wonder about man and what he can become. In the centuries since Socrates, men have conjectured and written and debated on the reasons why we behave the way we do. Man's attempt to understand himself was, until recently, carried on mostly by the poets, philosophers, and artists who were keen of vision and shrewd in abstracting principles from the mass of human experiences in which they personally were involved. These wise men summarized their personal experiences and taught them to their students as truths. Each new generation added bits of expe‑ riences to the body of available knowledge about human behavior. But this patchwork of guesses, opinions, insights, and convictions was full of contradictions and uncertainties. Men have approached the study of man somewhat like the fable of the four blind men who were "seeing" the elephant for the first time. Each of the four men felt a different part of the elephant with his hands and came to his own erroneous conclusion about the appearance of the entire animal.

Even today many intelligent people accumulate their own under‑ standing of human behavior in much the same way. If, for exam‑ ple, we are driving in a strange city and are involved in a collision by a careless driver, we are likely to conclude that "the drivers in that city sure are reckless." One or two unpleasant experiences with a member of a certain religious or racial group may be enough to convince us that all people in that group are undesirable.

By controlled observations we form "laws" of human behavior

While speculation about human nature is a very old pastime, scientific study of it is new. It has been only since around the middle of the nineteenth century that the *scientific method* of controlled observation or experimentation has been used to contribute to our understanding of the how and the why of human behavior. The physical, biological, and social sciences are all organized around principles obtained by a method of controlled experimentation called the *scientific method*. The scientific method is of tremendous importance because it can be used to solve everyday human problems as well as problems of science. The scientific method involves these steps:

(1) Clearly defining a question or a problem so that we know what we are trying to solve.

(2) Obtaining all of the known facts relating to the problem and suggesting some possible answers (hypotheses) to the problem.

(3) Checking each hypothesis or proving by a controlled experiment to see whether or not it is a solution to the problem. Repeating the same experiment to be sure of the result.

(4) If the experiment works out each time it is conducted, the solution to the problem can be accepted. If the experiment does not work out, a new tentative solution, or hypothesis, must be established and tested.

As part of their effort to understand how people are motivated, scientists using the scientific method expose human subjects to a motivating situation and carefully measure their reactions to it. The strength of the motivating situation is experimentally increased and decreased systematically and the reactions of the human subjects are systematically measured and recorded. For example, one such experiment attempted to determine how a situation of stress influences a person's ability to perform. By systematically increasing and decreasing the level of stress and measuring performance, it was discovered that a moderate amount of stress (in the form of distracting noise or light) actually increased the level of performance of human subjects who were involved in a simple task but higher degrees of the same stress were very disruptive and caused a much lower level of performance. In this manner, small bits of behavior can be studied and better understood in laboratory-like situations.

The attempt to study human behavior scientifically, as it actually occurs in life situations, is extremely difficult because so many of the influences upon human behavior cannot be controlled and cannot even be measured. For example, if we are trying to understand how a new sales talk will improve an underwriter's ability to close sales, we may simply compare results of his sales average before and after learning the new material. If we see that he closes more sales after learning the new material, we may feel that we have learned something new about motivating prospects. But how do we know that the increased volume of sales is not due simply to the fact that the salesman has gained more confidence in himself through experience?

While it proceeds with agonizing slowness, we have been gradually building up a structure of generalizations about human behavior which we may refer to as "laws." We use quotes around the word "laws" because our surmises about human behavior often do not have the same exactness as is true with the physical and biological sciences. We make a significant gain in our understanding of human behavior each time we can establish a new generalization. The validity and value of each new generalization, however, depends directly on both the accuracy and the frequency of our observations.

Generalizations apply to the mass, not to the individual

We know that we cannot understand human behavior in general by studying only one single individual. We recognize that people are so very different that understanding one person and being able to predict his behavior does not necessarily prepare us to understand and predict the behavior of any other specific individual. Therefore, we develop understanding of the nature of human behavior by observing great numbers of people under similar circumstances. An experienced salesman may conclude, after years of effort to sell his product, that "you don't make a sale by arguing with the customer." But this salesman may also tell us that he has one or two customers who never seem ready to buy until and unless they can engage the salesman in a rather furious argument for a while until the salesman "gives in" and allows the customer to feel that he has been victorious. The generalization, "never argue with a customer," is a perfectly valid generalization, but it applies to the majority of customers and probably not to everyone.

In a similar way, all of the generalizations about human behavior which we will discuss in this book can be applied only to the mass of people and not to every one. For example, we will say that a person is greatly influenced in his behavior by the standards of the group of which he is a member, but what we will really be saying is that most people are greatly influenced by the standards of a group of which they are a member. Any one single individual with whom we may be dealing *may* or *may not* be influenced greatly by the pressure from his group.

Generalizations guide the individual

It is somewhat annoying to anticipate reading a volume on human behavior and be told in advance that there are no fixed rules which can be applied to specific situations involving people. How are we to benefit from such general ideas and principles if we cannot be sure that they hold true for each individual? The benefit to us from being familiar with such generalizations is that we acquire more knowledge by which we can judge individual situations and, therefore, come closer to finding the most effective way of reacting. We will see that through a process known as "feed-back" we can pick up many clues as to how another individual is really reacting to our sales presentation so that we can improve the probabilities of motivating behavior change successfully. Essentially, generalizations or guidelines permit more intelligent trial-and-error efforts in motivation. The housewife makes the family budget stretch because she shops around before making a purchase. She finds out the range of prices, notes the quality of the merchandise available, and then decides which is the best course of action for her. Similarly, the more we are aware of the various possibilities involved in any situation involving human behavior, the more sensitive we can be to the one or two best possible solutions and the better we can budget our available time and energy. Having a generalized knowledge of human behavior does not, therefore, allow us to find fixed solutions to problems but certainly allows us to engage in more intelligent trial-and-error behavior.

Understanding basic concepts is our objective

The life underwriter becomes effective when he is able to change the behavior of other people. He must influence others to buy life insurance. He recognizes the necessity of a thorough knowledge of his product and its uses and submits himself to various technical training programs, lectures, seminars, and course work. What is not similarly recognized is that it is necessary for him to be just as conscious, deliberate, and intelligent in his efforts to learn the basic reasons for the behavior of his prospective clients.

Typical reactions on the part of an insurance salesman when sales are lagging are to make more calls, try more closes, change his market, or qualify his prospects better. These are good reactions, but they are often insufficient ones. What may well be needed is an *enlarged awareness* of some of the personal, social, cultural, and linguistic reasons why the prospect is not changing his behavior—why he is not buying life insurance.

The life insurance sale is a conversation with a purpose. And in this conversation at least two people are always involved. Individuals bring to this conversation a lifetime of experiences, prejudices, conscious and unconscious reactions, which influence the outcome of the conversation. Without an awareness of many such *hidden obstacles* to the sale, the agent loses effectiveness.

The reader may very well raise a question at this point. If understanding some of the basic concepts underlying human behavior will help us become better motivators of people, would further study of the behavioral sciences help us increase even more our

skill in motivating people? Our answer would have to be, "Well,
yes and no." Of course, a study of the behavioral sciences does
help us to do a better job of predicting and controlling the behavior
of other people. But it is possible to become a "nut" on psychology
and sociology to the extent that we think we must obtain almost
a professional background in these subjects so that we can properly
analyze everything that happens during the sales situation. It is
obvious that we might spend so much time educating ourselves
and so much time analyzing and trying to understand all of the
possible motives and influences in selling and motivating that we
might do very little actual selling. The life underwriter cannot and
should not take the time during a sales interview to try to analyze
all of the reasons why the prospect says what he says or why he
does what he does. It would seem appropriate, then, to strike a
balance between the two extremes of having very little information
on the one hand and trying to have complete knowledge and
understanding of the human being on the other hand. Finding the
happy medium or finding the proper balance between two extremes
is not only a solution to the question "how much should we study
human behavior," but it is also a solution to most of our life
problems.

PART ONE

MAN
IN DEVELOPMENT

People are alike in many ways, but the differences between them are astonishing! We are each truly unique individuals from our finger prints to our innermost thoughts. No two of us have had the same experiences, the same family background, the same frustrations, or the same victories. No two of us even experience new life situations in the same way. There is no one else just like us anywhere in the world. Our attitudes are different, our ways of expressing ourselves are different, and our reactions to problems are different. We have each spent our whole lifetime developing into a different, unique person.

This uniqueness of man is at the same time the most *stimulating* and the most *irritating* characteristic we possess. It is stimulating in that the many different viewpoints brought to bear on the problems of mankind have resulted in great gains in our technological and social worlds. It is irritating in that others often appear to be *too* different, too deviant in their behavior or much too peculiar for us to feel very comfortable with them. It is because people are different that we have a competitive society, leading to higher and higher levels of civilization. It is because people are different that we engage in wars of mutual destruction.

There are just enough similarities between men that we dare to form generalizations and laws about human behavior. We study these generalizations hoping that when we are dealing with another person, we can do a better job of *understanding* what he is doing or has done, a better job of *predicting* what he may do, and a better job of *influencing* his behavior in a direction pleasing to ourselves.

Individuals are relatively consistent in their behavior. We can expect that over a period of time our friends will tend to laugh at the same jokes, will be irritated by the same kinds of problems, and will vote for the same political parties. Banks are often robbed because of their consistent routine. The bank is "cased" by men who observe

what happens and when it happens until they see a pattern
in the events which helps them formulate some principles
of human behavior. On the basis of these observations, the
bank robbers confidently predict that the same thing will
happen at any given time. Knowing these principles
allows the "well-educated" bank robber to be successful
in his attempt to "motivate" people in banks to do things
for him.

The life underwriter is in the business of motivating
people to do things for him. To the extent that the underwriter is a well-educated student of human behavior,
he will more often than not be successful in motivating
his prospects to buy life insurance. To the extent that the
underwriter *understands* the similarities and differences
between his prospects, he will use a motivational approach
which best fits each prospect. Knowledge of how people
develop and how they defend and promote themselves will
allow the life underwriter to be more resourceful with
each of his *unique* prospects.

If the material which follows helps the reader to realize
the extraordinary complexity of the human being, and if
it stimulates him to continue his efforts to acquire understanding and wisdom in dealing with his fellow man, then
one of its purposes will have been realized.

If the material helps the reader see that he, as an individual, with his past experiences, his fears and doubts,
and his prejudices, is deeply involved in the motivational
processes of every sale, then a second purpose will have
been realized.

If the material stimulates the reader to *do* something
about his own blind spots, his fears and uncertainties, and
motivates him further to continue growing and developing as a man, then the third purpose will have been realized.

Our first step, then, will be an understanding of the beginnings of human development, and some of the basic

mental mechanisms which seem to operate in all of us. As we study Chapter 1, it will be important to keep in mind that these mechanisms are listed separately for discussion purposes only. In the walking, breathing, thinking human being they do not operate separately, but are always highly interrelated.

1

The Developing Self

Who am I? How do you, the reader of this text, answer that question? Are you saying your name to yourself? Are you thinking, "I'm a life underwriter"? Certainly, this tells us something of what you do, but there is more to the question "Who am I?" Are you a husband, a father, an uncle, a Rotarian, a Baptist, a voter, a traffic violator, a juror, an insurance agent, a failure, a success, a miser, an alcoholic, a golfer, a lone wolf, an organization man, a bigot, a commuter, a home owner, an apartment dweller? Many of these, and more too, describe each of us.

We are many things all at the same time. We wear many hats, and much is expected of us every day. But *why* are we all these things? Why did we choose to get married or remain single? Why do we make more money each year but somehow have less and less to save? Why do we vote Republican or Democrat? Why did we buy that particular brand of car or soap or cereal?

If we are to be successful, then knowing ourselves and understanding why people behave as they do are two of the most important accomplishments we can hope to achieve. All of us have an interest in human behavior. The life underwriter is interested especially because he needs to *understand, predict,* and *influence* the behavior of other people. All of us must adjust to other people, and frequently our most important job is to understand them, to know what their motives are, and to be able to predict what they are going to do, especially as it affects ourselves.

We need to have a reasonable idea of who we are and what we are so that we can introduce some planning into our lives and make the best use of our talents and abilities and experiences. The underwriter needs to know the "why" of human behavior because his job is principally to motivate the behavior of other people toward buying life insurance. The professional underwriter readily understands the need for a thorough grounding in the basic fundamentals of selling life insurance. This he takes for granted. What may not seem so obvious, however, is the need for such a basic background of knowledge and understanding of human behavior.

The Self—Who Are We?

All of us have some sort of *self-image* of ourselves. The way we think about ourselves, the things we believe about ourselves, all go to form a picture of ourselves, or a self-image. If we have reflected about the question that opened this chapter, we have seen that it is not easy to come up with a very clear picture of just who we are. Nevertheless, we do "see" ourselves as being a very definite kind of person. We may think of ourselves as being an intelligent, aggressive businessman. Perhaps we see ourselves as courteous and considerate, a person of integrity and honesty, a good husband and father, a witty fellow, etc.

We build this image over a period of years. The picture that we have of ourselves is formed mainly because of the way other people have responded to us in the past. If our parents have loved us, we come to think of ourselves as lovable. If our parents have not loved us, or if we were without parents, we may grow up with a feeling of low self-regard, a feeling that no one could possibly be interested in us.

We do certain things and avoid doing certain things because of the reactions of other people to our actions. Generally, we behave

in a way which gives us pleasure or satisfaction and avoid behaving in a way which decreases our satisfaction. We thus establish a kind of equilibrium in our behavior. We behave within certain rather well-established limits. It is our behavior within these limits which we come to think of as "ourselves." This is what other people refer to when they speak of our "personality." We behave the way we behave because we think that this is consistent with the picture we have of ourselves and with the picture we want others to have of us.

By the time we are adults, we have achieved a self-picture which is relatively stable and consistent. People who know us can rather easily predict our future behavior, and we ourselves know pretty much what we will or will not do under various conditions. As we grow older, we are likely to become less adventuresome and less prone to behave in a way which is grossly inconsistent with our self-picture. The common expression "I just can't see myself doing that" reflects this tendency to restrict our behavior in accordance with our self-picture.

Whatever our self-image happens to be, one thing is clear—we are the most important person in our life. If someone has taken a picture of us in a group and shows us a copy, our gaze is likely to center immediately on the picture of ourselves in the group. We may look casually at the other people in the picture, but when we locate *our image,* our attention is riveted to this spot. This is not to say that we do not have genuine feelings of regard and concern and interest in other people, but it is to suggest that we spend more time thinking about ourselves, being concerned about ourselves and protecting and satisfying ourselves than we do on any other person. This is not meant to diminish the stature of mankind or any one of us individually, but is merely to point out the natural and inevitable self-centeredness of our existence.

Being well-regarded by others is one of our most basic needs and we tend to live in a way which insures that we will continue to be well-regarded. The only way we know to do this is by living up to that picture of ourselves which we believe will result in pleasing others the most. Having established this self-image through a process of receiving praise and punishment, none of us is too willing to change the way we behave. We have established an

equilibrium in our behavior, and we don't want to "rock the boat." Thus, we develop a strong need to preserve the image that we have of ourselves. We need to avoid having our favorable self-picture disturbed. If we happen to stumble and fall while going up some steps, one of the first things we do is look around to see who saw us get into such an embarrassing position. We are concerned about how other people see us. We want to be sure that they get an "accurate" picture of us, and what we usually mean by "accurate" is that we hope others see all our good points and overlook our weaknesses.

When someone criticizes us, the favorable picture that we have of ourselves and that we hope the other person has of us is threatened. All of us find it difficult to accept criticism because we would like to view ourselves as being above criticism or reproach. It is difficult because it means that someone else doesn't have quite the same high regard for us that we have. It hurts to be criticized. We may vigorously deny that we refuse to accept criticism from others, and we may protest that we really want people to tell us what they think of us, but it still is painful to have anyone disturb our self-image. How do you feel if you happen to overhear a locker-room conversation between two of your friends as they are discussing you? If you hear some unflattering things said, you are likely to feel pretty deflated.

We defend ourselves—and we reject ourselves

The image we have of ourselves is important! When anyone threatens this self-image, our first reaction is usually to defend it. If we consider ourselves to be a very mature and careful driver but are somehow involved in an accident, our normal reaction is to find ways to blame the other driver. Even if it develops that we did cause the accident, we are still likely to defend our self-image by saying, "The sun was in my eyes and I couldn't see," or "I was watching the curb to make sure there were no children darting out."

It is so important to us that we defend our image that we sometimes go to rather absurd lengths to avoid seeing ourselves as we really are and, consequently, having to change our self-image. It is

very difficult for any insurance agent to say to himself, "I am a poor salesman," or "I am doing a very poor job of underwriting." We are more likely to say, "I had a poor production record last year, but I had a lot of trouble with rated cases, and one big case that I almost had fell through at the last minute." The implication is that we are really a pretty good life underwriter, but other things beyond our control have kept us from showing the best in ourselves.

Defending through aggression. We defend our valuable self-image in many ways. Perhaps one of the most important ways is that of *moving aggressively against that person or thing which threatens to diminish our self-image.* If someone were to tell you, "You are just a mediocre life underwriter," your reaction might very well be to say, "Oh yeah! what makes you think you're so hot?" If we can discredit a person who is making us uncomfortable, we have a better chance of retaining our self-image. We might say, for example, "It's all right for him to talk. He just sits there in the office and twiddles his thumbs while I'm out doing all the hard work."

The life underwriter has chosen as his life work an occupation which can be a source of great stimulation and satisfaction or at the same time, a source of frustration and even personal humiliation. If we are a salesman in a men's clothing store, or a department head in a large corporation, or a vice president in a bank, we may find it quite difficult to measure how well we are doing our job. But the life underwriter is made aware of his performance on a daily basis and in no uncertain terms. As he calls on a prospect, he runs the risk of being turned down, or he runs the risk of selling the prospect on the insurance but having the prospect rejected by his company as a poor risk.

The life underwriter's self-image comes under attack almost daily. It is not surprising, then, to see that the life underwriter may well react by some form of defensive behavior. If the underwriter fails to make the sale, he can always attack the prospect (in fantasy, if not in reality) by saying to himself, "That guy wouldn't buy because he's too selfish and doesn't care enough for his family." It takes courage to say, "That prospect didn't buy because I didn't have enough skill in presenting the ideas to make him write out a check for the insurance which he really needs." "The best defense is a good offense" seems to be the reasoning when we use this defensive method to preserve our self-image.

Defending through rationalization. Another way we have of defending ourselves is to find a reason for our behavior which sounds better to us than the real reason. If we fail to reach the Million Dollar Round Table, we can always say, "I could have done it if I hadn't spent so much time on work for my church," or we can fool ourselves by saying, "It's not really important to be an MDRT member. What does it mean anyway?" We might call this the sour-grapes mechanism; the technical term for it is *rationalization.*

Defending through regression. Growing up is a series of new adjustments to new problems. As soon as we learn good solutions to present problems, we are often thrust into new problem situations which require new adjustments. The kind of behavior that was appropriate in high school is no longer appropriate in college. College behavior doesn't always fit the business world. The life underwriter who becomes a manager or general agent finds that he must make still new adjustments to the daily problems he meets. It is inevitable that we sometimes make mistakes and experience failure rather than success. If the failure hurts badly enough, we are likely to retreat. Furthermore, we are likely to retreat in the direction of an earlier kind of adjustment or an earlier behavior pattern which is easier to maintain. This defense mechanism is referred to as *regression.* After a particularly hard day, when our self-image has been bruised a little, we are likely to think wistfully of the "good old days" when we had fewer worries. Our fantasy may even lead us to action as we stop by the local bar to visit the boys and "tie one on." In this setting, we are surrounded by friends who think well of us and this helps us think well of ourselves, too.

Regression is not altogether a harmful mechanism, for it does give us time to gather our strength and courage and try again tomorrow. It is when any of these methods of defense become habits or become a way of life that we are in danger of losing rather than gaining ground in our climb toward greater maturity.

Defending through compensation. If we fail at one thing, we can protect our feelings by excelling in something else. Thus, a life underwriter who is doing only a mediocre job can protect his self-image by excelling in club activities. We can compensate for a shortcoming in one area by excelling in another. This mechanism of defense is therefore referred to as *compensation*.

Defending through repression. To protect our self-image, we need to deny those things within ourselves which are not very flattering or are disgusting to us. When it is important that we "forget" something that has happened to us, we refer to this as the mechanism of *repression*. This is nothing more than an attempt to fool ourselves and preserve the self-image of which we are conscious. The "forgetting" that we do is unconscious in that we are not aware that we are pushing the unpleasant idea down into the unconscious. Consciously, we have forgotten, but unconsciously, we still know about it. More will be said about unconscious mental activity in a later section of this chapter, but with regard to this mechanism of repression we may say that the unconscious works in much the same way as does the fuse in the wiring system of a house. When the electrical load is greater than the system will stand, the fuse blows and interrupts the flow of electricity. When the load of uncomfortable mental activity becomes too great for us to bear, the conscious thoughts are interrupted by a repression, or a block in our ability to remember.

Defending through reaction formation. One way to make sure that certain ideas stay repressed is to stress the very opposite of what we unconsciously feel. The person, who unconsciously hates his children and must deny this to himself in order to preserve his favorable self-image, will frequently over-react by consciously displaying a great deal of affection toward them. This helps the parent consciously to believe that he has no hostile or unacceptable feelings towards his children. This defense mechanism is known as *reaction formation.* Shakespeare made use of this mechanism in his tragedy, *Hamlet*, when he wrote the queen's line, "The lady doth protest too much, methinks." We sometimes hear a person going out of his way to protest or deny that he has certain feelings even though no one may have claimed that he did.

These defense mechanisms are ways of behaving that we resort to in order to protect and safeguard our self-image.[1] They serve

[1] For a further discussion of defense mechanisms, see Percival M. Symonds, *Dynamic Psychology* (New York: Appleton-Century-Crofts, Inc., 1949), pp. 143-156.

the purpose of helping us to feel better about ourselves on a conscious level, but they have the disadvantage of making it harder for us to really know ourselves and do something about our shortcomings.

While a good deal of our time and energy is spent in defending our self-image, we occasionally do just the opposite: we reject ourselves. Some people do this to an extreme degree in that they ridicule themselves, punish themselves, and may even resort to that ultimate in self-punishment, suicide. However, a person who makes derogatory remarks about himself is not necessarily rejecting himself. If your wife surprises you with the comment, "I don't believe I'm a very good mother," the last thing she wants you to say is, "Well, yes, Mary, I believe you are right." Instead of rejecting the image she has of herself, your wife is probably searching for an overdue reassurance from you.

The self-image and motivation

It is amazing how much energy we spend in order to preserve the picture we have of ourselves. This desire to maintain a very favorable image of ourselves is perhaps one of the most powerful motivators of behavior. During the depression years, when many men lost their fortunes, their image of themselves was rather dramatically changed. They had thought of themselves as successful businessmen, when suddenly their fortunes were wiped out. Some men, rather than face this changed picture of themselves—rather than face the image of failure, humiliation, and defeat—killed themselves. If a businessman will throw himself out of a window rather than live with the image of failure, we can see how important it is to maintain a good image of oneself.

Not only are we concerned about maintaining our own self-image, but we are very much concerned about the image of ourselves that other people hold. We know that others do not see us as we really are, and in a way we are quite glad of it. Many of us feel that if our friends and neighbors really knew our innermost thoughts, they wouldn't be our friends any longer. There may well be much truth to this. Much of our behavior is strongly motivated by our *intense desire to look favorable in the eyes of other people.* This can be both a negative and a positive kind of motivation. If someone very important to us has a rather uncomplimentary image of us, we may decide to prove that he is all wrong by outdoing ourselves in achievement. On the other hand, we may react in the opposite way, saying to ourselves, "Well, I have the bad reputation; I might as well live up to it."

The parent who thinks his child is not to be trusted and who conveys this feeling to the child probably will encourage rebellion and untrustworthy behavior. The manager who thinks of his life underwriters as being lazy and ungrateful for all the help he has given to them may well demotivate his underwriters if he conveys that impression to them. Some outstanding general agents and managers seem to have the ability to see more in their agents than their agents see in themselves. This is not a false optimism. The general agent or manager simply holds the highest possible image of his men. When this impression is conveyed to the agents, they quite often outdo themselves trying to live up to the expectation of them. Similarly, a great deal of life insurance has been bought by policyholders who wanted to be sure that their life underwriter had a favorable image of them as individuals.

The fear of something happening to our self-picture not only affects how close we can get to other people, but also determines how effective we can be in motivating the behavior of other people. Every time we come in contact with another person, we expose ourselves to a potential source of damage to our self-picture. Whenever we talk to another person, there is always the question of whether we will succeed or fail in satisfying various needs or desires. Every time that the life underwriter calls on a prospect, he faces the possibility of either failure or success. When the life underwriter experiences failure or frustration in his work with other people, it is possible for some self-doubt to creep into his mind, doubt that he is really as good a life underwriter as he would like to think that he is. If we are courting a girl and ask for her hand in marriage, there is always a possibility that she will say no. If we attempt to be friendly and warm toward our next door neighbor, there is always a possibility that he will tell us to mind our own business. If other people like us and respond to us favorably, we congratulate ourselves on being nice people. But if people respond to us unfavorably or if we are hurt by others, we are likely to feel somewhat less sure of ourselves and wonder about the kind of person we are.

There is a way to avoid being hurt by other people. There is a way to avoid the various incidents in life which threaten to alter or diminish the favorable picture that we have of ourselves. We are not likely to be hurt or to have to change our self-image if we don't let ourselves get too "close" or too "involved" with others. We can hold people at arm's length, emotionally, and avoid being much disturbed if they happen to do something which bothers us. We can avoid damage to our self-image if we will only keep people from getting too close to us or getting to know us too well. Of course, we have to pay a price for this, because in addition to taking less risk of being hurt, there is also much less chance of our being loved.

All of us resort to a good bit of artificial behavior in order to keep people from getting too close to us or seeing through our defenses. But maintaining this distance from other people is expensive because it also keeps us from being able to motivate them to do as we would like them to do. This can become a kind of vicious circle. The fear of damage to our self-image can keep us from getting close to others, and failure to get close to them can result in frustration, which in turn threatens us with the self-image of failure and prompts us to maintain greater emotional distance from other people. If, however, we have the courage to expose our self-image to possible change and can move toward a challenge, we may find ourselves building a better and sounder self-image, one which simply needs less defending.

The self-image can be changed in a positive way so that the individual can "see himself" doing something that he previously thought was impossible. The story of the four-minute mile is a good example of how a person's self-image can affect his behavior. It illustrates how a change in one's self-image can overcome an obstacle and permit a person to do something that he had never before been able to do.

From 1864 to 1945 the record time for the mile run dropped from

4 minutes 54 seconds to 4 minutes 1.4 seconds. Despite the greatest of efforts, no one was able to break the four minute barrier in the mile run and people were beginning to say that it was an impossible feat. In 1954, Roger Bannister broke this four-minute barrier. He ran the mile in 3 minutes 59.6 seconds. A sportswriter describing the event said: "Roger Bannister opened the door" to other milers with his feat. Indeed he did, for only one month later John Landy broke this new record. Since then, more than two dozen milers have run the mile in less than four minutes.[2]

Why, after such a long period when no one could break the barrier, could so many men suddenly accomplish the heretofore impossible task? Undoubtedly, it was because these several men suddenly could "see themselves" running the mile in less than four minutes. Being able to see this possibility within themselves allowed them to accomplish what had been "impossible" just a short time before.

School teachers often report that a child who makes a 100 on a spelling test after previous months of very poor grades may have suddenly "seen himself" as a good speller. One sixth grade boy had been a poor speller until one day a substitute teacher praised his spelling efforts (which happened to be perfect that day), telling him, "You are a good speller." This comment opened the possibility to him that he was, in fact, a good speller. The boy went on in a later spelling contest to become the spelling champion for his city.

Perhaps the motivation of other people is not much more than changing their self-image. Certainly, the buyer of life insurance has to "see himself" owning more life insurance than he has. Change the image that someone else has of himself and you prepare him for a change in behavior. The insurance underwriter who is successful in understanding his prospect's self-image and deliberately inducing change in that self-image is likely to be a successful motivator. Rather than describe a salesman as a persuader or motivator of people, it is more to the point to describe him as an *image-changer*.

2 Frank G. Menke, *The Encyclopedia of Sports,* 2nd ed. (New York: A. S. Barnes Company, 1960), p. 1037.

How and Why We Learn to Be What We Are

The newborn infant has a lot to learn. He doesn't know how to care for himself or protect himself from harm. But he learns quickly. By the time he is five, the child has absorbed a tremendous amount of "know-how" and is well on his way to being a recognizable personality. The kind of person he becomes depends greatly on his early learning experiences. His childhood bumps and bruises, the love and caresses he receives, or doesn't receive, the victories and defeats he experiences, all help determine his characteristic way of dealing with the world.

The child learns to be human. Learning to be human may not be planned or even thought out in advance. But learning to be human is exactly what takes place. We inherit much from our ancestors, but we are the person we are largely because of the infinite number of minor and major learning situations we are exposed to as we grow and mature toward adulthood.

Early motivation: satisfying bodily needs

Much can be learned about human behavior and how it is motivated by examining what happens to each of us from the moment of birth. When the child becomes separated from the body of his mother, he immediately must take a more active part in the process of living. He must breathe for himself, and this he does, we say, by instinct. Instinctively, he begins sucking when placed at the breast. But from these first beginnings of life, the human infant begins a process of learning which stops only at death. When he is hungry and experiences discomfort, he cries. Through no effort of his, food is provided and his first need is satisfied. But in a short time, he is again uncomfortable. His automatic reaction is to end this discomfort without delay.

Gradually, the child "learns" that his "need" is satisfied in certain ways and he begins to direct his attention actively toward that source of satisfaction. The infant soon learns that when he cries or makes a fuss, things are provided for him which make him more comfortable. *This is the beginning of motivated behavior.* The first examples of motivated behavior, then, are activities which result from a physiological need. Motivated behavior which shows up at a later period in our maturation is behavior directed towards goals or satisfactions which we *learn* to need. These "needs" which we learn later might better be described as wants or desires. The role that these wants and desires play in determining human behavior will be explored at length in Chapters 5 and 6.

The growth of emotions

Another way in which we become the person we are is through our emotional development. Our lives have color and depth because of the presence of emotions. Because we are often aware of them, we know what it feels like to have the emotions of fear, anger, love, grief, pleasure, disgust, and many others. Like every other aspect of our psychological being, however, emotions can be felt and known consciously, or they may exist in our unconscious.[3] The first emotion that a child experiences is a general one of excitement. No matter what the stimulation may be, whether it is a loud noise, pain, or hunger, the infant in the first month or two responds in about the same way. There seems to be an over-all discharge of muscle activity. The other emotions that we know of seem to stem from this initial reaction of general excitement. By the time the infant is about three months old, we can clearly see the alternate emotions of distress and delight. By the time the child is two, we can observe the emotional reactions of elation, love, anger, disgust, fear, and jealousy.

The significance of emotions. Emotions affect every aspect of our lives. When we have embarrassed ourselves by making a stupid mistake in the presence of others, we are painfully aware of the emotional reaction that we have. We feel embarrassed, confused, and generally upset. Countless automobile accidents have occurred because the driver has just come from an emotional argument with his wife or boss. Emotions have a definitely destructive influence

---

[3] See page 50, "The Role of the Unconscious," for a definition of unconscious.

on human behavior, but emotions also are extremely valuable even in terms of our very survival. Emotions help us cope with various emergencies that may arise. They stimulate glandular and muscular activity and allow us to perform feats of strength and speed which would be impossible otherwise.

The emotional feelings that we experience have much to do with the way we develop preferences and aversions. We move toward certain situations because of a pleasant feeling that we have and move away from other situations because of unpleasantness. Much of our behavior is learned because it has resulted in pleasure. When we become aware of a feeling such as pleasure or pain, we refer to this as an emotion. If the feeling that we have is associated with the expectation of an increase or decrease in pleasure or pain, then the emotion is acting as a motive. It is the anticipation of a change in the feeling or emotion which is experienced that makes an emotion a motive with the power to move the individual in a certain direction. The role of the emotions in human motivation will be discussed at greater length in Chapter 5.

The physical effects of emotions. It is well known that emotions are associated with changes in heartbeat, breathing rate, and stomach or intestinal activities. The life underwriter who approaches the office door of a prospect may find that his palms are sweating, his heart is beating faster, and he feels a choking or constricting sensation in his throat. When we notice someone else blushing, we can feel certain that he is experiencing a fairly strong emotion. Because these various changes in physiological activity in response to emotions are beyond our conscious control, the lie detector has been used with great success to determine how the suspected criminal is really reacting to various questions presented to him. When we deliberately tell a lie or deny something that we know to be true, there is a tendency for the sweat glands in our body to increase their activity, for the heartbeat rate to increase, and for characteristic changes to occur in breathing patterns. The importance of the emotions in bodily changes is also illustrated by the fact that stomach ulcers seem to be related to a state of chronic emotional arousal.

Our perception of emotions. Emotions that we feel are expressed in overt behavior. Obviously, when we are pleased, we smile and when we are displeased, we tend to frown. Regardless of the accuracy of this method of measuring emotions, all of us notice this kind of behavior and tend to react accordingly. Sometimes we judge the presence of emotion by listening to the sound of a person's voice. There are many valuable clues to emotion contained in the sound of a voice that most of us fail to notice. A blind man, who must depend more on his sense of hearing than most of us do, often learns to be acutely aware of the expression of emotion in voices. The loudness of the voice, the change in the pitch of the voice, or simple tremors can be clues to the presence of emotional reactions.

The successful life underwriter has probably become very skillful in sensing the presence of emotional reaction on the part of his prospect and in varying his sales approach accordingly. We need not necessarily be aware of exactly what we are learning about the inner feelings of another person before we change our own behavior to be more effective with him. The ability to be in tune with another person in terms of understanding each other emotionally is usually referred to as *empathy*. The life underwriter who can be warm and can respond to his prospect as an empathetic, understanding individual is likely to be received more positively than his cold, unfeeling, and emotionally blind colleague.

Emotions add color to our lives. We have mentioned at the beginning of this section that it is emotion which gives our life color and depth. We live in a society, however, which deems it inappropriate for us to express ourselves emotionally to any degree. As the winner of a sports contest steps forward to receive his prize, we notice that he is trying hard not to show the joy that he feels. Why is this? When we suffer a keen disappointment we are admonished to "keep a stiff upper lip" and not reveal how sad we feel. Why is this? Why is it so embarrassing for us to tell another person how much he means to us? In this day and age, it is considered unmanly to shed tears of joy or sadness even at times of the most moving emotional experiences. Why is this?

As adults in our present society, we seem to have a need to deny much of that part of ourselves that we describe as emotional. Man is an emotional animal capable of rich experiences and feelings far beyond the possibilities of any other animal. Somehow we interpret expressions of vivid emotional feeling as a sign of weakness or human frailty. Is it not possible that our emotional experiences and satisfactions constitute instead one of man's greatest strengths? The great men of our time, the men who have contributed the most to the growth and advancement of civilization as we know it, have been predominantly men who were spontaneous, relatively unconventional, and even "eccentric." Such a man is often described as having great capacity for emotional feeling as well as great intellectual capacity. It seems that when we find it necessary to inhibit or overcontrol our natural spontaneous emotional expressions, we also control and inhibit much of our inventiveness or creativeness.

Conditioning

Everything that we know, and most things that we do, have been learned. We are what we are largely because we do have the ability to learn not only from our own experiences but from the accumulated experiences of countless generations before us. We can define learning as being any more-or-less permanent change in behavior which results from experiences from the very first day of life. The newborn infant seems to know how to suck when placed at the breast, but the infant does not know how to locate the nipple. When held in the arms of its mother at feeding time, he turns his head in a vague effort to find the nipple. This is a learning activity at perhaps the simplest level. The infant associates the acquiring of food with his body being in a certain position. This is a modification of an inborn reflex and is an example of conditioned-response learning.

Our first learning experiences are examples of conditioning, but conditioning continues as a learning process during our entire lifetime. The young child has no fear of height, but after he has fallen from a chair or a bed, he is likely to display fear the next time he is elevated. As we walk past the neighbor's house and are approached by their dog and are bitten, we are likely to start running. The next day as we pass by the house, simply seeing the dog advance in our direction is enough to cause us to start running. We have learned—we have been conditioned.

We behave in certain ways because we are reacting to some

stimulus or signal either from the outside or from within ourselves. This behavior is modified or conditioned when still another stimulus or signal produces the same behavior. We are conditioned or we learn to react to the new stimulus because it is somehow connected with receiving a reward or with avoiding a punishment or pain. When we put a piece of steak in our mouth and begin to chew, our salivary glands are activated by reflex action to facilitate swallowing and digesting. While we are chewing, we associate the pleasant smell of the steak with the chewing and the salivary action. Later on, just smelling a steak cooking is enough to make our salivary glands begin working. This illustrates how a new stimulus (steak aroma) becomes associated with an old stimulus (presence of food in the mouth) to produce the same behavior (salivation). This is another example of learning by conditioning.

For the adult life underwriter, behavior or sales activity can be modified or conditioned merely by a word of praise from his general agent or manager. It is important that the reward or the punishment occur at or about the same time as the behavior. If the difference in time between the two is too great, the individual will not see the connection and learning will not take place. It is more effective, therefore, to praise or reward an individual as soon after he performs a bit of desired behavior as possible.

Problem solving

We acquire all kinds of skills on a verbal and nonverbal level through our ability to solve problems. Probably most of the learning that takes place in our efforts to solve problems is on the basis of trial and error. When we first learn to shoot a rifle, we probably do not come very close to hitting the bull's-eye. With repeated trial and adjustment, however, we find that we become more accurate and have therefore learned a new skill. A principle involved here is that *learning takes place more effectively if we can be told the results of our efforts.* If as we are shooting at a target we are not permitted to see how far our mark is from the bull's-eye, not only are we not likely to learn to shoot, but we are more likely to become quite bored and give up the whole operation.

Learning how to be more effective in the sales interview is sometimes quite difficult because we do not know exactly how well we did or where we missed. Certainly, trial and error behavior can help a salesman learn new and more effective responses, but he may learn more effectively if he will ask someone else to accompany him occasionally to help him see what he is doing well and what he is doing poorly. As the salesman sees that a particular approach is effective, he learns to use that approach more often. As we shall see in Chapter 4, increasing our skill in listening will help us learn more quickly from experience. The better we are able to listen to our prospects and our supervisor, the more information we will hear in their comments which will help us know the results of our problem-solving efforts.

The principle of learning known as the *law of effect* tells us that *reward or punishment determines whether a given response will be strengthened or weakened*. This means that behavior which seems to lead to reward tends to be repeated, while behavior which seems not to lead to reward or seems to lead to punishment tends not to be repeated. From the results of controlled experiments, where it can be measured, we find that reward or praise is much more effective in stimulating individuals to learn and to perform more readily than is being ignored or rebuffed. Experience indicates, however, that it is probably easier for us to find the weaknesses or shortcomings in other people and to call these to their attention than to find their strengths or significant talents. Some general agents and managers are quick to call the life underwriter down when he has made a mistake, but find it difficult to give a pat on the back when it is deserved.

There are other principles of learning that have a bearing on learning academic material. When a great deal of material must be memorized, there is some evidence that it is learned more effectively in a number of brief study periods rather than in a single long study period of the same time length. It is also usually recommended that students look over the material as a whole first. This helps make the individual material more meaningful by relating it to the over-all purpose of the entire book or material. Self-recitation is also quite effective in learning academic material. If we try to restate the essential ideas in the material we are reading by putting it in our own words, we are more likely to learn and remember it. The more of our senses that we use in the original learning of the material, the more likely we are to be able to remember it. We can learn to recite a paragraph of material merely by reading it silently to ourselves, memorizing it, and then later recalling it. If this same paragraph is also read to us by someone else, we will remember it more easily. Reading the paragraph out loud ourselves further helps "stamp in" the memory. Writing the paragraph would give us still further assistance in remembering it.

Remembering

It is not news to any of us that we remember only a fraction of the things we have learned. Many ideas or concepts that we have learned during the school year just do not occur to us by the time the examination rolls around. Most of the forgetting that we do occurs soon after we have learned. Just how much is forgotten depends on many things. It depends first of all on *how well the material was learned in the first place.* If we learn something very well, and then continue to study it and *overlearn* it, we will remember it better and for a much longer time.

We remember material much better if we have learned it in *practice sessions distributed over a period of time* rather than after one intensive and long session. Students who cram for an examination may do fairly well if they take the examination shortly after their learning session, but a day or so later much of what they have "learned" is already forgotten.

Also, we tend to remember material much better if *it is meaningful to us.* Finding meaning in material, however, often depends on the way we adapt it. In this material on human behavior, the reader will remember much more of it and be able to use it more effectively if, at this very time of learning, he can relate it to his own personal experiences.

Forgetting. Forgetting occurs for several reasons. First of all, we can forget things simply through the passage of time. The *time that elapses* between the learning experience and our efforts to remember certainly has a bearing on how much we retain, but the *activities* that occur during this lapse of time have as much or even more to do with forgetting.

Forgetting occurs often because *new learning,* which takes place as time goes on, interferes with what we may be trying to remember. Let us assume that we are trying to memorize a speech this morning which we are to give at a meeting this evening. The things that we do during the day and the things that we attempt to learn and retain will tend to interfere with our ability to remember our speech when it comes time to deliver it. Material learned during the day which is similar to the speech will interfere more with the memory of the speech than material which is dissimilar to the speech. There is also some evidence that much less forgetting occurs during sleep than during the same amount of waking time. Since there is less mental activity going on during sleep than during the waking state, there is less interference in remembering material that may have been learned just before going to sleep.

As we have seen in the section on defensive mental mechanisms, we frequently "forget" because we do not want to remember. It is an *active purposeful forgetting.* We fail to remember, then, because there is some emotional disturbance present which we hope to relieve by forgetting. When the emotional difficulty is relieved, as through psychotherapy, the "forgotten" material may then be remembered.

Any *general anxiety* that we feel may keep us from remembering. All of us have probably had the experience of memorizing something for a recitation only to find that our mind is blank at the crucial moment. Memory is blocked in this instance probably because there are a number of other things filling our consciousness such as over-concern with our appearance or with the impression we are making on the audience.

The more carefully the underwriter prepares his work in advance and the more he practices his delivery, the less likely he is to forget essential points or ideas even if he is under unusual stress during the sales interview.

Remembering names. One of the memory difficulties we often have is that of remembering names. Although it may not seem so obvious to the reader, this is often because we simply are not very much interested in the person we are meeting. *Poor memory is probably just an example of poor learning in the first place.* Because most of us have this difficulty in remembering names, we are more than a little flattered when someone happens to remember our name.

It is quite important to the life underwriter that he make a special point of learning his prospect's name because of the sales advantages it gives him. We will remember names much better if we repeat the name as we hear it. Saying the prospect's name as soon as he mentions it or as soon as we are introduced to him is one way of reinforcing the learning experience and making it more vivid. If in the next few minutes of conversation we will use the prospect's name once or twice, this will further stamp in the impression and enable us to remember the name for a longer period of time. Some life underwriters are in the habit of writing down the name of any person that they really want to remember. We need not especially hide our effort to remember the name of the person we have been introduced to, for by making an obvious effort to remember, we are in a way complimenting the other person.

Perception: a Personalized Interpretation

"I saw it with my own eyes," said the witness testifying at the trial of an accused criminal. Rarely do we doubt the reality of what we see or hear. We take it for granted that what we see is in fact true. But doubt about this arises when two people "see" two different things while watching the same incident. The eye witness is of tremendous significance in establishing the "facts" regarding a murder trial. But every once in a while, an innocent man is electrocuted because, as it is later discovered, an eye witness made a mistake in what he reportedly saw. This makes us suspect that the human being does not always see what is there.

You and I both meet a man in the street. He happens to be a competitor of yours, but I do not know that. To me, he looks like a pleasant enough fellow, but as we walk on, you remark that he is a "sharpie" who cannot be trusted. Each of us has perceived him in a different way. Our perceptions of him were drastically affected by our own personal experiences. The next time I meet that man, he is very likely to look like a "sharpie" to me. In fact, if I talk to him for a few minutes, I'm likely to "find" all kinds of evidence to support the perception of him that I have learned to have. In other words, I am likely to "see" mostly those things which are consistent with the mental picture I already have of this person. Unless we are careful we will be *selective* in our *perception* and see only what we want to see.

Sensations and perceptions

We do *learn* to see. In fact, all sensations that we experience must be interpreted by us before they make sense to us. *We "see" reality through a screen of personal experiences, prejudices, and misconceptions.* Let us examine just exactly *how* we go about experiencing sensations and perceptions.

We must first be exposed to an object. From this object certain physical energies act on our sense receptors, that is, our eyes, ears, nose, skin, muscles, etc. From these sense receptors or sensory organs, nerve impulses travel to the brain. Here the nerve impulses are experienced by us as sensations. We are aware that there is some kind of object "out there." It is when we give these sensations a meaning that perception takes place. If we are driving down the street and begin to smell something burning, we have been made aware of something acting on our senses, that is, we experience a sensation. So far, we don't know what this sensation means. Our friend reports that it smells to him like a burning brake lining and suggests that the hand brake has not been released. Sure enough, this is what has happened. Because we now give some meaning to our sensation, we can refer to this as a perception.

Learning to perceive. We learn to perceive the world by *associating sensation with other information that we have.* Let us assume that a person has been born in Florida. As he drives his automobile along a highway while on a winter vacation trip in New York, he approaches an obvious icy patch on the pavement. Because he has had no previous experience with driving on ice, he may regard this as a matter of curiosity and not slow up his automobile. A moment later, much to his surprise, he has lost control of his automobile. He begins turning the wheel to the left and to the right, he applies his brakes and finds himself in a ditch. The next time this driver sees a patch of ice, it will have a different meaning to him. He will now see the ice in terms of past experience and because of his perception of the next icy patch, he will alter his behavior as a consequence of the meaning that is given to the sensation.

Errors in perception. We frequently make errors in perception. After his harrowing experience on the icy pavement, the southern driver may later on see a section of wet pavement that looks shiny and icy to him, and he may react by slowing down unnecessarily. Perhaps we have had the experience of reading a frightening mystery novel late at night and "hearing" someone jimmy open a window of the house. If we work up the courage to investigate, we may find that it was merely a branch of a bush scraping against the window. *We sometimes make errors in perception, then, because of preconceived ideas or expectancies.* We may be expecting to meet a dear friend at the airport terminal and think we see him in the distance with his back towards us. As we walk up to him and slap him on the back, we may be embarrassed to find that we have slapped a total stranger who bore a slight resemblance to our friend. Our perception has been distorted, then, by an expectation.

The *attitudes* [4] that we have towards an individual or toward a group of individuals can also affect our perception. The insurance prospect who has the attitude that all insurance salesmen are aggressively bothersome pests is likely to perceive even the mildest approach as being "pushy."

Our *needs* can determine our perception. The explorer lost on the desert without water is very likely to "see" a large lake full of clear, sparkling water just beyond the next rise. The life underwriter trying hard for a close may "see" that the prospect is about ready to buy and may press hard for the signature. If the underwriter has perceived incorrectly, he may ruin his chances of making the sale because of his poor timing.

Minimizing errors in perception. We have defined perception as an interpretation of sensation. *What can we do to avoid serious errors in perception?* How can we be sure that we are not completely distorting reality? How can we avoid seeing things as we want to see them and learn to see things as they really are? We can answer this question by looking for a moment at the method of observation which is practiced by scientists.

---

[4] Attitudes are discussed in detail in Chapter 6, pp. 220-225 of this volume.

First of all, in using the scientific method we are interested in getting as complete information as possible. We are not satisfied with one or two observations, but instead try to get many observations spread over a period of time. We record all information that comes to us, regardless of whether it pleases us or not. We are interested in knowing the truth of the matter, and not in merely supporting our own biases. We can check our own perceptions by *deliberately looking for other possible interpretations* of the facts.

If the prospect has refused to buy, and we think it is because he does not care enough for his family, we may try other interpretations, such as an inadequacy within ourselves in presenting the material, possible incorrect information the prospect may have, and the like. We can then see if we can find any evidence to support or refute these new interpretations. One of the main tools that the life underwriter has to help him in gathering evidence to test these interpretations is that of listening. In a later section, we shall discuss the importance of real listening and find ways to improve our listening ability. We will see that it is possible to improve our listening ability by learning to listen more accurately and with less distortion of facts.

Frames of reference

We have seen that perception is determined partly by the needs that we have at any one time. A second main determinant of perception is our frame of reference. This is sometimes referred to as a "mental set." What this means is that things are perceived in relationship to the larger or over-all setting in which they occur. If a life underwriter tells us that he is the top producer in his company, we can interpret this only in reference to the size of the company, the number of other underwriters in the company, etc. A very tall man is likely to describe a friend of his of average height (5'9") as being short. Another individual who is 5'3" may describe this same friend as being a little taller than average. *We perceive characteristics of other people, then, according to our own frame of reference.*

The frame of reference is learned. We form various concepts of classes of subjects such as people, occupations, etc. and we judge new experiences according to these learned concepts. A small farm to a Texan may mean 3,000 acres. A suburbanite might describe his 1½ acres as a small farm. These two men have different frames of reference.

Establishing a frame of reference is useful. We judge and evaluate other people on the basis of our past experiences and unless we have formed some frame of reference, we will find ourselves in utter confusion whenever we have to make new decisions or judgments. The general agent or manager who was able to produce only $300,000 or $400,000 worth of business a year as an underwriter may think that he has a top-notch man when his agent goes over the $400,000 mark. Another general agent, who was formerly a Million Dollar Round Table member, may feel that he is not succeeding unless most, if not all, of his agents pass the million dollar level.

The changeability of our frame of reference. Our frame of reference can change with time. The life underwriter who sold a half million dollars worth of business last year may have felt quite satisfied, but this year he may feel it is no special achievement. His frame of reference has changed. But our frame of reference is also resistant to change. The various stereotypes that we have are examples of frames of reference which are relatively unchangeable. If we have stereotyped people of a certain nationality as shrewd and clannish, we are very quick to "see" these characteristics in their behavior, whether they exist or not. If we happen to observe kinds of behavior in a person of this nationality which do not fit in with the stereotype that we have, we tend to dismiss this evidence because it has very little meaning to us. The danger here should be obvious. Anytime that our frame of reference is unyielding to change, we are very likely to be considerably misled by our perceptions and not be "in tune" with reality.

The vital significance of our perception

The way we form our perception can be a matter of life and death. If we make a left turn in front of an oncoming car because we perceived its being farther away than it really was, then we have made what is perhaps our last mistake. *We cannot know any more about objective reality than that which we allow ourselves to know.* If because of pride, ignorance, prejudice, misconceptions, intense personal needs, or the presence of a strong emotion, we grossly distort the information that comes to our senses, we alone will be the loser. We would not attempt to cross Times Square or any other busy intersection with a blindfold on. Neither, then, should we attempt to move through life without trying to minimize our distortions of reality. We see other people only through ourselves. We are prisoners of our own frame of reference. Our perceptions are formed through learning experiences. We can make our perceptions more accurate or more in line with objective realities only by efforts to relearn.

It would be a mistake to leave the subject of perception without stressing the fact that mental processes can be either conscious or unconscious. We can perceive a stimulus, that is, we can give meaning to a sensation, without even being aware or conscious of having made this perception. We can unconsciously perceive hostility in another person, but when questioned, would conscientiously deny it. The operation of the unconscious part of our psychological being will be discussed at greater length in a later section.

Emergence from Dependency

The concept of personality is something that we know a lot about, and yet each of us would find it difficult to define exactly what he means by the term. The word personality has been used in a number of different ways. We speak of an individual as having a "good" personality or a "lousy" personality. We may say of a friend, "He's *really* got personality." Used in this sense, the word personality is another way of describing our like or dislike for someone. Each of us, then, will attach a slightly different meaning to the term personality. The kind of personality that one person might think is good would be far different from what another person would judge as good. The frame of reference that we have affects the way we think of this concept of personality. *We use the concept of personality, then, in our efforts to judge or evaluate other people.*

Another way in which we use the term personality is to assist in characterizing or describing another individual. We may talk about another person's personality when we mean the special unique patterns of traits and abilities which go to make up that individual. We may say that a man has a practical personality, or a theoretical personality, or a businesslike personality.

While it is difficult to define the term personality with any precision, we offer the following definition as coming close to the sense in which the word will be used in this book. We say that a person's personality is his characteristic way of reacting to various life situations and to the underlying influences which cause them. *Personality is the dynamic organization of wants, desires, abilities, drives, etc. within the individual which help determine his unique way of adjusting to his environment.*[5]

A person is what he is because of two broad influences: his heredity and his environment. Both influences are important. Our personality, or the way we habitually react to the world, is affected by such things as our physical size and weight. We are not suggesting that a short person has inherited a different kind of personality than a tall person. In our society, however, a short man is reacted to by those around him in a different way than is a tall man. If we are referred to all of our lives as "shorty," "shrimp," or "squirt," our outlook on life is likely to be different than if we are continually asked, "How's the weather up there, Stretch?" Almost invariably, the fat man in our society is the brunt of a good many jokes. It is not a surprise that a good many overweight people adopt the role of the clown or buffoon. *While inherited characteristics play a part in shaping our personality, we are what we are largely because of learning experience.*

[5] For further reading on the relationship between personality and motivation, the following texts are suggested: Carl I. Hovland and Irving L. Janis, eds., *Personality and Persuasibility* (New Haven, Connecticut: Yale University Press, 1959); A. H. Maslow, *Motivation and Personality* (New York: Harper & Row, Publishers, 1954); H. A. Witkin, *Personality through Perception* (New York: Harper & Row, Publishers, 1954).

The growth of our personality

How do we get our personality? How do we become one type of person and not another? Unfortunately a clear comprehensive answer is not possible, but we do know some of the influences which mold us and shape us and give us our personality. In any discussion of human behavior, we find that we must return again and again to a consideration of childhood and the impact of early experiences. The formation of our personality begins there.

When the infant is born, he is essentially without a personality. Within the first year of life, the child learns to want to please his parents. He wants to be cared for. He wants to avoid any loss of love. With this as a stimulus, the child begins to form his personality. He adopts much the same attitude towards the world that his parents have. He begins to imitate his parents' speech patterns. He even tends to sit, stand, and walk in the same way as his parents.

The child begins his life by being completely dependent on his parents, or on their substitutes. This almost complete dependence continues for at least the first five or six years of the child's life. We don't have to wait that long to notice efforts on the part of the child to exert his independence. The first efforts to manipulate and explore his surroundings before the child is a year old represent this need to exert himself and learn for himself or to be less dependent on his parents. The drive to emerge from this total dependence and move towards the relative independence of adulthood appears to be one of the driving forces which underlies the formation of our personality. Some individuals never seem to lose a strong feeling of dependence on their parents. Other individuals appear to be so independent that they may be unable to work cooperatively with other people. Somewhere in between these two extremes most of us find some balance and try to maintain it. In our efforts to establish ourselves as a unique, relatively independent individual with our own drives and goals, we *emerge as a personality*. This drive to emerge as an independent individual is rewarded by an ever-increasing personal freedom, that is, a greater control over our surroundings so that we achieve more satisfaction and less dissatisfaction. We emerge with a clearer idea of who we are, of what other people expect of us, and, of course, what we expect of ourselves.

As we shall see in Chapter 2, the role of our family, our school group, our community, and our culture in general plays a tremendous role in shaping and molding us as individual personalities. Most of the time we are not aware of these influences which so affect our behavior patterns, but the life underwriter who is in the business of changing the behavior of other people will find that he can work more effectively if he makes himself aware of the manifold determinants of human behavior.

The formation of values and attitudes

The formation of values in the growing individual becomes the core from which particular patterns of behavior emerge. What are values? How are they formed? Why should we be concerned with values?

We might define values as those broad standards of behavior or those concepts and ideas which an individual considers to be important and meaningful and which govern his daily behavior. One man's system of values might include the value of human dignity, personal freedom, honesty, equal justice for rich and poor, etc., while another man may value the concept that money is more important than social approval, that establishing power over people is the only "truth," that the end justifies the means, and that we should look out for ourselves first and "the heck with everybody else." You can be sure that these two men will not only see the world in a different light, but their whole pattern of attitudes, beliefs, and *behavior* will be different.

The success that the life underwriter has may depend upon the similarity between the values of his clients and his own values. The life underwriter, therefore, who has the ability to select prospective clients with value systems similar to his own may systematically increase his chances of successfully motivating the prospective client to buy life insurance. However, achieving a broader understanding of human behavior and, specifically, a broader and deeper understanding of values and attitudes may allow the life underwriter to extend this "natural" range of prospective clients.

Most typically, we begin to learn our value system from the first group of which we are a member, that is, our family. The pickpocket who teaches his son how to help out in this activity is teaching a certain value to his son. Until he runs into a contrary view, this boy will feel that the ideas he has been taught are right and good. Probably the most important lesson that we learn in our early years of life is *what to value*. In order that we may get along with any number of other people with any degree of cooperation, we must all reach some agreement concerning what is to be of value—what is to be rejected or accepted. While complete and unanimous agreement as to a value system is not necessary for cooperation, there must be a general sort of agreement.

Depending upon an individual's value system, certain attitudes and beliefs are embraced and others are rejected. If we hold to the value of white supremacy, we will find it difficult to adopt attitudes of nondiscrimination regarding racial problems. If we highly value obedience to superiors and to the law, we will find it difficult to entertain ideas of cheating on our income tax returns. The attitudes we form, which rest on our value system, are like built-in circuits which tend to predetermine what our behavior will be like in various situations. Attitudes can be very general or very specific. We engage in certain *characteristic kinds of behavior* (personality) because of a broad foundation of attitudes. For example, if you have a favorable attitude toward one political party, you are likely to cast a vote for that party's candidate. Because of your favorable attitude towards the party, you are likely to cast a vote, not especially because you feel strongly about that one individual, but because your favorable attitude has become very *general* to include all individuals who say that they represent your favorite party.

An individual's specific attitude may be that life insurance is a racket, and so he refuses to buy. The life underwriter, of course, is concerned about how he can change such a negative attitude toward life insurance. This exact problem will be considered at length in Chapter 6. However, understanding how values and attitudes are formed is valuable background information for the life underwriter as he attempts to influence or alter the values and attitudes which he meets in his prospects.

Independence and interdependence as a goal

Independence. The human being appears to be motivated towards gaining greater and greater control over his environmental limitations. The newborn infant feels a sense of comfort and security when held tightly by his mother, but the older child struggles and resists when he is held. The older child wants to be given more and more responsibility and feels considerably put upon if he is curbed or restrained. The emergence of personality and the growth of values signal a movement towards independence and away from the absolute dependence of the infant. We look forward to the time when we can "stand on our own two feet," "stand up and be counted," and "be out on our own." In the childhood years, this drive towards independence exists along with a continuing drive for dependence on the parents.

In the normal human being, independence as a goal gradually increases in importance as dependence gradually decreases. By the time that we are adults, we do not want to be dictated to. We want to determine our own destiny. We want to be independent. Probably no one of us, however, ever succeeds in giving up some need to be dependent on other people. Many general agents and managers feel that they want to hire life underwriters who are "self-starters" and who can depend on themselves for inspiration. In practice, however, it is the rare life underwriter who can maintain a high level of activity and inspiration without occasionally depending upon his manager for a boost in morale or a few leads.

Too independent? Ordinarily we think that as a man matures he becomes more independent and less dependent upon others. But is it possible to be *too* independent? The underwriter who resists supervision and who wants no one to accompany him on calls may be revealing a natural healthy desire for independent action. But he may also be revealing a need to mature still further. What looks like mature independence is often a rather childish rebellion against authority. Rebellion, for the sake of rebelling, may be a reaction formation to which the individual resorts in order to cover up a more basic immature dependency that he still yearns for. Some of the rebellion that is so apparent during the teen-age years is often nothing more than a testing of the limits, or in other words, a plea to the parents to assume more control over the children.

The distinction between independence and dominant aggressiveness on the one hand and immature rebellion on the other is an important one for the general agent to make in his efforts to select life underwriters for his agency. A general agent or manager may become quite excited when a candidate life underwriter speaks up and talks back to him during the selection interview. The manager may think such behavior indicates a strong aggressive man who will control later sales interviews. The man who asserts himself just for the sake of asserting himself or for arguing or rebelling against an authority figure is likely to be relatively ineffective in the sales interview. He is likely to argue with his prospect, win the argument and lose the sale.

Interdependence. It is doubtful that independence should be considered as the ultimate level of emotional maturity for the adult. Certainly we need to grow away from being dependent on our parents, but if we stop maturing at the point of being "independent," this often means that we are trying to "go it alone," without the healthy and stimulating influence of help and ideas from other people. We would suggest that a further phase of maturity for the adult might be to establish himself as an *interdependent* individual. By this, we mean an individual who can, of course, accomplish things on his own, but also reaches out to others for help. Such an individual would be dependable, but could also be dependent on other people for emotional and intellectual stimulation.

It is characteristic of the individual who has not matured to the point of interdependence that he feels it a weakness to admit ignorance by asking questions or getting directions from other people. Interdependence as a goal, and as a level of maturity, describes a way of relating to others by being both dependent on them for ideas, love, and assistance, but, at the same time, being dependable or responsible and in that sense, independent.

The way the parents of a child respond to his drives for independence, and the way the life underwriter's manager reacts to his dependency and independency needs will determine in a large measure the extent of growth and development which occurs in that individual. Too much domination of the child by his parents may force him to grow up as a weak, dependent, passive individual, or as an overly independent or rebellious person. Neither of these extremes would represent a high degree of maturity as the child grows to adulthood. Likewise, too much control exerted over the underwriter by his manager can keep the underwriter from developing as a person and as an agent.

Inevitably, the general agent or manager is in a superior position to his underwriters. The manager controls a number of things which are important to the underwriter. The manager can decide whether the agent keeps his job or not. He can give or refuse to give him office space, secretarial help, etc. The agent must depend on his manager for information, training, supervisory help, etc., and, of course, must depend on his manager to be fair and honest. Such a situation may encourage some agents to become emotionally dependent on their manager in the sense that they ask the manager for help in planning their day's activities, in closing sales, in filling out expense reports, etc. The more emotionally dependent on the manager the agent becomes, the less likely he is to develop the habit of keeping himself on a work schedule and the less he will develop initiative and the kind of creative thinking so essential in successful life insurance selling.

It is important to some general agents or managers that their underwriters be emotionally dependent on them. This is often an unconscious desire, but the effect on the life underwriters is negative just the same. One general agent was frank to admit that he wanted his underwriters to "respect me and look up to me." This general agent flatly stated his unwillingness to be bothered by "those prima donnas who try to throw their weight around." What he was revealing, although he was not conscious of it, was that he was essentially afraid of strong, independent men, and was selecting agents for his agency who would be "yes men." This particular general agent not only failed to select agents who did an average job, but found it impossible to retain even those men doing a less than average job. The home office ultimately removed this man from his position as general agent because of lack of production from his agency.

Man: Rational and Irrational

The life underwriter attempts to sell insurance to a wide variety of individuals. Some may be college professors, some may be laborers, some may be businessmen, and a great many may hold routine jobs in large corporations. Each of these individuals is likely to vary a good deal in terms of his intelligence. Some of them will be of superior intelligence, a good many will be average, and some may be below average in intelligence.

Intellectual capacity is an important facet of human behavior, and it is an especially important factor for the life underwriter to consider because his success in selling life insurance depends at least partly on his prospect's ability to comprehend the various statements that he makes. Most life underwriters have learned to give a logical, well-organized sales presentation and are usually well prepared to answer more technical questions about the policy if it becomes necessary. Life underwriters often find that a prospect does not buy even after a most careful and detailed analysis of the prospect's needs and a most logical sales presentation explaining exactly how these needs can be met.

We are becoming increasingly aware that people do not always do things for logical reasons. There may be, instead, *emotional reasons for buying.* The life underwriter, then, deals with individuals who vary in their ability to comprehend, who are motivated for emotional as well as intellectual reasons, and who buy or fail to buy for conscious and also unconscious reasons. This section will cover some of the essential facts concerning the growth and development of our rational thought processes as well as the growth and development of the irrational or unconscious ways of thinking.

In our society, however, everyone is expected to be logical and to be able to give a reasonable explanation for his actions. Consequently, it will usually be poor psychology for a salesman to point out that a prospect is acting in an emotional rather than in a logical manner. Many people take this as an insult. Consequently, the underwriter must take into account the fact that people often act on the basis of emotions, but he must not indicate to his prospects that he considers them to be illogical or unreasonable.

The growth of intelligence and reasoning

The life underwriter hopes that as he presents his material to the prospect, the prospect will be able to do a certain amount of reasoning and come to a conclusion. It might be well, therefore, to consider several questions. How do we think? How do we form conclusions? How does reasoning influence behavior?

We are not born with an ability to be logical or rational in our thinking. The normal human being is born with a brain which has the capacity for learning very complex mental activities, but our thinking and reasoning ability depends largely on maturation and learning experiences as we grow toward adulthood. Thinking is regarded as the most complex of all man's ways of behaving and the one kind of behavior that, more than anything else, distinguishes man from all other animals. All of us are not born with an equal capacity to learn and think. Intellectual ability seems to be distributed among the general population in much the same way as other characteristics such as height and weight. Look at a group of men standing together and you will notice that most of them are between 5 ft. 6 in. and 6 ft. tall. A few are taller than 6 ft. and a few are shorter than 5 ft. 6 in. but the average seems to be around 5 ft. 9 in. In the same way, a little over 50 per cent of the general population is grouped between the I.Q. scores of 90 and 110, while 83 per cent would fall between 80 and 120 I.Q. points.[6] The implication of this to the underwriter is that he will be presenting his ideas to people who have varying degrees of ability to comprehend the meaning of what he is saying. While the underwriter must never make the mistake of underestimating a person's intelligence and making this estimate known to the prospect, neither should the underwriter assume that his prospect can grasp insurance ideas and facts as readily as he himself. A prospect who fails to understand the material being presented or the logic behind the salesman's argument may refuse to buy, not because he has no need, but because he doesn't understand the proposal and will not admit that he doesn't understand it.

[6] David Wechsler, The Measurement of Adult Intelligence, 3rd ed. (Baltimore: The Williams and Wilkins Company, 1944), p. 40.

Our intellectual capacity also changes somewhat during our life-time. Intellectual or mental growth increases year by year as we are growing up until we reach the age of about 16 or 17. After this age, there is very little, if any, increase in our basic capacity to understand and think intelligently. Starting in the early twenties, there is even a tendency for intellectual capacity to decrease slightly year by year. The sixty year old man usually will not be as quick and facile in his intellectual abilities as he was as a younger man. At the same time, however, increased knowledge and experience in a particular field may allow that individual to in-crease his ability to solve problems in that field. The decline in reasoning and thinking ability seems to be a matter of speed. The older man must simply take a little longer to learn and under-stand something.

One of the best single indicators of a person's general level of intelligence is his vocabulary. The more intelligent the person, the more extensive his vocabulary is likely to be. Of course, educational opportunity also has something to do with the size and complexity of a person's vocabulary. There is also a tendency for the more intelligent person to have a better memory. Again, many other things besides our intellectual capacity influence our ability to remember. As we have noted, we more easily remember those things in which we are interested and find it practically impossible to remember those in which we have very little interest.

Thinking and reasoning, of course, depend upon what has been learned previously. Reasoning is distinctly a mental activity which may be thought of as a kind of trial and error process. When we are given a problem to consider, certain previous experiences which seem to be related to this problem are called to mind. These are tried out mentally and some discarded and some retained. This process continues until a likely solution is arrived at out of the individual's fund of past experiences.

The process of reasoning involves at least five different activities: (1) a problem is recognized, (2) a problem is adequately described, (3) a number of possible solutions are suggested, (4) the possible solutions are examined to see how they might bear on the problem, and (5) observation or actual trial and error behavior is begun which will lead to the acceptance or rejection of each of the possible solutions.[7]

Reasoning, like every other human activity, is subjected to error caused by personal desires, biases, or conscious motives. We occasionally see someone reasoning out the solution to a problem but arriving at a false solution because of unwarranted assumptions that may not have been critically examined. For example, an underwriter may propose an insurance plan for a father which is a reasonable and logical way of providing for the education of his children. The logic of the plan may be lost on the prospect who feels that, although his children should be educated, they should work their way through college just as he did. The underwriter's assumption that the prospect wants to provide money for his children's education is, therefore, unwarranted.

In order to be effective in our thinking and reasoning activity, we need to be relatively free from rigid assumptions or even false assumptions. If the behavior of the prospect seems unreasonable to the life underwriter, it may be that the underwriter has made assumptions about the prospect's desires or financial needs which are unwarranted. We can do some checking on the validity of assumptions through the process of inference. If we see that the prospect is following a certain trend of thought, we may ask ourselves, "What assumptions must he be making in his own mind for him to think that way?" We may then proceed to ask the prospect if he thinks that this or that is true and perhaps we will be able to remove a possible block to the sale that has been existing in the mind of the prospect.

Because of the possibility that the life underwriter's entire presentation may be based on a faulty assumption, or that the prospect's understanding of the underwriter's presentation is based on a faulty assumption, we emphasize once more the importance of listening ability on the part of the life underwriter. If the life underwriter is essentially self-centered and is preoccupied with his own presentation and his own financial needs, he may not be in a

[7] Understanding how the child develops in his thought processes gives us clues as to possible faulty thinking which may occur in the adult. The reader is referred to Jean Piaget, *The Language and Thought of the Child* (New York: Humanities Press, Inc., 1959).

position to detect mistakes in his own logic or reasoning ability, or faulty thinking on the part of his prospect.

The role of the unconscious

We have made repeated references to the existence of what is called the unconscious part of our mind. We have been referring to mental and emotional activities that are somehow beyond the level of our sense of awareness. As we talk about the unconscious, we may get the impression that it is a specific part of the brain, but this is definitely not so. Referring to the unconscious is merely a way of recognizing the existence of mental activity which has force and influence but which is somehow beyond our ability to observe or measure. The concept of the unconscious is strictly an inference. By this we mean that we *assume* that such a mental mechanism as the unconscious exists because of the kinds of behavior that we reveal.

We are aware that there are a number of things about ourselves that we do not reveal to anyone else. We may reveal to our closest friends or associates some of our more embarrassing experiences or our innermost thoughts, but even to them there are feelings and past experiences that we cannot bring ourselves to reveal. Many times we try to hide our feelings from other people. We pretend to be interested in what someone else is saying even though we may be bored. We may actually feel terrible, but will tell an inquiring person that we feel fine. Thus, in many ways, we hide from the rest of the world some of our true feelings and thoughts. In somewhat the same way, we hide certain feelings and thoughts even from ourselves. We say that these thoughts and feelings are unconscious or that we are not aware of them.

At any one time during the day, we are conscious or aware of only a very limited number of things which pertain to us and to our past experiences. If we want to, however, we can call forth many memories or feelings which are at the moment unconscious. We have all had the experience of meeting an old friend and being unable to recall his name. At that moment, we are not conscious of his name. In a few moments, however, his name may suddenly occur to us. We can say, then, that when we first met our old friend, his name was somehow "buried" in our unconscious. If someone were to ask us what we were doing exactly one year ago today, most of us would find it difficult to give a very good answer. But if we were reminded of one or two events which happened to us a year ago, this would possibly be enough to stimulate further memories, and if we made enough of an effort, we might be able to recall an amazing number of facts which had, until a moment ago, apparently been forgotten.

Many experiences in our past are apparently impossible for us to recall even though we may try very hard to do so. Under hypnosis, however, we find that we are able to recall and verbalize experiences dating back even to the first two or three years of our life. This gives us a hint as to the vast and almost endless amount of material that must somehow be collected and stored in what we have been referring to as our unconscious. The importance of this concept of the unconscious is that our present behavior can be influenced by unconscious feelings and thoughts as much as, if not more so, than by thoughts or experiences of which we are conscious.

The example of the iceberg has been used frequently in an attempt to compare the conscious and the unconscious parts of our psychological being. The part of the iceberg which floats above the surface of the water and which is visible constitutes only about one eighth of the total mass. This visible part of the iceberg has been compared to our conscious mind, while the submerged part has been related to our unconscious. We might carry this example one step further. The iceberg has achieved a kind of equilibrium as it floats in the water. The weight of the ice above the surface of the water creates a pressure downward while the buoyancy of the submerged ice creates a force upward. In somewhat the same way, there is an opposing force between the conscious and unconscious parts of our mind. Ideas and feelings in the unconscious may be struggling to reach the surface of consciousness only to be forced down again by our need to avoid recognizing their existence.

If, while we are watching an iceberg, we see it suddenly begin to roll and shift in the water, we infer that something has happened to the ice below the surface to cause a change in the center of gravity. In the same way, we infer unconscious mental activities by noticing obvious changes in behavior. What might seem like slips of the tongue are often reflections of unconscious desires or impulses.

We can suspect the influence of some unconscious mental activity when we notice that a certain bit of behavior doesn't seem to be appropriate or doesn't seem to follow from something that has just occurred. When we feel depressed or excited for no apparent reason, we may conclude that we are being influenced by unconscious impulses or interests. Dream activity that we experience is an expression of unconscious mental activity although usually a heavily disguised expression. An interpretation of dreams by a professional person can frequently tell us much about ourselves that we could not otherwise know.

One of the interesting things about the functioning of the unconscious is that we can react to another person with unconscious hostility of which we are unaware, and the other person can perceive our hostility unconsciously without his being aware that he has perceived it. When this happens, the two individuals feel strangely uncomfortable with each other, but neither has any idea of what might be causing his discomfort.

Unconscious mental activity can distort our perception and cause uncomfortable gaps in our ability to remember, but *the unconscious is also one of mankind's most valuable and helpful assets.* As we shall see in the later section on creativity, the unconscious can be of immense help to us in solving problems or in resolving conflicts. Inventors, writers, and other creative individuals often have the experience of attempting to solve a problem consciously and logically only to meet with frustration and failure, but after a certain period of time, with no apparent conscious effort, the solution or idea that they have been searching for suddenly leaps into awareness. Many of us have had the experience of waking in the morning with the solution to a problem which we did not have the night before when we went to sleep. There is much evidence that our unconscious works for us in many helpful ways.

The human brain has been compared in some ways with our

latest and most advanced automatic computing machines.[8] It has been suggested that we actually solve many problems by feeding information to our brain in much the same way that information is fed to a computing machine through tapes. The unconscious then goes to work "with a mind of its own," so to speak, and grinds out an answer for us.

Frustration and conflict

When we begin to open a door and find that it is stuck, our automatic response is to push a little harder to try to open it. If that doesn't work, we may back off and give it a kick. We may even say things to it. Depending on our mood, we may continue to pound on the door, we may stand in silent rage, or we may search for another door which opens.

One of the most common reactions to frustration is aggression. Let someone drive in front of us and block our progress while we are rushing to an appointment and our thin veneer of civilized behavior may be peeled off with a blast on the horn or an angry shout. The prospect who offers ridiculous objections or who becomes insulting may give rise to feelings of anger within the underwriter. This reaction to frustration can prevent the underwriter from thinking objectively about the prospect's problems and from going any further with the sale.

We react to frustration by increasing the amount of energy we bring to bear on the cause of the frustration in order to overcome it. This increased energy can be in the form of senseless rage *or* it can be in the form of increased interest, ingenuity, and persistence in finding adequate solutions to the problems. This second use of the increased energy level often results in real progress or invention. It is the healthy and constructive way to rise to a challenge.

This constructive response to frustrations seems to depend on the level of emotional maturity of the individual *and* on his background of knowledge and skill which makes creative problem solv-

---

[8] For an interesting and very readable discussion of some similarities between the human brain and computers or servo-mechanisms, see Maxwell Maltz, *Psycho-Cybernetics* (Englewood Cliffs, New Jeresy: Prentice-Hall, Inc., 1960).

ing possible. The life underwriter can make more constructive use of the frustrations he often encounters by becoming more competent both in insurance matters and in his understanding of human behavior. Instead of kicking on the door that blocks his efforts to motivate his prospect to buy, the underwriter *can* learn to see quickly other doors leading to the sale.

The life underwriter is an expert in the field of frustration. He experiences some of it every day. He also is aware of what frustration does to him. He sees that it occasionally makes him angry, it may make him retreat, it may make him regress, and it may make him feel just plain depressed. Each of these reactions is fairly typical of our inability to reach a desired goal or object. Frustration, or the inability to obtain satisfaction when we have been motivated to move in a certain direction, leads to a tension or condition of stress which we call *conflict*. The tension we feel when we are torn between two or more equally attractive goals, or when we are motivated to avoid two or more painful situations, is another example of conflict.

It is typical that during a state of conflict we experience indecision and perhaps vacillation, moving first in one direction and then another, while not knowing exactly what it is that we really want to do. Each of us, as individuals, has his own characteristic way of reacting to conflict. Some of us attempt to resolve the conflict immediately by making a snap decision and moving, even if we are moving in what may be the wrong direction. Others of us make such a move only after a long period of deliberation during which we suspend practically all activity until we have made the decision to move in one direction or another. Most people fall somewhere between these two extremes. In Chapter 7 we will discuss how ethical considerations influence the decisions we make.

A common example of conflict which most life underwriters experience is expressed by the words "call reluctance." Life underwriters must make calls. Only by making a great many calls can the life underwriter be assured of his success in selling life insurance. But a desire to make the call can exist simultaneously with a reluctance to make the call. The life underwriter wants to make a sale, but he is afraid of being turned down. If he does not make the call, he will not make the sale, but he won't be turned down either.

Call reluctance invariably centers around the underwriter's fear of being rejected as an individual. The fear of rejection affects us all, some more than others. As we saw at the beginning of this chapter, we acquire a concept of ourselves especially by noticing how other people react to us. If as a child we are loved by our parents, we tend to regard ourselves as worthy of love. If we are trusted, we are more likely to be trustworthy than if we are not trusted. It works the other way, too, in that the less respect we have for ourselves, the less respect others will have for us. Most of the conflict that we experience in everyday living centers around this fear of personal rejection. What is this fear of rejection? How did it get started? What can be done to overcome it? To answer these questions, and to get a better understanding of frustration and conflict, we need to consider some things that commonly occur in our childhood.

Many parents find that an effective method of disciplining their children is to show love and affection to the child when he is good and take away love when he is bad. The child who has broken his mother's favorite vase may be told, "You are a bad boy. You are clumsy and stupid. Go up to your room and stay there till I tell you to come down." The child soon learns that when he fails to perform according to expectations he will be shut away from the love and affection of his parents. There is nothing that hurts more than to be deprived of the love of an individual, particularly when one is greatly dependent on that person for physical and emotional security. The child learns to behave well, not so much because of the correctness of the behavior itself, but because of the love which he will receive after his "good" behavior. This fear of rejection for wrong behavior can be so great as to become generalized to include other adults who resemble the parents in that they are in positions of authority. Such adults might be the schoolteacher, the policeman, the judge, the boss, and even the prospective buyer of life insurance. The latter is in a position of authority because he can say "yes" or "no" to the agent and can deny him something that he wants very much.

Some parents minimize this fear of rejection by responding differently to their child's behavior. They may well say to the boy who has just broken a vase, "You have just done a bad thing. Even though I love you, I cannot allow you to do such a thing." Such a parent might even continue to punish the child by denying him some special privilege. When the parent makes a special effort to show the child that he is not a bad child, but has done an unacceptable thing, the child can realize that his parents' love for him is not dependent on the specific things that he does or does not do. Such a child can feel a sense of worth that would be denied the child of the first parents. This second child, if he grew up to be an insurance agent, could more readily see that his failure to sell insurance to a prospect meant that the prospect was rejecting the *idea* of insurance and not rejecting the insurance agent personally.

In the sales situation, the salesman puts himself in the position of being accepted or rejected by the life insurance prospect. Of course, there is much more to the sales situation than this, but if the life underwriter sees it only as a matter of being rejected or accepted personally, he will probably form a habit of call reluctance. It is not easy for us to admit that we are afraid. But fear is with us in some form every day. The life underwriter is not likely to tell his general agent or manager that he is afraid to make calls. The life underwriter may not even recognize this fear that he has about making calls. But if fear is the source of conflict between making calls and not making calls, then efforts by the general agent or manager to help the life underwriter organize his time and build a prospect file may not help very much to overcome this conflict.

Surprisingly enough, we can take big steps to overcome such fear if we will only recognize it and especially if we have the opportunity to discuss it with a sympathetic listener. Like any conflict, call reluctance can be overcome if we are willing to move toward the problem, recognize it as a problem, and try out different possible solutions to it. It is when we bury our heads in the sand and try to deny that we have fears that we are likely to get ourselves into real trouble.

The life underwriter who sees that the call on a prospective insurance client is a social experience rather than a business venture is much more likely to experience the frustrations of personal rejection. The stress of approaching relative or total strangers day after day, in addition to the stress of fear of personal rejection, forces many otherwise well-qualified life underwriters to abandon the field of selling life insurance. If the life underwriter can make the distinction between being turned down personally and having his ideas turned down, the stress of making calls will be reduced.

Conflict and anxiety

Our reaction to conflict can be anything from momentary indecision to a total breakdown or collapse. Underlying all conflict is that vague state of uneasiness, unrest, and even terror, which is called *anxiety*.[9] Anxiety and fear are somewhat alike, but anxiety is a vague anticipation of an unknown danger, while fear is a more direct reaction to a specific and identifiable object or situation. Anxiety gives rise to feelings of hopelessness and impotence, while fear most often generates some specific actions to escape from the danger.

Anxiety is distressing and is something we very much want to avoid. Because of this, anxiety is a powerful motivator of human behavior. When we accidentally or on purpose behave in a way which *reduces* the level of our anxiety, this behavior is *rewarding* to us and is *learned*.

Since anxiety is often unconscious and is vague as to its origin, we may not be able to do much about it. But if we can turn our anxiety into a fear, then we can begin to plan ways of overcoming this fear. If we can locate the source of the disturbance, we can move toward it and attempt to cope with it. The underwriter who is unconsciously afraid to make calls will feel anxiety without knowing why. When he can discover that he is afraid of being personally rejected by the prospect and can *admit* this to himself, then he will know the source of his discomfort and can make plans to overcome the fear. Someone else can often see what is making us anxious when we ourselves are blind to it. The more mature the underwriter, the more likely it is that he will go to his general

[9] For further reading on the functioning of anxiety see Rollo May, *The Meaning of Anxiety* (New York: The Ronald Press Company, 1950).

agent or manager and ask for help in observing or locating such sources of disturbance.

The underwriter will occasionally feel anxiety not only before calling on a prospect but also while in the presence of the prospect. Some of the more obvious signs of anxiety are rapid breathing, rapid heartbeat, a tightness in the stomach, sweaty hands, clearing of the throat, sudden itches that must be scratched, belching, and even sudden feelings of weakness and fatigue. One way to avoid or temporarily reduce such anxiety is not to make the call at all or to postpone it. Not making the call is a little too obvious, however, and we might not be able to allow ourselves this method of reducing anxiety. That is, if we unconsciously don't want to make the call but can't consciously admit this to ourselves, we must pretend to ourselves that we really *do* want to call on the prospect: we must at least "go through the motions." Postponing the interview reduces the anxiety and gives us a reasonable sounding excuse, too. We can say, "I need to get the car greased first," or "The prospect is probably too busy to see me now, so I'll call on him later." Expressions like "the hot door knob" are used to illustrate the reluctance a salesman may have to enter the office of his prospect and make his sales presentation.

Anxiety and humor

Either cancelling or postponing something in order to reduce or avoid anxiety is a common method of adjusting to everyday problems, but it is not a very mature or constructive method. Facing and coping directly with the anxiety-arousing situation can often be too painful for us to attempt. A useful compromise between these two extremes is the use of humor.

Humor can be an anxiety-reducing mechanism. Man's ability to look ahead and imagine things frequently builds up anxiety within himself. Man's ability to create humor helps reduce this anxiety and restores a balance. If we can find some humor in our own situation when things look black, we generally feel better. The toastmaster who gets his tongue twisted in introducing the distinguished speaker and who can laugh at his own mistake is probably healthier emotionally than the toastmaster who broods for days after making such a mistake in public. The nervous salesman with sweaty palms and shaking hands who can chuckle at himself and say, "Boy, you'd think I was walking the last mile," is probably well on his way towards overcoming his anxiety.

A sense of humor frequently disappears when a person begins to suffer from mental illness. (This, of course, does not mean that a person who, from our point of view, lacks a sense of humor, is mentally ill!) Humor helps us see life situations in a different, larger, and less tragic, perspective. Because of this, humor can help to prevent mental illness and to regain mental health.

An agency manager once used humor to help an underwriter overcome severe call reluctance. The manager suggested to the underwriter that as he entered the office of a particular prospect, he should picture how the man might look if he were sitting behind his desk without his pants on. The image concocted by the underwriter was naturally very funny. When he did enter a prospect's office and remembered his manager's suggestion, he approached the prospect in a smiling, light-hearted mood. Interestingly enough, the underwriter was no longer uneasy.

The suggestion by the manager actually did two things to help the underwriter find some relief from his anxiety. First, it introduced humor into an otherwise anxiety-arousing situation. Second, but perhaps more important, it focused the underwriter's attention not on himself but on the prospect, where of course it should have been. While we may question this manager's particular suggestion, the end result of using some form of humor was successful in overcoming call reluctance.

The delicate equilibrium and its control

From infancy to manhood we engage in countless learning experiences, meet with countless frustrations, and are faced with countless conflicts which must somehow be resolved if we are to move forward. Generally, we try to move in the direction of receiving pleasure and away from receiving pain or punishment. We are often in conflict because we need things which are themselves in conflict or opposed to each other. We are often in conflict because various people who are important to us want us to live in ways which conflict with each other. As we become uncomfortable for any reason, we are aroused to activity which we hope will make us more comfortable. Human growth and development, then, may be thought of as a never-ending cycle of establishing an equilibrium, having an equilibrium disturbed, and finding it necessary to establish a new equilibrium. We are balanced somewhere between doing what we want to do and what other people want us to do.

If we are to get along reasonably well with other people who are important to us, it is necessary that we strike a balance between doing what we want to do and doing what they want us to. We can do this by compromising, and by attempting to emphasize the points on which we agree with another person and to minimize the points on which we disagree.

In spite of our best efforts to maintain an acceptable equilibrium or balance between the many forces which bear upon us, we often find that we are not maintaining a satisfactory equilibrium. We are "off balance." Statistics show that approximately one out of ten persons will at some time be hospitalized for severe mental illness. This means that their balance will be disturbed sufficiently so that they cannot take care of themselves in our society. One out of four families will at some time or another have a member in a mental hospital. It is estimated that at least 50 per cent of the patients visiting a general medical practitioner are suffering from mental or emotional illness or from a physical illness closely associated with a mental illness.

When our delicate equilibrium is disturbed and we find it difficult or impossible to maintain a healthy balance in life, something has happened to our control mechanism. As we have seen, this equilibrium becomes disturbed if certain vital areas of our psychological life are repressed or unconscious. If our perception of the world is grossly distorted, we will be receiving faulty information and will fall into the trap of nonlogical thinking. Maintaining our equilibrium depends to a large extent upon our ability *to observe our own behavior scientifically, to understand the causes and consequences* of our own behavior, and *to readjust our behavior* on the basis of new information. We block ourselves from doing this by the existence of prejudice. We block ourselves from maintaining a good equilibrium because of a foolish reluctance to express ourselves emotionally and a reluctance to expose ourselves to deep and rich emotional experiences. Acquiring a deeper understanding of human behavior and its endless possibilities and variations will help us maintain a more effective equilibrium throughout life.

2

Society Shapes the Individual

Over the years, each one of us develops a *unique* and *identifiable* way of behaving that is called our personality. We each develop into a person unlike any other person. We are individuals. We do not stand alone as individuals, however, but instead are buffeted by a sea of forces and pressures. In one sense, we are free to come and go as we please, but in another sense, we are blocked by visible and invisible barriers. These forces and barriers are *social* forces and *social* barriers.

Man is a social animal. He lives, works, and creates in groups. He is made more free from the restrictions of his environment because of the help he gives and gets in groups. But, at the same time, he is hemmed in and held prisoner by his group memberships. Man is an animal that can care more about the good will of his group than about his life. He is stimulated to great heights of creativity by the approval or perhaps the love of other persons. But the influence of others can also demand the opposite of creativity, slavish conformity.

In Chapter 1 we talked principally about the growth and development of man as an individual. In that discussion, however, we could not describe the various behavior patterns or mental mechanisms without referring to the influence of other people. *The influence of society upon man's growth is intense and manifold.* If we are to understand man, we must understand the influence that the groups of which he is a member exert upon him. We must understand the *environmental forces* which daily shape and direct man's behavior. It will be difficult for us to grasp adequately the full significance of this environmental pressure upon all of us because we are so close to it ourselves. The difficulty of understanding this pressure should not make us hesitate, but should help us realize the intriguing complexity of man.

Kinds of Environment

Man is a product of his heredity and his environment. What constitutes our environment? We should consider three different kinds of environment: (1) natural environment, (2) physiological and psychological environment, and (3) social environment.

When we speak of *natural environment,* we include the specific climate in which we live, the weather, topography, natural resources, animal life, plant life, and even bacteria. This natural environment, of course, involves certain dangers against which we must protect ourselves. Within the United States, there is a great diversity of things that make up natural environment. The climate in the northern states contributes to ways of living, ways of dressing, recreational activities, etc., which are quite different from those found in the states of the South.

Conditions which exist within us, that is, *physiological and psychological conditions,* also rather directly cause differences in our behavior. The individual born with a physical or mental deficiency is subject to environmental determinants of behavior that would never be experienced by the normal or average individual. A person born with a cleft palate, crossed eyes, brown skin, etc., will invariably arouse significantly different reactions in people around him than will a person who is more "normal" or less conspicuous. Temporary internal disturbances, such as indigestion, high blood pressure, anemia, are part of an individual's environment and as such influence his behavior.

A third kind of environment, *social environment,* is difficult to measure in its influence, but is probably more important and extensive in its influence on the human being than the other two kinds. Most of this chapter will be devoted to this so-called social environment.

Social environment consists, of course, of people. We are obviously influenced by the person next to us on the bus, by our neighbor, by our family and friends. But our social environment also includes many people we never or seldom see, such as the mayor of our town, the manager of the radio or TV station, the local censor of the movies, etc. There are literally thousands of people who affect the way we live, although many of them do so indirectly.

An even broader and more far-reaching influence on the way we behave is known as our *culture.* The influence of our culture is powerful precisely because it is a subtle, often unseen, force which is hard to pin down. Because our culture plays such an important part in every human relationship, including the interchange between the underwriter and his prospect, it becomes an important subject of study for the person who wants to be more effective in motivating people.

Culture: Man's Ideas

The concept of culture

What is culture? [1] The word culture has acquired a good many different meanings and is consequently a confusing word to use. Culture is popularly thought of as a special training or refining of the mind or manners and the acquiring of certain tastes. Used in this sense, we might say of an individual that he is "cultured." Another meaning of the word has to do with *a way of life for a group* of people. Culture in this sense includes *the behavior patterns which are learned, the attitudes which are transmitted from one person to another and which were created by man.* It is in the latter sense that culture will be discussed in this chapter.

---

[1] For background reading on culture the reader may want to read Ruth Benedict, *Patterns of Culture* (Boston: Houghton Mifflin Co., 1934).

Culture is a collection of ideas. Culture is the pattern of ideas and habits in men's minds which gives them the solution to many of their current problems. Culture is that part of a person's surroundings, or environment, which is socially created. Culture is made up of all the achievements of all the people who have ever lived within a certain area to the extent that these achievements have been remembered or recorded or somehow communicated to people who are now living.

One tiny facet of our culture is the idea of "ladies first." [2] In another culture, the woman walks behind her husband. Other facets of our culture are underground sewers and chlorinated water, the rule that a man may have only one wife at a time, the hot dog and the ice-cream cone, the Sunday drive, the new model car every year, Superman, soap operas, free elections, large hospitals and mental institutions, the concept of life insurance, taxes, and an almost endless list of things. Like a jewel with an almost infinite number of facets or surfaces, our culture is a compound or collection of material things, ideas about material things, and ideas about ideas.

The acquiring of culture

One's culture is acquired or learned. We start to learn about our culture as soon as we are born. Every parent is aware of the fact that his baby, soon after birth, begins to imitate his behavior. As a matter of fact, the parent sometimes learns much about himself by noticing the way the child has been imitating him. The child learns through imitation. Much of what the parent teaches the child about his culture is taught consciously. We make a conscious effort to teach our children "good" eating habits, toilet training, ways of dressing, and the like. Yet, we are unaware of much of what we teach our children about our culture. Our culture moves us to behave in certain ways without our being conscious of it. We pass these behavior patterns on to our children, likewise being unaware that we are teaching them.

We begin to learn our culture principally from our experiences

---

[2] This is also known as a cultural trait.

in the family group. A child is taught what he is allowed to do or forbidden to do by the kind of reaction his parents show to his various actions. For behavior which the parents approve of, the child receives rewards in terms of smiles or even gifts. But if he does things which he should not do, he very quickly discovers that his parents are disturbed by his actions and react to him with displeasure. This is a kind of punishment. Trial and error learning is an important part of the child's efforts to assimilate his culture. We are a product of our culture. What our society thinks is good and right, we also will tend to think is good and right.

The significance of culture

The influence of culture is of tremendous importance in motivating men to act socially. Culture is all around us and moves us in both obvious and mysterious ways. Culture is as ever present as the air that we breathe. We cannot actually see the wind as it blows. We can only see the effect of the force of the wind. When the wind blows hard, we automatically lean in the direction of the wind to maintain our balance. We grab our hats or hold down our skirts, and we do these things almost without realizing it. In the same way, our culture exerts pressures upon us and we almost automatically move in response to these pressures. If we could somehow develop a conscious, objective view of cultural pressures, we could be more aware of the influence that they exert. The study of culture allows us to do that very thing. It is obviously impossible to have a complete understanding of one's own culture: too much of it is unconscious. But the more we can learn about the seen and unseen things which influence us individually and as group members, the more we can predict and control not only our own behavior, but that of other people as well.

Culture can be thought of as a balance wheel. It allows a large group of individuals to exist with a minimum amount of disruptive variation. We can expect, for example, that as we drive down the street, most of the other drivers will stop for red lights and stop signs, and in the American culture, will drive on the right side of the street rather than the left. The fact that cultural patterns exist allows us to do a much better job of predicting human behavior.

Individuals who come from a common cultural background are likely to have similar responses to the problems and situations they face. Culture provides many ready-made solutions to the problems that each of us face every day. This is a tremendous advantage for each of us, of course, since it eliminates much trial and error experimentation that we would otherwise have to go through in order to find our own individual solution to problems of daily living. Culture, then, makes our society more *consistent*, more *predictable*, and more *economical* in the sense of conserving human time and energy.

One characteristic of a people within a certain cultural pattern is that they usually feel that someone with another cultural pattern is inferior. This emotional attitude that one's own race, nation, or culture is superior to all others is called *ethnocentrism*. Ethnocentrism appears to be characteristic of all cultures in all parts of the world. The difficulty involved in being ethnocentric, however, is that it is not an objective point of view. The life underwriter who feels that his particular religion, class, background, or even his way of dressing is superior to that of his prospect may keep himself from a full appreciation of his prospect as an individual and consequently may fail to understand him as a man. This failure to understand his prospect may contribute to a failure to make a sale.

Cultural diffusion

When we consider our own culture to be the best in all respects and fail to learn from other cultures and subcultures, much is lost. There is not much in our American way of life that is exclusively "American." Much of what we do and much of what we are has been borrowed from other cultures and from other times. The following description helps us understand this process of cultures contributing to one another, sometimes referred to as *cultural diffusion:*

> Our solid American citizen awakens in a bed built on a pattern which originated in the Near East, but which was modified in Northern Europe before it was transmitted to America. He throws back the covers made from cotton, domesticated in India, or linen domesticated in the Near East, or wool from sheep, also domesticated in the Near East, or

silk, the use of which was discovered in China. All of these materials have been spun and woven by processes invented in the Near East. He slips into his moccasins, invented by the Indians of the Eastern woodlands, and goes to the bathroom, whose fixtures are a mixture of European and American inventions, both of recent date. He takes off his pajamas, a garment invented in India, and washes with soap invented by the ancient Gauls. He then shaves, a masochistic rite which seems to have been derived from either Sumer or ancient Egypt.

Returning to the bedroom, he removes his clothes from a chair of southern European type and proceeds to dress. He puts on garments whose form originally derived from the skin clothing of the nomads of the Asiatic steppes, puts on shoes made from skins tanned by a process invented in ancient Egypt, and cut to a pattern derived from the classical civilization of the Mediterranean, and ties around his neck a strip of bright-colored cloth which is a vestigial survival of the shoulder shawls worn by the seventeenth century Croatians. Before going out for breakfast, he glances through the window, made of glass invented in Egypt, and if it is raining, puts on overshoes made of rubber discovered by the Central American Indians and takes an umbrella, invented in southeastern Asia. Upon his head he puts a hat made of felt, a material invented in the Asiatic steppes.

On his way to breakfast he stops to buy a paper, paying for it with coins, an ancient Lydian invention. At the restaurant a whole new series of borrowed elements confronts him. His plate is made of a form of pottery invented in China. His knife is of steel, an alloy first made in southern India, his fork a medieval Italian invention, and his spoon a derivative of a Roman original. He begins breakfast with an orange, from the eastern Mediterranean, a cantaloupe from Persia, or perhaps a piece of African watermelon. With this he has coffee, an Abyssinian plant, with cream and sugar. Both the domestication of cows and the idea of milking them originated in the Near East, while sugar was first made in India. After his fruit and first coffee, he goes on to waffles, cakes made by a Scandinavian technique from wheat domesticated in Asia Minor. Over these he pours maple syrup, invented by the Indians of the Eastern woodlands. As a side dish he may have the eggs of a species of bird domesticated in Indo-China, or thin strips of the flesh of an animal domesticated in Eastern Asia which have been salted and smoked by a process developed in northern Europe.

When our friend has finished eating, he settles back to smoke, an American Indian habit, consuming a plant domesticated in Brazil in either a pipe, derived from the Indians of Virginia, or a cigarette, derived from Mexico. If he is hardy enough he may even attempt a cigar, transmitted to us from the Antilles by way of Spain. While smoking he reads the news of the day, imprinted in characters invented in Germany. As he absorbs the accounts of foreign troubles, he will, if he is a good conservative citizen, thank a Hebrew deity in an Indo-European language that he is 100 per cent American.[3]

Customs and mores

Customs. The types or patterns of behavior that we learn from our culture are referred to as customs. Customs are patterns of behavior which are relatively well organized and which repeat themselves. The need to eat is not learned but is a biological necessity. But the manner in which we satisfy this need does depend on our cultural training or custom. It is the custom in the Orient not to eat the products of the cow. Horse meat is eaten in Europe, but not in the United States. Various insects may be eaten by Indians in Brazil, but it is not the custom to eat this particular food in Europe or America. The way we use our knife and fork is regulated by custom. The way we dress at mealtime is another behavior dictated by custom.

Customs exert much control over the way we behave in specific situations. It is the custom for men to remove their hats in an elevator in the presence of women. But this custom varies according to the environment in which the elevator is located. It is the custom to wear certain clothes when invited to a formal dinner or dance. While an individual violating the custom would not be jailed or fined, he probably would never be invited again.

Mores. When the customs involve more important activities, such as avoiding marriage with close relatives, physically harming another person, or stealing the possessions of others, the punishment for violating these customs goes beyond mere social disapproval to imprisonment and even death. These more important customs that must not be violated are usually referred to as mores.

One important characteristic of cultural mores is their dynamic quality. Cultural patterns change with time, and so do our important customs change, even those that carry with them violent punishment for nonconformity. Something that is "right" at one time may be very "wrong" at another time. To make another person a slave is wrong today, but was right in our country a century

[3] From The Study of Man by Ralph Linton. Copyright 1936, D. Appleton-Century Company, Inc. Reprinted by permission of Appleton-Century-Crofts.

ago. Just a few years ago, a woman could not be seen at a public bathing beach without being fully clothed. Now it is correct to wear a bathing suit which reveals most of the body. Just a few years ago, being a member of the Communist Party was not highly censured in this country. Today, however, membership in the Communist Party is regarded as a serious matter and is cause for public censure. It is so important today that individuals who were members of the party twenty years ago, but who have since renounced their membership, may still be chastised to the extent of being disgraced or of losing their jobs.

Cultural lag

It is characteristic of a culture that it is in a process of constant change. Culture is dynamic. Different parts of our culture appear to change at different rates of speed. In the last fifty years we have seen tremendous changes in the material and technological portions of our culture. Changes in our social organizations, or in our ability to get along with one another, seem to occur much more slowly than those changes in our material environment. The lag in time between man's technological ability and the effectiveness of his social institutions, that is, his ability to control the problems which arise because of advances in our material culture, is called *cultural lag*. Changes in our material culture occur more rapidly and perhaps are accepted more readily because results from such changes are more easily recognizable.

The life underwriter will come in contact with many individuals who place a higher priority on being up-to-date on the latest model of the family automobile than on being up-to-date in their social responsibilities toward their family. We see another example of cultural lag at the present time when, although man has achieved space flight, it is still impossible for large groups of people of different skin color to work together successfully.

The American Culture

When we listen to a politician tell us that, if he is elected, he will do everything in his power to maintain "the American way of life," just what does he mean? He is talking essentially about our total culture.[4] Because the phrase includes so much, it has relatively little meaning. Perhaps one of the most outstanding characteristics of our nation is the amazing diversity of its people. America constitutes not one culture, but a great many. Rather than talk about "the American way of life," it is more accurate to speak of the American *ways* of life. As a nation, we are tied together by a common language and a common form of government. But regional differences in customs, values, opinions, and attitudes vary so much that we can understand the American way of life only by studying its variability. Within any one region in our country there are likely to be a number of races and nationality groups. These various subgroups have their own characteristic ways of thinking and acting. We can think of these groups as cultures within a culture, and we refer to them as *subcultures*.

From the beginning, America has been heterogeneous in its composition. Immigrant groups making up the American population have originated in various European and Asian countries, such as Germany, Sweden, Italy, Russia, Greece, England, China, Japan, etc., and each of these groups brought with them unique cultural practices. With the passage of time, there has been a certain mixture among these subcultures, but some regions of the United States still contain predominantly German or Swedish, Italian or Chinese groups which can be recognized as distinct subcultures with their own customs, mannerisms, vocabulary, values, and goals. "Chinatown" is an example of a small subculture within the larger culture of San Francisco within the still larger culture of California.

Each prospect which the life underwriter calls on is a *product* of the total American culture (or foreign national culture, if foreign born) plus several smaller subcultures. Each of the cultural influences have shaped the prospect's way of thinking, his way of responding to events (such as the visit of the underwriter), his beliefs, attitudes, prejudices, preferences, and perceptions. The

---

[4] Additional reading on the influence of cultural patterns on the behavior of Americans might include: Saxon Graham, *American Culture* (New York: Harper and Row, Publishers, 1957); Harold Hoffsommer, *The Sociology of American Life* (Englewood Cliffs, New Jersey: Prentice-Hall, Inc., 1958).

prospect reared in an upper-class home in Utah, who has grown up in the Mormon church, who was an Eagle Scout and is currently the president of a leading civic club in Los Angeles, will not hear the same things said by the underwriter as will the prospect born in the Bronx of low-income parents of mixed religions, who was a member of a street gang known as the "Avengers," educated in a trade school for "exceptional" children, who manages a ladies' ready-to-wear shop and is now the vice-president of the same civic club in Los Angeles.

These two men are different personalities partly because of their different cultural backgrounds. At the present time, they may be wearing almost identical suits, support the same candidate for mayor, and may both appear on a list of prospects obtained by the underwriter from the same client. But their different cultural backgrounds have given them a different slant on life, and, of course, a different way of reacting to motivational appeals from the underwriter. The underwriter who has an awareness of cultural variations within our own over-all culture and who realizes the impact of these variations on his own effectiveness as a motivator will have an edge over his colleague who does not.

Group Influence on the Individual

We are what we are largely because of what we have learned from our culture. We acquire our culture through the teaching activities of various groups of which we are a member. It is through a group that a child learns to behave in certain ways. It is through a group that a child becomes civilized and able eventually to *contribute* to later group activity as well as to *receive* knowledge from the group. When someone asks you, "Who are you?" you are most likely, after giving your name, to identify yourself as being a member of a group. Depending on the occasion, your answer may be, "I am an American citizen, I am a life underwriter, I am a Democrat," etc. Upon reflection we realize that we are members of not just one or two or three groups, but as many as forty or fifty different kinds of groups.

Varieties of groups

We can, for example, be a member of these kinds of groups: a generation, a community, a religion, an ethnic group, a country, a family, a neighborhood, a region, a social class, a nation, a state, a county, a ward, a political party, a club, an industrial or work group, or a pressure group. Occasionally we are members of groups which might be called *informal groups,* such as the passengers on a commuters' train, shoppers in a department store, patrons of a theater, or a crowd watching a building burn.

A person's behavior is likely to change a great deal depending on the groups of which he sees himself a member. A man may behave very differently at his secret lodge meeting than he does when he puts on his uniform and participates in a public parade. We accept rather boisterous behavior in an individual during a parade or party, but on the next day in the office we are annoyed by such behavior. Knowing something about a man's specific group memberships allows us to know quite a bit about the man himself. More significant, such knowledge *increases our ability to motivate and influence his behavior.*

We deceive ourselves if we think that we are individuals who can stand apart from our society or group memberships. From infancy we are molded by the customs and beliefs of our family group. As we enter any kind of school system, we are again members of a group which has far-reaching influence on our behavior pattern. At any time in our life, unless we are on an island completely by ourselves, we are pressured and molded by the influence of groups. Group pressure can cause us to change our opinions. A group may control rewards and punishments which are important to us, and thereby exert a powerful influence on us. A group forces us to conform. Of course, we also gain much from our membership in various groups. One of the main ways that we have of enhancing our self-esteem and, of course, establishing higher status is through our various group memberships. We wear a school sweater or a class ring or a lodge pin partly because we hope other people will think better of us when they know that we are a member of an important group.

The group defined

A group may be defined as consisting of two or more people between or among whom there is a pattern of social interaction. A
group is recognized as such because of a particular type of selective
behavior. A group may be formal or informal. The formal group
usually has rules and regulations which are written down and
well understood and is characterized by a good deal of organization and structure. The informal group, such as friendships, cliques,
etc., is less well organized and the rules of behavior are implicit
rather than explicit.

The importance of understanding groups

The life underwriter usually deals with individuals, but these
individuals are members of various groups. Knowing something
about groups as such and how they function is important for two
reasons: (1) because of the influence of the group on the individual,
and (2) because of the influence of the group on the way our
whole society functions. Our society is made up of groups whose
makeup is determined in part by the individuals in the groups. A
neighborhood group, which is organized in the sense of holding a
certain view regarding community matters, can exert great influence and pressure on city government. In the same way, pressure groups influence the members of our legislature who in turn
pass laws affecting all of us.

In addition to his biological needs and his need for some kind
of physical protection from the elements, a man apparently also
has a *strong drive to belong to a group*. He feels more secure
within a group and he also apparently needs to feel that he is
personally important and significant to those groups of which he is
a member. When an individual joins a group, he brings to it his
unique contributions, abilities, experiences, and so forth. It is
usually an advantage for the group to include him as a member
just as it is personally advantageous for him to be a member.

While he gives much to the group, he also must give up something of his own desires in order to be a satisfactory member of

the group. He cannot always do what he wants to do, but must sacrifice some of his personal desires in order to enjoy the benefits of his membership in the group. At the same time, it is important for the group to recognize to a certain extent the individuality of its members. This adjustment of the individual to his group and the adjustment of the group to the individual is referred to as a *fusion process.* In a later section on conformity and creativity we will see some of the intensely important ramifications of the conflict between the individual and his group.

The Family Group

One of the important groups of our society with which life underwriters are most often and most intimately involved is the family. The life underwriter plays a rather important role in influencing the present living standard of families and also the later continuation of the family group after the main income producer has become incapacitated or is deceased. As every experienced underwriter realizes, all families are not alike in terms of their basic attitudes or structure. To some heads of the household, their family is their most important possession, while to other husbands and fathers, there may be very little concern about their family's existence or their continuance as a family group. In some families, the husband and father is the dominant figure, while in other family groups the mother assumes this role. These are some of the many things the life underwriter must consider as he plans his sales approach to the family.

The family defined

The family group may be considered a social institution which is centered around the primary interests of sex, affection, and the care and rearing of children. Ordinarily we think of a family unit as including a married mother and father and their children. The term family is also applied to a group involving one parent and the children, the husband and wife without children, a common-law married couple with their children, and a group of closely related people such as brothers, sisters, cousins, or aunts living together in the same place. The family is an extension of its surrounding culture. The family is the first source of authority for the children.

The changing function of the American family

In this country the family as an institution is undergoing very marked changes in the functions which it performs. Patterns of family life have been changing gradually, corresponding with the shift in this country from an agricultural to an industrialized nation. In the early years of our nation, the family was much more of an economic group than it is now. The husband and father very frequently performed his work in the home or very near to it and quite often the entire family participated in this "business." This type of family unit is still found in certain parts of the country, especially in the rural communities.

The increased urbanization of our society along with the techniques of mass production has not only increased the available material goods and services which can be used by the family, but has changed standards of living and the way family members relate to each other. As the various functions of the family change, the role of the children in the family also changes. In the predominantly rural culture of the nineteenth century, children were an economic aid to their parents. This was true partly because it was difficult to hire adult help. Children could be put to work at no cost. In modern urban culture, children are probably as much an economic liability as anything. More and more education is required to train children for a more complex economic system. There is less tendency for children to be employed by their parents or to help their parents in their old age. Perhaps the greatest satisfaction that parents have today is the affection they receive from their children rather than any economic return.

While it is a culturally accepted assumption that parents are vitally interested in their children's future education and welfare, actually many modern parents may be reluctant to sacrifice today for the comfort of their children tomorrow. This attitude would perhaps not be admitted to a stranger such as the life underwriter but may be a factor in the sales interview nevertheless.

The function of the family is changing, too, in regard to its role as an educational institution. Less responsibility is being assumed by the family for the teaching of the children. There appears also to be a tendency for the parents to give to public school systems and churches the responsibility for teaching the child in the areas of basic values and religion as well as in formal education.

Generally speaking, the home and family have become less and less the place for recreation. Various members of the family find their recreation with more organized "institutions" such as motion pictures, radio and television programs, state parks, various clubs, and other associations.

Partly as a result of its changing function in these several areas of economic, educational, and recreational life, the family has lost a large part of its control over its members. Whereas the father was the principal authority figure for children for many years, modern children receive much of their discipline from other men and women, outside the home, especially during the school years.

The changing roles of mothers and fathers

The role of the man in the family is also undergoing definite changes. At the turn of the twentieth century, the father was most often the unquestioned head of the household and the source of authority. Legally the wife had very little status. The man was able to make all decisions regarding money and property and his wife was considered to have almost no legal rights. The man owned and controlled any property his wife might have contributed to their marriage and family, and he also controlled anything which she earned after marriage. While the legal status of the American wife and mother in a few of our states is no different now, generally speaking it has changed considerably.

More and more women are receiving higher education and training for business activities. Such women frequently see their role of homemaker as drudgery and they view it with resentment. There is an increasing tendency for women to participate in various activities outside their home and family unit. Of course, this changing role of the wife in the American family has much to do with the growing market for insurance on the life of the wife. The growing tendency for the wife to help provide the family income and the necessity to work after the husband dies creates a growing insurance need.

In many ways, the wife and mother of the family unit is less and less dependent upon the family for many of her satisfactions. There is less dependence of the woman on her mate for security. Women probably not only have more choice in the kind of men that they pick for husbands but are more free to follow a career or occupational pursuit of their choice. This increased independence in women's role as a wife and mother has brought with it some confusion in her own mind as to what her role should be. One of the most frequent conflicts existing within the American wife and mother is the degree to which she should be either homemaker or career woman. These conflicts and uncertainties tend to weaken the structure of the family group.

Women are becoming more and more important in decision-making especially with regard to decisions to make purchases for the family. More and more, the family structure is such that the husband and wife share the responsibility for making decisions. It is important for the life underwriter to be aware of the role the wife plays in making the decision to purchase life insurance. Misunderstanding this rather vital part of the family life of his prospect may well cost the underwriter a sale.

The Position of the Individual in the Group

"All men are created equal." This is one of the beliefs that we hold to most strongly in our American culture. What we mean by this is that men are equal in the sense of being valuable in and of themselves and in their right to equal opportunity. While in practice we do not always behave as if we believed this, especially in regard to various minority groups, generally this is part of the philosophy of life held by most Americans. In all other ways, however, we are quite different from each other. Of course, it is obvious that we do not resemble each other in appearance, in height, in weight, or in other physical dimensions. We differ also in terms of our various positions within the different groups of which we are members. The position that we may occupy in a group can be thought of as our *status* in that group. We know that as we were graduated from high school, we enjoyed a very high status as members of the senior class. But as we moved on to college we found ourselves at the bottom of the ladder again in the status of freshmen. As we go on through life and become members of various groups, we find that our status in the group varies depending on our abilities, our length of time in the group, and perhaps our "social background." We occupy a high status in some of our groups and a very low status in others. The position that we occupy in any group is of vital importance to us and helps determine our individual behavior.

Our stratified society

One of the obvious facts about our society is that we are divided into various groups depending on our income, actions, beliefs, attitudes, values, and occupations. One way of discussing the various layers in our society is by use of the concept "social classes." Generally we can divide our society into upper, middle, and lower classes. This classification can be further extended to an upper-upper class, a lower-upper class, an upper-middle and a lower-middle class, and an upper-lower and a lower-lower class.

Each of these various classes has somewhat different value systems, different interests, and different goals for which the members are striving. In general, the so-called upper classes in America are individuals of greater than ordinary wealth. The occupations of people within this class would include bankers, corporation executives, attorneys, physicians, engineers, and business proprietors. In the upper class, family background and family tradition are of great importance. Upper-class family members are often long-time residents of the communities where they live.

Occupation is an important element in determining our social status and may be one of the best single measures for determining our rank in the community. In the mind of the public, all familiar occupations in the United States carry with them definite prestige values. In an opinion poll to determine just what these values were, a Supreme Court justice, a physician and a state governor were ranked at the top in terms of prestige and the shoe-shiner, street sweeper, and garbage collector ranked at the bottom.

In comparing the various social classes with each other, it is often found that there are differences in such things as the denomination of the church attended. People of various classes apparently tend to eat different things, buy furniture of different styles, and dress differently. While social studies indicate that the tastes of people in a similar class do show tendencies to be alike, there is so much overlap between classes that it is impossible to predict an individual's taste merely by knowing something about his class affiliation.

Families of the lower, middle, and upper classes tend to emphasize different ideas and values in rearing their children. The behavior and value patterns of the middle class have been studied much more extensively than those of the lower and upper classes. The middle-class family, for example, tends to stress achievement. It is probable that middle-class families take a greater interest in the development of their children and stress the importance of being recognized for superiority in at least one, and hopefully many, things. There is a strong "future orientation" in the middle-class group. Middle-class parents are very much concerned about what other people think and tend more to discipline their children to conform with conventional standards.

In lower-class families, there is often less emphasis on achievement, less concern with the children's position or status, and more of a tendency to emphasize present needs and wants rather than the future. There are greater expressions of aggression in the lower-class group and less regard for social and moral standards. Upper-class families apparently emphasize following the family tradition. Achieving excellence in social and recreational activities is also stressed.

As we have seen, a great many factors must be considered in determining an individual's class position within his society. Various studies show that people generally have a clear idea of their social class. Most of us, in other words, have an opinion as to the class in which we should be placed.

Class mobility

The prestige which goes with any certain status or class is not always related to the amount of effort or exertion which is necessary to reach that status. An individual born into a very wealthy and notable family enjoys great prestige but only through an accident of birth. One of the common beliefs of the American value system is that upward mobility is possible for anyone who is willing to work hard enough. However, studies show that only a small percentage of the population ever makes any kind of rise in class status.

The gap that separates one social class from another—called *social distance*—is occasionally transcended or bridged by certain individuals. It is possible, for example, for the son of a laborer to be graduated from medical school (perhaps with the assistance of the GI Bill) and after graduation obviously to belong to a very different social class than his father. This movement is an example of class mobility. The example given here happens to be a relatively rare occurrence, for only about four per cent of the children of laborer families are able to reach a professional status in life. Perhaps the most important way of moving from one class to another is through education. Another way, of course, is to marry someone from a higher class. There are definite barriers to class or social mobility, however. A man may be passed over for promotion from vice-president to president of a company because he "doesn't have the right background." Not only is the man's own social background a barrier, but the social background of the man's wife also can become a barrier to his promotion within the company.

The social class to which the life underwriter belongs probably has much to do with the group of prospective clients with which he can be successful. It seems likely that the greater the distance between the social class of the life underwriter and the class of his prospects, the less ability there will be for the underwriter to establish rapport with each prospect and the more likelihood there will be of greater tension between the two individuals.

The roles we play

Status refers to a position that we hold in an individual group. An individual's relative status in a group has sometimes been compared to the "pecking order" among chickens. An observer in the barnyard will notice that the various chickens peck each other according to some rather rigid rules. At the top of the order is one chicken that pecks but is not pecked by any other chicken; at the other end of the scale is a chicken that is pecked but in turn does not peck any other chicken.

This pecking order with humans may be illustrated by the se· quence of a man who is chastised by his boss, who comes home to criticize his wife's cooking, who in turn slaps the children, who kick the dog, that chases the cat, etc. If we think of the social status that we enjoy as a collection of rights and duties, then a person is performing a *social role* when he puts these rights and duties into effect. The concept of role and status cannot be separated. Carrying out a role in society is something like performing in a play. As Shakespeare put it:

> All the world's a stage,
> And all the men and women merely players.
> They have their exits and their entrances:
> And one man in his time plays many parts.[5]

Most of us are members of a great many different groups, and since we have a rather distinct status within each group, we consequently have many roles which we play from time to time. We may play the role of the strong, dominant, aggressive life underwriter during the daytime, but change to the role of the meek, respectful husband as we come home to our wife in the evening. We may play the role of the dashing, sophisticated, brilliant con· versationalist while chatting with a pretty girl at a cocktail party, but later may play the role of the gruff, inarticulate male when called upon for our opinions at a P.T.A. meeting.

[5] William Shakespeare, *As You Like It*, Act II, scene 7.

To be a member of any social group we must behave to some extent as the other members of the group expect us to. If we fail to play the role as it is outlined to us, we may simply be expelled from the group as a result. If an individual steps out of his role, that is, if he behaves in ways that are not expected of him, we feel that he has somehow made a mistake, has "gotten out of hand," and needs to be "brought back into line."

The more important our group is to us the more rigidly we are likely to persist in playing the role that is expected of us. But the role that we play is more than just a series of activities. Our role includes an appropriate emotional response. A funeral director may make all the necessary arrangements to insure a decent and dignified burial of his customers, but if he hums and smiles while doing this because business is good, those who observe him are likely to feel that he is not properly "playing his role." The mother who takes excellent care of her children but who does not show the expected emotions of warmth and love will give others the impression that she is not properly playing her role as a mother.

When we talk about the role that we play in life, we are referring to a pattern of behavior that is appropriate or expected in a given situation. In using this term role, we are not speaking of it in the same sense as the role that an actor plays, because most of the time we are not particularly aware that we are playing a role. We only become aware of our expected role or that of someone else when the role is not played as it should be.

When we enter a new group, we are frequently unaware of exactly what our role should be. The members themselves may not be consciously aware of the expected role that we should play. There is usually agreement, however, when the expected role is not followed. As with conformity in general, deviating from the expected role draws increased attention to ourselves and generates some activity on the part of the group to force us back into the expected role. Many of our social standards and of our role expectations are in the form of unwritten rules, but deviation from these rules is recognized and often punished just as swiftly, if not more so, than our well-known and clearly stated civil laws.

How we learn our roles

We learn what to do in a given situation, that is, we learn to play a certain role, largely by watching what other people are doing. We can see this kind of *learning by imitation* most clearly in children. Every father knows how his son tries hard to imitate him in behavior, in posture, and even in dress by clomping around in his father's shoes. As we join a new club, we alert ourselves to the particular customs and manners of the other members so that we can "fit in" with the rest of the group.

To borrow Emerson's metaphor about groups and their leaders, we might say that the insurance agency is the "lengthened shadow" of the man who heads it. This is on the one hand a description of the group and the way it is structured, and on the other hand, an important principle of motivation. The careful, cautious general agent or manager who emphasizes service to the policyholders is very likely to "teach" this role to his agents. The general agent or manager who likes to do things in a big way, who stresses the importance of membership in the Million Dollar Round Table and who himself obviously follows a very high standard of living will be indirectly teaching quite a different role to his agents. An example of behavior is set by the general agent or manager and is copied by the agents, usually without awareness on the part of either.

A second method of learning a role is *learning by instruction*. If the general agent or manager consciously and deliberately encourages his agents to be dissatisfied with their present standard of living, he is actively attempting to change the role expectation they have of themselves. Such new role expectations are generally taught by the general agent or manager in an appropriately subtle way. The general agent or manager may become more direct in teaching a role, however, when he tells his agent, "If you want to become a million dollar round table member, you've got to act like one." The general agent or manager may continue, then, to instruct his agents as to ways of dressing, ways of talking to prospects over the telephone, and may even give instructions as to the kinds of automobile that would be appropriate for making calls.

Learning a role by imitation or learning because we have been told to behave in a certain way is not always successful, precisely because of the fact that proper *playing of a role* demands not only the right kind of behavior but also the *appropriate emotional response.* The agent who tries to play the role of a fast-moving, highly successful, dominant, and aggressive writer of large cases may not feel comfortable doing this, emotionally, and thereby defeats his own purpose. Quite often, we learn a new role only after a good bit of actual experience on a practical level.

Role conflict

All of us play many roles, and some of these roles are in direct opposition to each other. This does not normally cause difficulty because we can separate our several roles, either in time or in distance. We see by the newspapers how it is possible for a man to play the role of the dutiful husband to two different wives as long as the wives are in different cities. A problem arises when the distance between the two wives is reduced or eliminated!

The role that an agent plays at the company's conventions varies according to whether or not his wife accompanies him. If his wife is along, he may play the role which seems appropriate to his wife but seems strange to his fellow agents, who are familiar with the man's role-playing activities during previous conventions when his wife was not with him.

We play one role as the father of our children and quite a different role when we in turn visit our own parents. Such a visit to the grandparents is often strained, precisely because we feel compelled to play two conflicting roles. We may experience conflict with the roles we must play in another important area. The agent may be well aware of the role he must play in order to sell insurance with his company. If, however, he is in doubt as to the quality of his company or if he feels that the policies he must sell are inferior to others that he knows about, he will feel a certain amount of personal conflict. The life underwriter, under such circumstances, may find it difficult to carry out, at the same time, the expected role of a life insurance salesman and the expected role of an honest, decent individual of integrity.

One obvious way to escape the conflict which may arise over the divergent roles that we play is to remove ourselves from at least one of the situations demanding the conflicting role activity. One agent had this kind of experience. He had been born, reared, and educated in a fairly small town and was well liked in town by almost everyone. He had been an outstanding student and had achieved modest success as an athlete. He discovered, however, that even after three or four years of hard work, he was just not succeeding as a life underwriter. Various businessmen in town continued to think of him as an outstanding high school student even four years after he had left high school. He himself had a tendency to continue to see the business leaders as adult, parent-like figures that he had looked up to as a growing boy. He was attempting to play the role of the adult life underwriter, but at the same time other people saw him in the very different role of a well-known high school student. This conflict in roles, which was adversely affecting his production, was resolved only after the life underwriter moved away from his home town. The next year, even though he was in a strange environment, his production almost doubled and the satis- faction he found in life underwriting increased many fold.

Sex roles

We are pleasantly aware that there are differences between male and female. The biological differences are important, but of at least equal importance are the differences in the way society expects men and women to act.[6] Much of masculinity and femininity is learned, and these learned reactions are roles. Depending upon our sex, we learn how we are expected to behave from our very earliest family experiences. Boys and girls are expected to behave differently, as this nursery rhyme tells us:

> Sugar and spice and all things nice,
> That's what little girls are made of.
> Snips and snails and puppy dog tails,
> That's what little boys are made of.

[6] The interested reader is referred to the following text: Margaret Mead, *Male and Female* (New York: William Morrow and Co., Inc., 1950).

In our culture, boys are taught to be aggressive, adventuresome, and bold while girls are taught to be refined, clean, careful, and passive. We know that males and females are not born with these traits, but instead learn them. We know this from studying a number of other cultures and finding in some almost an exact reversal of what we consider to be the normal male and female roles. In our culture, men tend to have greater prestige than women. Men are considered more practical. In business positions, men and women doing the same work are rarely paid the same salary, with men enjoying the advantage. In our culture, we expect men to be dominant and women to be submissive.

The woman who elects to become a life underwriter may find some conflict in roles between what is expected of her as an aggressive sales person and what her society expects of her as a feminine individual. Men generally have much more freedom of action than women, who are expected to be more conforming. In sexual behavior, a double standard exists whereby a woman is more severely punished for violating the sex taboos than a man would be.

Our concept of what is properly masculine and feminine changes with time. The popular wrist watch as worn today by almost all businessmen was considered not long ago to be a sign of effeminacy. Today, it is not unusual to see a husband pushing a cart in the supermarket, holding a baby in one hand and doing the grocery shopping with the other. Such behavior just a few years ago would have been ridiculed. A woman has much greater freedom to choose her occupation today, but this very freedom often creates a serious conflict in her mind between the values of motherhood and homemaking as opposed to the values of a career and service outside the family.

Achieving a sense of adequacy as a male or a female becomes a motivator of tremendous importance in our culture. A woman may well feel that she has not fully achieved her sex membership until she has been able to conceive and give birth to another human being. While the male achieves a similar sense of adequacy with the birth of his child, his actual paternity must always remain inferential. Because adequacy as a sexual partner has been so emphasized in this culture, many men seem to need to prove their potency over and over again. Much behavior which might otherwise seem to be motivated by a sexual drive is probably actually motivated by a need for reassurance that one is adequately playing the expected sex role.

The suspicion has grown in the minds of some general agents and managers that the successful life underwriter probably has a stronger sex drive than most men, and in some agencies this inferred "fact" may play a role in the selection of new life underwriters. It is probably true that a man in good health and with a high level of energy works harder in all phases of life than does someone else who may be chronically fatigued. The individual striving to prove his adequacy through sexual adventures may also attempt to prove this through success and "conquering activity" as a life insurance salesman. It would be erroneous to assume, however, that a man with a strong sex drive (and it is doubtful that this could ever be definitely known about a candidate) would necessarily become a more successful underwriter. There are too many other factors which have a bearing on the ultimate success or failure of each individual underwriter.

Social Control

All societies have a need for some kind of social control. In our discussion of culture we found that it contains not only many rules for behavior but also methods of punishment for any individual who breaks these rules. The way social control is exerted depends much upon what the group believes to be correct behavior. We know that the individual who deviates from the expected behavior of his group may be viewed with suspicion and perhaps even thought to be dangerous. The pattern of pressure which a society exerts to maintain order and insure adherence to rules is known as its *system of social control*.

The reluctant pupil

Social control is exerted upon the child from the very moment of birth, and the agency which exerts this control is the family.

The child learns in a few short years those rules of conduct and solutions to problems which mankind has learned and refined over a period of centuries. The child learns to be civilized. But the child is a reluctant pupil. He wants to "do what comes naturally" but finds that his parents want him to do other things. This struggle between the individual and his groups continues without letup all during his life. For any group of individuals to work cooperatively with each other for mutual benefit, there must be a way of predicting one another's behavior and there must be a certain amount of social cohesion. The mechanism of social control helps insure that the child grows from being the reluctant pupil to becoming the willing teacher of others. For this transformation to take place, it is important that each individual "internalize" the system of social control. In the same way that the over-all culture is internalized, the method of disciplining and minimizing devious behavior must come primarily from *within* each individual. Without a high degree of willing cooperation and self-control, our civilization as we know it could not exist.

The reluctant pupil learns to be civilized because of the existence of mechanisms of social control. There are two main types of social control: (1) *physical control*, and (2) *motivational control*. In order to enforce conformity to the group norm, an individual may be threatened with removal and may actually be forcibly removed from society. The individual who tries to force himself into a line of people waiting to buy a ticket may be physically controlled by this group. One method of controlling extreme deviant behavior in our culture is that of execution.

Direct physical manipulation as a means of social control is used extensively with very young children, but as the child grows older is replaced more and more with techniques of motivation. Most adults have a desire for recognition and status in their various groups. The desire to achieve and maintain this status is the factor which allows motivational social control mechanisms to operate effectively. A word of disapproval or perhaps complete silence at the least suggestion of deviant behavior can be enough to keep an individual from straying too far away from expected behavior.

The social rebel

There will always be rebels exhibiting deviant behavior in our society. An individual may rebel because he has inadequately absorbed or incorporated his culture. He may rebel because of an unusual amount of aggression stemming from overly severe frustrations in childhood. An individual may rebel because of a deficiency in mental ability and a consequent deficiency in the ability to learn or incorporate the mechanisms of social control. An individual may rebel because of the natural desires of human beings to explore, manipulate and control their environment. The individual who deviates from the group norm of behavior will be punished or rewarded depending upon the value that the group places upon the behavior. The individual who deviates by running the mile faster than anyone else in the world is highly acclaimed. Severe punishment is administered to the individual caught deviating through acts of stealing, murder, and the like.

Behavior which is punished in our culture may be highly rewarded in one of our subcultures. For example, the member of a street gang who is the most skillful in robbery or is the first of the gang to commit rape may be held in the highest esteem by the other members of the gang. In our present society, which is highly complex and huge in sheer numbers of people, the pressure of a small individual group cannot be relied upon as a means of social control. A larger institution is necessary and this institution is government. State and federal government is a necessary system of social control basically needed because of the competition of individuals. In the American culture, individuals are taught that they should compete for various goods and services, but an unregulated striving for these goals would jeopardize the stability of society. The larger institution of government, then, exercises a control and regulation which would be impossible through smaller local groups.

The dilemma of social control

While it is important that society exercise some measure of social control over its individual members, this very pressure on the individual to conform to the group's standards of behavior may discourage the kind of individual initiative, innovation, and creativity which is often the very basis of real advancement in our civilization. As a society becomes larger and more complicated, more exacting methods of social control are required. There may, therefore, be a tendency for group thinking to be emphasized and praised more extensively than individual thinking. Society must exercise enough control to maintain a relative stability, but must not go so far as to curb the deviations from present standards of behavior which may themselves lead to contributions towards a future more effective and perhaps even more stable to society.

Conformity and Creativity

Social control or authority is necessary to prevent a society from disintegrating. But every invention, every innovation, every improvement in the way things are done is a rebellion against existing knowledge and authority. This presents mankind with a dilemma. Each one of us as individuals is faced with the same kind of dilemma.[7]

We pay a price

A successful underwriter pays a price for his success just as surely as he does when he purchases any material thing. The underwriter gives up much of his personal freedom to do the many things he enjoys in order to do those things which he must do to sell life insurance. The underwriter may pay the price of a greatly diminished family life, the price of giving up active participation in sports or other activities, and the price of having to attend to many irksome details. In somewhat the same way, we all pay a price for being part of our contemporary civilization. We

[7] For a provocative discussion on the dilemma we experience in reacting to pressures to conform, read Robert Lindner, *Must You Conform?* (New York: Holt, Rinehart and Winston, Inc., 1956). For a discussion of different kinds of conformity in our changing way of life, see David Riesman, *et al.*, *The Lonely Crowd* (New Haven, Connecticut: Yale University Press, 1950).

pay a price for being a recognized member of our society. We pay
a price to gain the advantage of group effort. We pay a price to
grow up and mature as useful citizens.

We compromise. We must conform to the dictates of our society
and yet we must develop our individualism and realize our greatest
potential in our own unique way which may be, in some ways, a
departure from strictly traditional ways of doing things. We must
find a healthy balance between the pressure to develop our individuality and the pressure to become "socialized." This balance
is not easy to achieve. We find ourselves exposed to pressures
which force us to behave "the way it's always been done" but at
the same time urge us to "stand on your own two feet."

We give up freedom. In the present American culture, we prize
individuality highly. Freedom of the individual is one of the basic
concepts of our democratic form of government. More than any
other culture in the world, Americans praise and reward individual
thinking and effort. But too much individualism brings not reward
or acclaim, but punishment, chastisement, and even enforced
separation from the rest of society. If we believe that each individual reaches greater heights of accomplishment primarily by developing and accentuating those talents and capabilities which he
has, then the development and nurture of human potentialities becomes one of our greatest goals as a nation. We must give up some
freedom to become members of a complex society, but we must
be sure that we do not give up the freedom to be creative.

The origins of conformity

The pressure to conform begins on the first day of life and continues until the last. Much of this pressure is unconscious. It is the
business of our culture to check or to control the behavior patterns
of individuals. The family acts as the agent of the culture and
teaches the child to conform. To the child, his parents are the
ultimate in authority. It is through his parents that he is taught and
his values and attitudes are shaped. It is the parents' job to insist
on the child's conformity. His conformity is enforced, first of all by
direct control, manipulation, and compulsion from the parent. It is
the eventual aim of this parental pressure to help the child develop

an inner compulsion to conform. This inner compulsion develops on an unconscious level. The formation of this inner compulsion to conform is possible because of the existence of *anxiety*. Anxiety, an unknown or unrecognizable fear, is a normal part of being human. As the child misbehaves and is punished by his parents, he does not always see the connection between his behavior and the punishment. He does know that somehow he has made his parents displeased and this is an upsetting experience to him. If he can discover the kind of behavior which will please his parents and act accordingly, his anxiety will be reduced.

The value of conformity

Reduction of anxiety. Conformity for the child and for the adult is a way of obtaining relief from anxiety. Most of us feel comfortable when we are in harmony with the things around us. A new situation, an unknown situation, a changing situation, force us to learn new solutions and new ways of behaving. In learning anything new, there is usually a period when we feel uncertain, confused, and quite unsettled. It may be more comfortable for an individual to conform to an existing pattern of behavior even if it is not as effective as a newer or revised pattern might be, in order that he does not have to undergo the anxiety of new learning and adaptation. Conformity does aid the individual in avoiding or minimizing some of the anxiety that he experiences.

Economy of energy. Conformity to existing cultural patterns means a great economy of energy and thought for the individual. Countless generations before us have worked out good solutions to recurring problems. By conforming to existing patterns of behavior, the individual can solve these recurring problems almost automatically. In establishing a new club, we automatically follow the rules of parliamentary procedure that have been very carefully worked out beforehand. This undoubtedly avoids a great deal of confusion, misunderstanding, and loss of time that would occur if we were to attempt to work out our own way of organizing club meetings. We do not have to "invent the wheel" each time we want to use one!

The dangers of conformity

Encourages mediocrity. The pressure of conformity may be one of the more important factors that keep a life underwriter from doing more than a mediocre job. Some managers and general agents appear to be more interested in forcing their agents to conform to standards regarding number of calls made, number of applications submitted, and hours worked than they are in encouraging their agents to give better service or make more money. The manager who is disturbed by a deviation in behavior of an agent may unknowingly select only mediocre or unimaginative underwriters and systematically eliminate the harder-to-control but more creative underwriters. The smaller the agency, the stronger will be the pressure on each individual underwriter to conform to the explicitly expressed standards of behavior of the agency. The manager's own "need" to conform will have a direct bearing on his ability to help his underwriters grow and develop. If an underwriter comes to his manager with a new idea for merchandising life insurance, the manager might quickly say, "Well, I don't know. We've never done it that way before." At this moment, this life underwriter may either give up in his efforts to create new ideas or he may decide to go with another agency where the individual challenge is greater.

The general agent or manager can give lip service to the desirability of developing creativity in his underwriters, but at the same time actively discourage innovation or departures from the norm by his behavior or by unexpressed negative attitudes towards the agent's behavior. To one manager, for example, it was important that he have "one big happy family" in his agency. He stressed in many subtle ways the importance of the various underwriters "getting along well with each other." His agency, in fact, resembled a social club more than a business office. At the same time, the manager wondered why it was that the production of his agency had been on a plateau for so long. This manager demanded conformity to norms of social behavior at the expense of stimulating a desire among his life underwriters to try out new ideas, explore new markets, and reach new records of production. We see again the importance of an individual's understanding his own behavior as well as that of others, if he is to maximize his influence on them.

Causes loss of ideas. We are in danger of losing ideas because of the pressures to conform. The classical story of the persecution of Galileo illustrates this point. Galileo, only a little over 300 years ago, dared to question some of the assumptions and the logic of his time which had been formulated by Aristotle and which had remained relatively unchanged for centuries. But Galileo was a pioneer—he dared to question existing authority. Galileo felt that even though particular "facts" had been handed down from generation to generation as being the truth, and were assumed by all to be correct, they could still be questioned. Furthermore, he felt that they should be investigated by systematic and controlled observation. For example, he challenged existing belief by stating that the earth was not the center of the universe, and that the earth itself moved. These ideas were so upsetting that church officials forced him to swear publicly that he had made a mistake. Because of the pressure of conformity, one of the greatest thinkers of all times was confined to his home and discouraged from any further deviance in thinking.

We can also see the effects of conformity on the members of a top management group in a company. Because an executive wants very much to be promoted, he may well decide to take the "safe and sure route" and plan his work so that he avoids "mistakes" rather than plan to maximize his creative contribution to the business. The cost of ideas which may be lost because the president or board of directors will not tolerate mistakes or "deviant" thinking must be enormous. In our public schools, the "good" or "well-adjusted" child is often the one who follows directions and who avoids asking strange or unusual questions. The bright or creative child is often punished because he misbehaves by wanting to try new things or read new and different books. This may be the kind of influence which discourages a bright child from using more of his natural creative ability. What countless ideas or inventions must have been lost because of this early pressure on an impressionable mind to conform rather than to create!

How conformity works

Conformity reduces variation. The pressure of conformity tends to reduce the variation in behavior of individuals in that group. When individuals are apart from a group, they will give more diverse opinions and judgments than when they are with the group. The effect of the group is to exert a restraining or a conservative force on the behavior of members of that group. It is often observed in business management that when a company is managed by committee rather than by individuals, the company tends to be more conservative and more cautious in its policies.

Conformity reduces extremes. The pressure of conformity tends to eliminate extreme variation. As the individual behaves in a way that is further and further away from the group norm, the pressure for him to return to the group increases. Minor deviations from the group pattern can be tolerated, but as the deviations become more extreme the group will take action and may even take the life of the deviant. The degree to which the group will permit nonconformity depends on the kind of social situation in question, the status or standing of the individual in the group, and the actual behavior involved. College students are often permitted to perpetrate minor crimes against other individuals or groups which would be severely censored or punished if these things were done away from the university. The rash of panty raids is an example of such "permitted" behavior.

Influence of the group. The size of the group of which one is a member has a bearing on the force of conformity which is applied to him. The larger the group, the more deviant the behavior can be and still remain accepted by the group. In a small town, for example, there is usually far less variation or deviation from the group pattern than would be found in a large metropolitan center. A Greenwich Village can exist in New York City, but would not be tolerated in a small town.

The pressure of conformity on the individual, of course, is related to the degree of attachment that the individual has for the group. When the attachment is loose, the pressure of conformity may produce some overt changes in behavior, but less change or even no change in inner convictions. When the individual greatly values his membership in the group and is afraid of being ostracized, the group is likely to have a more permanent effect on the individual's inner convictions. Personal convictions which are influenced or changed by the pressure of such a valued group are likely to remain changed. Conformity and behavior which is enforced by a larger group or a group less important to the individual is very likely to lose its hold once the influence of the group is removed.

New agencies of conformity. While the family is probably the most important pressure-enforcing conformity in the individual's early life, it does not retain this power to influence behavior in general. In earlier phases of our developing American culture, the family and the community and also the church were the main agencies of social control. At the present time, however, these have been replaced by new agencies of conformity or social control, such as business and governmental groups. While it is less true in smaller communities, a man's economic group probably exerts greater pressure on him than does his family or his church. If a business has a closed-shop agreement, a man cannot even get a job unless he agrees to join the union. The union may even exert pressure on the individual member to support certain political candidates. At the management level, executives often find that their business exerts a pressure of conformity which extends even to the choice of their marriage mates. An executive may understand, if he has not been directly told, that if he expects to rise very high in management, he must be sure that he marries "right."

Creativity

The life underwriter is in a character-building profession. He is in a profession where he can influence other people toward a more mature attitude regarding their family and also their community. *It is likely that the underwriter who is mature, flexible, and creative can do a much better job of rendering a professional service to his clients than the underwriter who is afraid, rigid, overconforming, and uninspiring.* The underwriter who is prepared to understand and accept the individuality of his prospect and his insurance needs, and who has the courage to consider new and different ways of providing proper insurance coverage is likely to provide a more genuine professional service to his prospect than the underwriter who mechanically sells a package plan. It seems important that the life underwriter learn how to use more of his creative ability. It seems important that the life underwriter learn not to conform to tradition slavishly, but *to conform intelligently* and *to deviate from conformity intelligently* when it is appropriate.

Creativity has much to do with persuasion. In any effort to negotiate or to reach an agreement with an individual, failure is most often caused by rigidity on the part of one or both individuals involved. The more flexible and creative the underwriter can become, the more effective as a persuader of other people he may become. The underwriter who adopts one sales talk and sells one form of insurance may achieve a high degree of success because he works hard at this method. But what about the literally hundreds of prospects that he fails to sell? Is it not possible that using a more flexible, a more creative approach will allow him to do an even better job?

The nature of creativity. Creativity is the capacity to innovate, invent, or place elements together in new ways.[8] Some individuals appear to be more creative than others. But all of us possess a certain degree of creativity and all of us have the ability to make better use of the creative capacity that we possess. *Creativity is probably not so much an inherited trait as a product of life experiences.* The creative or deviant person has been a subject of great interest throughout the ages. It is the creative individuals who are frequently discredited by their contemporary groups, but who provide us with the significant advances in our technology and in our social institutions. What is it that gives rise to creativity? What stimulates creativity?

There are at least two basic theories as to the nature of creativity and why it emerges. The two theories seem to be rather directly opposed to each other. One theory of creativity is that it emerges only when a person has solved his basic problem of biological survival and security in his social group. It is supposed that only when

[8] A collection of papers on creativity is found in H. H. Anderson, *Creativity and Its Cultivation* (New York: Harper & Row, Publishers, 1959).

the individual has achieved security, that is, when he is fed, clothed, safe from harm, and loved by others can he be free to innovate and create.

A second major theory regarding the emergence of creativity is that it is itself a response to major dissatisfaction in important desires. In support of this theory it has been suggested that the world's greatest creative leaders come from very unhappy or unsatisfactory environmental conditions. Highly creative people often come from broken homes. Furthermore, it can be seen that in the history of creative people, there has been perhaps more than the usual amount of freedom in their early lives. This may have come from the loss of their parents when they were young or perhaps because of a real absence of parental coercion. When the child does not have firm direction from adults, it apparently becomes more necessary for him to create and invent his own solutions to problems.

The importance of creativity. Why is it important for the life underwriter to know something about the creative process? At the present time in our culture we are faced with widespread, deep, and rapid changes in our society and changes in our ability to control our environment. This is a time of change. It is a time when we can rely less and less on tradition and on precedent. The life underwriter is associated with a field of activity which is itself deeply concerned with change. Perhaps no other industry has been quite so much interested as the life insurance industry in examining itself and finding ways of changing and improving the nature of its service to its clients.

An understanding of the creative process is important because of the assistance which it can give us in handling difficult problems associated with this kind of change. Insight into the process of invention or innovation can increase the effectiveness of the adult intelligence. It is important that the life underwriter examine himself to see how his own possible fear of change or fear of deviating from the group may be keeping him from achieving real and genuine creativity or self-realization. The strength of our nation has come largely from the pioneering or inventive nature of its people. The decay of our nation, according to some contemporary writers, may very well follow from men's reluctance to continue these pioneering, creative efforts.

The growth of creativity. In scientific studies which have been made on the stimulation of creativity, it has been found that creativity emerges in a situation of informality and in an atmosphere of acceptance and freedom rather than in an atmosphere of criticism and rejection. Some of the characteristics that seem to be highly related to the growth of creativity are a basic personal security, intelligence, flexibility, spontaneity, humor, originality, ability to perceive a variety of essential features of an object or situation, playfulness, radicalness, and eccentricity. Some traits or characteristics which appear to be opposed to the development of creativity are thoroughness, excessive concern with neatness, personal rigidity, too much control, reason, logic, respect for tradition and authority.

It has been suggested that creativity is a process of (1) *preparation,* (2) *incubation,* (3) *illumination* and (4) *verification.*[9] Certainly before creative work can be done, much preparation must precede it. No painter ever painted a masterpiece without years of hard work and preparation. No inventor ever created a new device without much basic preparation in his field. In the same way, the life underwriter cannot expect to be creative in business without *thorough preparation* and a sound background of knowledge in life insurance.

Creative individuals report that when they are trying to solve a problem or create something new, there is often a period of time in which they feel somewhat confused, indecisive, or at least in a state of suspended decision-making. There seems to be a need to "lose themselves" or somehow relax and not try too hard to drive towards a solution. The word *incubation* fits this state of mind. It is a time when the individual is able to be very free in his thinking and free of restrictions and criticisms from other individuals.

The third step in the creative process, *illumination,* is illustrated by the fact that we often grasp the solution to problems or think of an idea quite spontaneously. We "see the light." Haven't we all had the experience of waking up in the middle of the night with the solution to a problem on which we had been reflecting without success? The more spontaneous an individual is in his behavior and thinking, the more likely it is that he can *allow his unconscious*

---

[9] Wallas, G., *The Art of Thought* (New York: Harcourt, Brace & World, Inc., 1926).

thought processes to work for him and to help him achieve creative effort. Creativity through a process of deliberate, conscious, calculated effort seems rarely to occur. The well-ordered, plodding individual who follows established routine may achieve fair success in life and may avoid mistakes, but he may also avoid the discovery of new solutions.

The last step in the creative process, *verification*, is the step which permits constructive creative gain, rather than simply a hair-brained notion. The new idea, once created, needs to be tested or subjected to systematic observation (as through the scientific method) in order to make sure that it is a true advance over tradition rather than sheer rebellion against existing authority.

The right atmosphere. The general agent or manager can help his underwriters become better and more creative problem solvers if he will listen to their ideas objectively and with understanding, help them find workable ways of putting the ideas into action, and do this with an absence of petty criticism or ridicule. To establish an atmosphere which helps his agents grow in their creative ability *the manager or general agent must himself be in the process of growing and developing creatively.* New ideas in prospecting or in solving the insurance needs of the prospect are more likely to come from those agencies headed by a man who is strong enough to try new ideas without being afraid that he will "look silly" if they don't happen to work out. The manager who follows the rules to the letter and operates his agency in the same way that it has been operated in the last twenty years may not be able to recognize a genuine advance in thinking when it does occur.

Behave yourself or be yourself? From the earliest time that each of us can remember, we have been told to behave ourselves. Our parents told us that when we were little and our bosses (and even our wives) tell us this now. "Behave yourself." What this usually means is that you must stop what you are doing and do what they want you to do. Of course, it is necessary that we behave ourselves, for conformity to standards prevents chaos and inefficiency. But nonconformity can also be quite important! In addition to behaving ourselves, we can probably accomplish far more in our lives if we will only *be ourselves*. Being yourself means realizing more and more of your potential as a human being. In each of us there is a good deal of falseness or artificiality in our behavior, not solely because it is demanded of us by group pressures to conform, but because we are in one way or another afraid, insecure, or lacking in self-confidence.

We are often aware of when we are being artificial and when we are being genuine in our behavior. But by a curious maneuver, we repress recognition of much of our false behavior, or if we do happen to notice it, put it out of our minds immediately and try not to think about it. If the life underwriter pretends an interest in his client which he does not feel, the client is likely to realize this. The belief in life insurance as a product can also be pretended only with difficulty. In any individual's effort to be himself, to realize more of his potential, and to make better use of the creative ability which he has, it is important that he practice being honest with himself and with other individuals. It takes courage to be yourself, but the rewards for doing this are great.

Being human

Man seems to have a drive to improve himself, to get somewhere, to amount to something, and above all to become a person who knows who he is and how he fits into the larger scheme of life. We asked the question, "Who am I?" at the beginning of Chapter 1. This is a hard question to answer. But the fact that man asks himself this question and is concerned about the answer spells out for us the meaning of *being human*.[10]

Being human means painting a picture for no other reason than just to look at it. Being human means wondering why grass is green and why objects fall down rather than up. Being human means wanting to be with other human beings and at the same time wanting to be alone. Being human means experiencing a desperate urgency to understand others and to be understood in turn. But above all, being human means to want to transcend the limitations of time and space, to rise above the natural restrictions which keep

---

[10] The concept of growing and developing into a healthier and more productive person is discussed in a series of papers appearing in C. R. Rogers, *On Becoming a Person* (Boston: Houghton Mifflin Co., 1961).

all other animals at the mercy of their surroundings, to control our destiny rather than be controlled by it.

Man becomes human in the company of man. Man grows by helping man to grow. Man grows to the extent that he can visualize his potential. Man visualizes his potential to the extent that he can look at himself without flinching, can see what is there and can share his observations with his fellow man. Man has the choice of growing toward greater humanness or of ignoring his potentialities. Each of us has this choice to make!

PART TWO

MAN
IN COMMUNICATION

The life insurance interview is a conversation with a purpose. In this conversation at least two people are always involved. There are, then, at least two sources of confusion and misunderstanding which can operate to keep this conversation from achieving its purpose. These two people bring their own experiences, prejudices, blind spots, and conscious and unconscious reactions to the conversation, and distortion of communication is frequently the result. How does this happen? We often hear only what we want to hear. What we say may not be the same thing that the other person hears. The same word can mean different things to each of us. The meaning of words is like shifting sand, and can be every bit as treacherous.

Words have tremendous power. Words permit us to pass on knowledge from one generation to another. Words make it possible for men to work together cooperatively and to accomplish much more than they could individually. Words help us become civilized. But words also lead marriages to the divorce court and nations to war. We tend to be prisoners of words.

Listening is a skill and a very active process. There are many reasons why we may be poor listeners, but for effective communication it is essential that at least one party to a conversation be a good listener. The scientist does not "listen" only to the data which he wants to hear; he is interested in ascertaining the whole truth. The good listener must adopt this same attitude. The life underwriter normally will present his sales talk to prospects who may be very poor listeners. This obstacle to the sale is greater if the underwriter himself also happens to be a poor listener. In a conversation involving two poor listeners, we can expect very little behavior change to occur.

How can we communicate more accurately? How can we move people with words? How do words affect our own values and the way we think? How can we become more

effective listeners? The discussion in this section will help
the reader not only find answers to these questions, but
will provide him with the tools necessary to become more
effective in fighting the battle against confusion which
is involved in all communication between men.

3

Communication:
Talking and Listening

Man is a social animal. He lives and works in groups. As we have seen, he learns from groups and he achieves his greatest efforts through group activity. Mankind has achieved great things in overcoming the natural limitations of his environment. Through the centuries, he has provided efficient shelters from the elements and has found weapons against disease so as to prolong his life span. He has found ways to overcome gravity and has perfected efficient ways of providing himself with adequate food. Mankind has done these things not merely because he has formed himself into groups. Other species of animal life such as apes have also formed themselves into groups, even a kind of community life. We cannot even say that man is unique among animals in his ability to communicate with one another, because lower forms of animal life are also able to do this. Mankind has achieved his unique position among animals because of his unique ability to use a *language*. Man's supremacy stems from his ability and desire to formulate a system of abstractions and symbols, called language, that stands for the world of reality.

The Role of Language

Language is distinctly human

There is nothing more human than the speech of an individual or of a group of individuals. In studying different ape societies (apes and chimpanzees being among the closest to man in intelligence), it has been found that different vocal sounds apparently have separate and distinct meanings for the individual animals, and this forms a kind of communication. Lower forms of animals apparently do have an ability to communicate some kinds of meaning through their natural sounds and bodily movements. But man is the only animal that can communicate abstract ideas and that can transmit them from one generation to another in order to avoid costly trial and error and advance what we know as civilization. Lower forms of animals are bound by time, that is, there can be no communication about things that happened in the past or will happen in the future. Man, of course, is able to do this. Lower forms of animals can communicate only about things or objects that actually exist. Only the human animal can communicate about abstract ideas and concepts which may not exist in fact or reality. The uniqueness that man enjoys in the use of language is not because other animals are incapable of forming the basic speech sounds. Other animals and even birds such as the parakeet are able to make individual sounds which closely resemble words. But man's unique language ability stems rather from his innate or inborn capacity to use symbols to represent things and to use his imagination to find meaning in these symbols.

Language is the cement that binds people together. Language is what makes us human. It permits us to form societies and allows us to learn from the mistakes and successes of others. Language is one kind of cultural behavior and one which is learned. Language is, in fact, the reason that cultures or societies continue to exist at all.

Symbolism and imagination

A symbol is something that stands for or represents another thing. For example, the cross is the symbol for Christianity. Words are symbols which stand for objects, qualities, or ideas. Man's ability to use symbols allows him to form *bridges of understanding* between his fellow creatures of the same generation and from one generation to another. But the use (or misuse) of these very symbols can become insurmountable barriers between men. Many of mankind's problems have to do with the fact that we don't all "speak the same language" either in a literal sense or in the colloquial sense. It is within our power to determine whether the language we use becomes a bridge allowing us to transcend frustrating conditions or becomes a barrier to our own growth and development as individuals and as a society.

Language is not the only form of symbolic expression that man uses, but it is the most important form. Without speech there would be no human social organization. Without language, we would have no laws, no rules of behavior, no science, literature, music or religion. It is the continued use of this ability that makes it possible to perpetuate our culture. Without the use of symbols, there would be no culture, and man would not be much different from other animals.

Just as symbolic behavior which we call language has made mankind "human," so each individual, as an infant, becomes human only as he learns to make use of symbols or language. Until the infant learns to use speech, his behavior cannot be distinguished qualitatively from that of an ape or baby chimpanzee. As we have seen, the family is the chief teacher of culture to the child. The child learns about his culture through the use of language as a means of communication.

Man's unique ability to make use of symbols in his efforts to communicate gives him an advantage of incalculable value over all other animals, but this same advantage can become a tremendous disadvantage because of the very nature of symbolic expression. A symbol represents or stands for an actual object or an idea. Note that we say the symbol *stands for* the other thing; it is not the other thing itself. As we say the word "chair," the listener will invariably form a mental picture of some kind of chair, possibly the one he is sitting in. The word "chair" is a symbol which stands for the real object.

Through the use of language it is possible to transmit images from one mind to another in somewhat the same way that television pictures are transmitted. As we walk into an appliance store and look at the array of television sets for sale, we may perhaps see a dozen sets all tuned to the same station and all receiving apparently the same image at the same time. The transmission of images from the television station to the set is accomplished with a minimum of distortion. When one speaker talks to an audience of a dozen people, however, all of these people do not receive the same mental images as a result of the transmission of symbols from the speaker to the audience. Instead, these twelve individuals will quite likely receive twelve different images. If the speaker mentions the word "chair," one listener may picture a soft, comfortable, overstuffed, well-worn leather chair in his den, another may think of the device used for electrocution, while still a third may immediately think of a position at a university.

Man's ability to use symbols to represent things can be a source of great understanding, but also a source of immense and sometimes tragic misunderstanding. *In communication between individuals, one of the few things that we can be absolutely sure of is that the receiver will never get exactly the same message that the speaker is attempting to send.* There is no way that we can communicate with another person with complete accuracy. There will always be a certain amount of distortion in the message picked up by the listener or receiver. Different individuals give different meanings to the same symbol and this fact is of vital significance to the life underwriter who makes his living by motivating men's behavior through the use of symbols.

Learning the language of symbols

Just as our culture teaches us how to behave, so our culture teaches us the use of symbolic communications, or language. The child learns to speak by imitating his parents. Learning to talk is primarily a matter of trial and error with many repetitions being necessary before a recognizable speech emerges. The child who is born deaf learns to talk only through an extremely difficult process. Because he cannot hear the sounds, he cannot use imitation as a method of learning. Thus, the child who learns to talk without a sense of hearing never completely escapes a harsh, unnatural tone of voice.

When we learn to bat a ball or shoot targets or reach for things and grasp them, we are depending upon an elaborate *system of feed-back of information*. As we reach for a pencil on the desk, a whole network of muscles and nerve impulses are called into play. If our hand overshoots the target, we automatically compensate for this and adjust our muscle effort so that our hand does grasp the pencil. We do this easily and smoothly when we have a constant and reliable source of feed-back information. If we close our eyes and reach for the same pencil, we see that we engage in a good bit of groping and poorly coordinated movements directed towards the goal. Even though our eyes are covered, we still have a source of feed-back information in our sense of touch and also in the muscle sense which is called kinesthetics. As soon as we touch the pencil, we know that we can grasp our fingers around it and move it.[1]

In the same way, in learning to speak, we need the information which comes to us from our feed-back mechanism. Feed-back is important not only in learning a language, but in continuing to speak normally as well. The child tries first one pronunciation and then another until he sees that he is rewarded by his parents. He has then learned a new word. With adults, unless we have a steady feed-back of information about the sounds that we utter, our speech patterns are likely to become distorted and virtually unrecognizable. We hear ourselves speak when we are talking to someone else.

[1] Cybernetics is a science which includes the study of feed-back mechanisms and their operation in the machine and in man. Further theoretical background and some practical applications may be found in the following texts: Norbert Wiener, *The Human Use of Human Beings: Cybernetics and Society* (Garden City, New York: Doubleday & Co., Inc., 1954); F. H. George, *Automation, Cybernetics and Society* (Piqua, Ohio: Leonard V. Hill, 1959); and G. T. Guilbaud, *What Is Cybernetics?* (New York: Criterion Books, Inc., 1959).

If there is some interference with our ability to hear a feed-back of our speech, that is, through outside noise, earplugs, etc., our pattern of speech immediately takes on a different quality. Our voice may become higher-pitched, we may speak with greater volume, and we may do a good bit of slurring and mispronouncing of words.

In one scientific study on the effect of this kind of feed-back information on the quality of speech, the subjects were asked to speak into a microphone which was plugged into a tape recorder. As the speech was recorded on the tape, the message was immediately played back to the subject through the earphones that the subject was wearing. The pickup head of the tape recorder was arranged so that it could be adjusted along the length of tape as it passed through the recorder. In effect, this allowed the experimenter to delay the return of the speaker's voice to the speaker's ears. When the subject spoke, and he heard the sound of his own voice delayed for just a tiny fraction of a second, this delay in voice feed-back was enough to cause a complete breakdown in his ability to speak at all. At first, the subject reacted by gradually slowing his rate of speech. Then, he either stopped completely or continued to verbalize a single word by stretching it out so that it became a wail or almost a scream. This study had to be done with care because of the very upsetting psychological conditions which it presented to the subject. Many of the subjects became extremely disturbed and remained so for some time after taking off the earphones.

We have illustrated the importance of a feed-back mechanism in terms of the actual presence of sound which comes back to the speaker. This we might call *phonetic feedback*. But another kind of feedback is important in learning a language, and that is *semantic* feedback. We learn to use our language by speaking it and then by seeing the effects of our speech on other people. If we cannot see how other people react, or if we are too insensitive to notice how they react, distortions may occur in our ability to communicate which are just as severe and dramatic as those discussed in the above paragraph. Learning a language is much more than memorizing the dictionary definitions of words. As we shall see in a later section, words mean much more than the simple explanations which are in the dictionary. The life underwriter may feel that he has already learned to speak, and to use his native language. But learning to speak and communicate with others is a skill which must be learned and relearned and refined on a daily basis if we are to eliminate sources of error in communication and become more effective in motivating others.

Learning the language of movements

The infant expresses its feelings by sucking, biting, licking, spitting, wetting, etc. Many of these movements which are so eloquently expressive are retained by adults as a kind of *silent language*. Certainly the adult expresses extreme disgust by spitting. Even the very basic movements of breathing are expressive in nature. Breathing in tends to be associated with the acceptance of a thing, while breathing out is a rejection of it. When we are delighted with something going on, we frequently gasp and draw in breath. But when we are disgusted or angry, we are very likely to snort or expel air violently.

The clenched fist suggests anger. The open palm expresses acceptance or nonviolence. We express a positive and usually warm attitude towards another person when we extend our open hand for the conventional handshake. The thumb turned up or down meant the difference between life or death to the gladiators of ancient times. Depending on which finger of the hand it is, a single raised finger can mean either an admonition, a command, or extreme aggression and rejection. An understanding of this silent language is important to the life underwriter because these movements can drastically alter the meaning of the spoken word. A slight smile, a wink of the eye or even a slight clearing of the throat can suddenly change the entire meaning of our communications.

The eye, "the window of the soul," sometimes shouts very loudly during the insurance sales situation. While it is not true that a shifty-eyed person is necessarily a criminal, many people in our society feel that something is wrong with a person who cannot or will not "look me in the eye." We are often uncomfortable when talking to another person if that person has on dark glasses which hide the movement and the expression of his eyes. Once again, *a source of feed-back information is denied us,* and we are uneasy because of it.

The life underwriter, in doing his work, establishes a contact with his prospect. This contact is primarily verbal, but it almost surely includes some physical contact and a good deal of eye contact. Without being entirely sure of the reason, most of us realize that we can sense coldness or warmth in another individual because of his eyes. There is probably that moment in every successful life insurance sale when a rapport, or a feeling of understanding, develops between the prospect and the life underwriter. There is a "twinkle in the eye" which occurs when two men understand each other. It is most difficult to have this twinkle in our eye if we do not feel it emotionally. We cannot achieve this twinkle in the eye if we are hiding or being defensive or trying to evade answering a question that someone has put to us. *This eye-to-eye, man-to-man, very personal contact that the life underwriter establishes with his prospect undoubtedly has as much, if not more, to do with the successful outcome of the sale than anything else which takes place.* The life underwriter who pretends to smile and understand something that the prospect has said, even though he does not understand it, is very likely to betray himself and to communicate a kind of deceit to his prospect.

Movements and gestures and facial expressions are undoubtedly the oldest and most basic means of communicating ideas and feelings. We can do much to control what we say. We may simply remain silent, although this very silence can be expressive. But telltale bodily movements are often much more difficult to conceal or camouflage. Despite the popular advertisements concerning the extreme pleasure to be gained in taste and smell from cigarettes, it is all too true that cigarettes represent a psychological crutch for many people. At moments of stress, a man reaches for his package of cigarettes. Much of the manipulation of the cigarette package, the matches, the lighter, etc., is an attempt on our part to conceal nervousness and anxiety from other people and even from ourselves. If we can be very busy doing something that is culturally acceptable, we may be able to hide a slight tremor of our hand or a tense position of our body. Extreme surprise or alarm is sometimes dramatically revealed by an actor on the stage by the dropping of a dish or by some physically clumsy act. In everyday behavior, we communicate much by the shuffling of our feet, by dropping things, or by gripping something until our hands appear white.

We learn this language of bodily movements through experience. This language is heavily colored by the culture in which we live, by the subcultures in which we live, and by the many hundreds of personal experiences that each of us has had in growing up. The life underwriter who is *more aware* of the variety of human behavior and the influence of different cultures and subcultures will be in a much better position to *"read" the silent language* that his prospect is using in communicating with him.[2]

The Process of Communication

The extent of communication

In every day of our lives we are communicating with someone or with some thing. We ordinarily think of communication as being limited to the passing of an idea from one person to another through some form of language, but man communicates in many ways. Communication is involved in almost all of our experiences. When you wake in the morning, it is usually because of the alarm clock which has communicated with you that it is time to get up. The sound of rain on the window is a communication from the elements to you which may mean that moving about during the day will be difficult, or that the golf game is cancelled, or that the newly spread grass seed is washing away and another few hours of work will be needed in the yard. Your reaction to the communication of the rain may be to get up feeling in a bad mood or to roll over in bed and go back to sleep.

Later, communication over the breakfast table, for instance, may likewise have much to do with the success or failure of the day. While you are trying to wake up with your first cup of coffee, your

2 For further study, see Edward T. Hall, *The Silent Language* (Garden City, New York: Doubleday & Co., Inc., 1959).

wife may communicate to you that the gas tank in the car is nearly empty as a result of her shopping trip and you had better get it filled up before starting out for work. If this communication is incomplete—if you do not hear it or remember it—the price for this error in communication may be many wasted minutes as well as frayed tempers later on.

Driving the car to work illustrates another kind of communication. We use our muscles to turn the steering wheel and keep the car going in a straight line. But the steering wheel communicates back to us through our muscles. We keep the automobile in position on the highway not so much because of our visual perception of the car in relation to the center line, but as a result of our muscle sense and what it tells us. As mentioned earlier, this receiving of sensations from the activity of our muscles is known as *kinesthesis*.

As you drive toward the office and approach an intersection with a traffic light, there is again communication from a machine to you. If the light is green as you approach the intersection, but you notice that it suddenly turns to yellow, this communication may be interpreted by you as meaning that you should speed up and beat the red light. The driver coming on the cross street who also sees the yellow light may receive the communication that the green light is about to go on for him and may decide to get a "jack rabbit" start through the intersection. The effect of this kind of communication from a machine to man can result in anything from inconvenience to death. Yes, communication is all around us.

The life insurance sale is a study in communication. The life underwriter has a story he wishes to communicate to his prospect in order to effect a change of behavior in that prospect. As any impartial observer will notice, what the life underwriter *says* is not always what the prospect *hears*. Communication is a complex business. The life underwriter who has a sound knowledge of communication, its laws and its mysteries, will surely be in a better position to influence and control the behavior of those with whom he comes in contact.

The vital importance of communication can be appreciated from the following incident which took place during the Korean skirmish. An isolated United States military unit was being pinned down by enemy fire. Forward United States observers reported the enemy position to United States artillery which commenced firing. Because of a misunderstanding of the observers' information, the United States artillery fell short of its mark by 300 yards. The United States artillery wiped out one of its own company of men with the exception of three survivors. Fortunately for most of us, errors in communication have consequences which are less drastic than this. We must understand people and how they use language if we are to understand what they mean when they talk. Unless we understand the person to whom we may be communicating, we will fail in our attempt to send a message to him that he can understand.

The elements of communication

Communication is the passing of information from one place to another. Communication must involve: (1) a sender of information, (2) the information or the message itself, and (3) the receiver of such information. Without all three of these elements, communication does not take place. If we attempt to speak to a deaf person, we may in fact send an intelligent message, but if it cannot be received, then we have not communicated. Errors and misunderstandings can occur in all three elements of communication. We communicate with other individuals because we expect to effect some change in their behavior. If we do not see the expected behavior change, we must carefully inspect each of the three elements of communication for sources of error.

For example, if the underwriter has made an appointment with a prospect through the prospect's secretary, and the prospect is not in at the appointed time, there are several questions which must be asked: Did the underwriter really say the date that he thought he did? Did the secretary write down the message and give it to the prospect? Did the prospect read the same message that his secretary wrote or did he misread the date? Did the prospect choose to ignore the message? Before the underwriter gets all upset on being "stood up," he should at least try to find out where the communication failed. The most common reaction, however, is to assume that our message did not get through only because the receiver or listener was at fault in not understanding the message or because he was willfully ignoring the communication.

Most of the material in Chapters 3 and 4 has to do with the role of these three elements in the success or failure of communication. The life underwriter spends much of his working day communicating with other people. It is vital that he understand not only the sources of error but also the steps by which he can improve the effectiveness of his communication. But not all of his efforts to communicate are with other people. The life underwriter also communicates with himself. This communication with himself is potentially the most disruptive because the sources of error and the effect on his own behavior are far less obvious than is the case when he communicates with another individual.

The forms of communication

We have seen that man communicates with machines and machines in turn communicate with man. The life underwriter is more concerned, however, with the problems involved in communication with other people. Communication between one person and another takes place on a *verbal* and a *nonverbal* level and on a *conscious* and an *unconscious* level. All four forms of communication are used by the life underwriter as he presents his proposal to a prospective client. The underwriter may be conscious that he is using words to sway the prospect to purchase life insurance. He may be unaware of the fact that certain of his mannerisms are offending the prospect and making the sale less likely. It is possible that the unconscious, nonverbal (nonlanguage) communication from the underwriter to the prospect is more powerful and a greater motivator of human behavior than the conscious, verbal communication.

Verbal communication. Within the first year of life, the infant may begin making sounds which are words or which sound like words standing for the things that the infant wants or needs. The beginning of verbal language is a matter of trial-and-error learning. The child makes a sound when it wants its milk and may or may not be understood. The closer the child gets to the sound of the word "milk" the faster it is probably delivered to him. The child soon learns to associate certain sounds that he makes or that his parents make with an actual object of value. This is communication on a verbal level.

The enormity of the child's task in learning to speak his native language can be better understood if we imagine ourselves suddenly dropped into a foreign country with a language we had never heard before. We would go through a period of confusion and would undoubtedly try to use some kind of sign language to indicate to the native our various desires. The task is even greater for the child, because he must *also* grasp the complicated concept of language itself, that is, that sounds or words are symbols for things and ideas.

As the child learns his native language, he naturally makes many mistakes of interpretation. Even as adults, we use many words even though we may not be entirely sure of their specific meaning. The English language contains about one million words and most of us in our lifetime learn to use only a small fraction of this number. There is a close relationship between an individual's general level of intellectual capacity (IQ) and his ability to acquire and use a great many words. The learning of a language is a private affair. Each of us acquires the use of the hundreds of symbols that we call words because of the experiences that each of us has had with words and the things the words stand for. Because we learn words according to our own individual experiences, it is no wonder that each of us attaches slightly different meanings to the same word. Such individual interpretation of the common words that we use can become a formidable barrier to communication. This will be discussed at greater length in Chapter 4.

We will mention in passing one other tremendous obstacle to communication involved in the verbal transmission of ideas. The *words* that we learn to use for different experiences we have had or different objects *never completely describe the experiences or the objects for which they stand.* When we are concerned about what a word does stand for, we normally resort to the dictionary as the authority. But the meaning of a word or phrase is not only its dictionary equivalent but is also the effect its use has in any given situation. We have certain emotional reactions to words which are not included in its dictionary definition.[3]

Nonverbal communication. We have seen how the child learns to acquire human characteristics through his ability to learn and make use of verbal symbols or language. Communication on a nonverbal level is probably just as important, if not more so, in shaping the early behavior patterns of the child and the later experiences of the adult. Andrew Carnegie is reported to have said, "As I grow older, I pay less attention to what men say. I just watch what they do." One of our cliches expresses this same idea: Actions speak louder than words. Even silence is often more eloquent in meaning than words.

Referring to one's associate as "an old buzzard" will mean one thing when said with a smile and quite a different thing without the smile. As we talk we emphasize or modify the meaning of our words by our facial expressions, our bodily movements, gestures, pauses, inflections, and even significant omissions of certain words. Researchers in the field of nonverbal communication estimate that our *gesture language* may include around 700,000 distinct and different signals. Our largest dictionaries contain fewer words than this.[4]

Contained in every spoken word there is always nonverbal communication: the *pitch* and *timbre* of an individual's voice, the *speed* with which he speaks, the way he *pauses* between words. People who have made a study of speech patterns and habits find that they can tell much about an individual's emotions and thoughts simply from the sound of his voice. A person who is blind frequently compensates for this deficiency by becoming more keenly attuned to the voices of others and the emotional qualities that are revealed.

[3] Words, the meaning of words, and their impact on man is the subject of the science of general semantics. The following are references: Wendell Johnson, *People in Quandaries: The Semantics of Personal Adjustment* (New York: Harper & Row, Publishers, 1946); John Magee, *The General Semantics of Wall Street* (published by the author, 1958); S. I. Hayakawa, *Language in Action* (New York: Harcourt, Brace & World, Inc., 1941).

[4] The English language contains many words which are not found in the dictionary. Esoteric, technical terms used in various occupational and professional fields, colloquial expressions and many slang words may be in common use by various groups of people but will still not appear in a dictionary.

Just as we can "read between the lines," so can we hear between the words when we are spoken to. When we are attempting to communicate with a blind person, we often feel some uneasiness. Possibly this is because we realize that the blind individual can "hear" more as we talk than most people can.

When we talk, we use facial expressions, gestures, bodily movements, etc. to augment and supplement what we say with words. These bodily expressions are often used as a kind of camouflage to hide our true feelings or thoughts. We probably have all at one time or another said to someone that we are very glad to have met them even though we didn't mean this, and have attempted to prove our pleasure by smiling very broadly, and shaking his hand, making it a point to look very much pleased. A person who could not see this physical show of apparent interest might very well detect in our voice the actual distaste or disdain that we really feel.

Nonverbal communications, such as the way the life underwriter wears his clothes, the way his desk looks, and his personal mannerisms such as biting his fingernails or squinting his eyes, all undoubtedly affect the total message that his prospect receives. A man's clothes and the way he wears them literally "says something" to those who see him. His clothing tends to say, "Look at me. I'm successful," or it might say just the opposite. If, when a life underwriter is meeting with a prospective client in the former's office, the underwriter allows himself to be interrupted by phone calls, he will unwittingly communicate to his client that these interruptions are more important to him than the client is.

It is probable that the successful life underwriter does a better job of communicating with the prospect and understanding the prospect's communications on this nonverbal plane than does the unsuccessful underwriter. The successful life underwriter seems to "know" when the prospect is ready to buy. This same underwriter may find it impossible to explain to someone else just how he "knows" when this moment is at hand. It is likely, however, that this successful life underwriter is picking up from the behavior of his prospect faint clues which indicate the general mood and feeling that the prospect is experiencing.

The manager or general agent communicates a great deal to his leading life underwriter nonverbally when he gives him a private office. He communicates even more when he authorizes this agent to have a rug in his office. The underwriter who makes an evening call on a prospect in his living room, and who in an unguarded moment looks aghast at the dust and dirt that he observes in the room, might just as well pack his briefcase and leave. He has communicated something to his prospect on a nonverbal level that probably can never be corrected on a verbal level.

The physical distance that we maintain between ourselves and other people is a part of nonverbal communication. Generally speaking, we get close physically to those individuals whom we like and we maintain much more distance between ourselves and those we dislike. Let us assume that a life underwriter has decided to make a call at the home of a prospect. After he knocks on the door, the woman of the household may answer. If the underwriter happens to be standing very close to the door at this moment, the woman may very well feel threatened or disturbed, either consciously or unconsciously. If, as the door is opened, the underwriter will take a step backward as he is announcing his name, this may relieve any anxiety that the woman may feel. This, of course, would be especially true if the woman happened to be alone in the house at the time. In a standing conversation, the distance between the two people may either facilitate or disrupt communications. Perhaps all of us have had the experience of meeting someone for the first time and having them stand too close to us as they talked. If some· one does stand too close to us, according to our own frame of reference, we are likely to feel vaguely uncomfortable even though we may not realize exactly why.

Most salesmen are aware that the desk in a man's office is a very real psychological barrier as well as a physical barrier. The desk in the office is an important status symbol. It represents authority, position, accomplishment, prestige, protection, etc. Some salesmen attempt to seat themselves beside their prospect if at all possible. They feel that they can, somehow, get closer to the prospect emotionally as well as physically. This, however, can be interpreted by the prospect as an invasion of his own private space. As a result of this invasion, the prospect's defenses may be raised to the point that it is impossible for the underwriter to get through to him. It is likely, however, that if the prospect *invites* the salesman to sit behind the desk with him, he will probably be more receptive to what the salesman says than if he asks the salesman to sit across the desk and away from him.

We are all very well aware that we can mislead people and state an untruth through the use of our language. We can also be quite deceptive in our nonverbal communications. The man who walks by throwing out his chest and swaggering may be trying to convince other people that he is a very sophisticated and poised fellow, even though he may feel quite uncomfortable and inferior within himself. Just as we are often tripped up in our verbal lies, so can we be discovered in our nonverbal deceitfulness. Attempting to prevaricate in nonverbal communications may make our behavior so artificial that an observer may mutter to himself, "Boy, is he a phony!"

Some general agents and managers place great emphasis on hiring life underwriters who are dominant personalities. They feel that a man's natural dominance is an important factor in his ability to make a sale. Undoubtedly, there is much to this. It is likely that a dominant individual may control his prospect not so much by what he says as by the way he says it. The dominant life underwriter has usually had a lifetime of experience in compelling people to action. He usually feels strongly that the prospect will do as he says and will buy the life insurance. When we are in the presence of such a dominant personality, we very often unconsciously do without question whatever he wishes us to do. Of course, like anything else, if a dominant personality exaggerates his behavior and becomes instead a domineering person who attempts to bully those around him, he may find that he is antagonizing people so much that they will not follow his "command" to buy.

Conscious and unconscious communication. To further complicate the matter of communication, nonverbal expressions may be conscious or unconscious. The underwriter who is tense and ill-at-ease may appear on the surface to be poised and relaxed. The prospect, however, may very well detect this tension on the part of the underwriter and may himself become quite uneasy because of it. One of the completely fascinating things about the human being is that he may detect such unconscious signals on the part of someone else without even being conscious of it himself! In other words, two individuals can communicate with each other without either of them being aware that communication is taking place. It is probable that many life insurance sales are lost because the life underwriter unconsciously reacted to his prospect with hostility and the prospect was dimly aware that he didn't like the life underwriter and didn't feel complete confidence in him.

At this point, the life underwriter may very well ask, "If I don't know that I am creating a negative impression, how can I do anything about it?" The answer is not a simple one, but it can be said in general that the more an individual does to advance his own personal growth and development, to free himself from prejudice, stereotypes, false pride, etc., the more likely he is to be able to have a genuine *self-regard* and a genuine *regard for other people*. A genuine regard and respect for the prospect (even though he may be of a different religion or color) will be communicated just as readily as tension or hostility might be. The more the underwriter makes himself aware of the *possibilities* of conscious or unconscious communication, the more effective he can be in using techniques of communication to influence his prospect.

Words and Communication

The meaning of words

Words allow us to love and hate each other. Words allow us to build societies and to destroy each other's societies. Words can be "mightier than the sword." Words cause mental illness, and words help us become sane again. Word sounds are only vibrations in the air, but they make us think or behave in certain ways. Words mean something to us because we give them meaning.

"*Webster says.*" When we come across a word that we don't know the meaning of, we invariably turn to the dictionary to find its definition. Webster says that the word definition is "1. the act of defining, determining, distinguishing, or explaining. 2. A brief description of what a thing is. 3. An explanation or statement of what a word or phrase means or has meant. 4. A putting or being in clear, sharp outline." Referring to a dictionary gives us only the barest notion of the full meaning of a particular word. The meaning of a word or phrase is not solely its dictionary definition but is in addition the hidden or obvious reaction that its use brings about in any particular situation. We use words to interest people in what we are doing, to threaten them, to protest, and so forth. We know that very often the words that are used are less important than the fact that something has been said at all.

Words have a *denotation* and a *connotation*. The denotation of a word is that direct, explicit meaning or reference to an object, especially as it may appear in a dictionary definition. The connotation of a word is an idea which is *suggested* by or *associated* with a word or a phrase. We would define the word "mother" as meaning a female parent, but the connotation of the word "mother" is that of love, care, and tenderness.

When we use words to communicate, we usually do not stop to consider the various possible denotations and connotations which the words may have. The life underwriter may explain to a prospect and his wife that a certain settlement option should be chosen so that the wife have a monthly income rather than a lump sum at the death of the husband. The connotation that this may have for the wife of the prospect could be a feeling of being overcontrolled or restricted and lacking freedom in her ability to do any financial planning of her own. She may feel unfavorable toward the purchase of the policy and directly or indirectly block the sale. If the life underwriter is lucky enough to have the wife verbalize this connotation, then a possible objection to the sale may be averted. If, as is often the case, the prospect or his wife have private connotations which they do not reveal (possibly because they are not aware of them), the life underwriter may have inadvertently said something which will effectively block the sale and may be powerless to correct it. These nonverbalized objections are sometimes called "hidden objections." As we shall see in a later section, active and intelligent listening on the part of the life underwriter can help him discover many of the personal connotations which his prospects may have in response to the verbal communication between them.

Loaded words. A word can have the impact and shock of a rifle shot. Daily we read about people who are injured or perhaps killed by the handling of a gun that was thought not to be loaded. We often injure another person by the use of a certain word even though we might afterward say, "I didn't know it was loaded." Words can have what is called an *emotional loading*. This means that certain words carry with them an emotional response for the listener. The words female parent do not have nearly the emotional loading for us that the word mother has. A word acquires an emotional loading through association. If we use a word or hear a word used at a time when our emotions are aroused, the emotional tone of the situation can then become attached to the word itself. We react much differently to the sentence, "My boss and I had a misunderstanding and we both decided it would be better for me to move on," than we do to the phrase, "I got fired."[5]

Our language is full of euphemisms, which are words or phrases that are less expressive or direct and are considered less distasteful and offensive than other words. The life underwriter may find that he must refer to the husband's eventual demise by saying, "when he is no longer here," or "when he passes on," rather than saying, "when he is dead." There are advantages and disadvantages in the use of such "soft-pedaled" expressions. When the life underwriter really does want to "shake up" his prospect, it may be advisable to use the most pointed, most direct language possible concerning the prospect's eventual death or incapacity. The life underwriter, to make his point, may say to the prospect, "Without this additional coverage, it's possible that you may prevent your family from having all the things that you would like them to have," or he could say, "If you don't buy this coverage, you will cheat your family." The impact of the latter phraseology is much greater. The disadvantage of being indirect in what we say is that our real intent or meaning may be lost "in translation." Many a manager or general agent has failed completely to get his point across to an underwriter because he used such a roundabout or inaccurate way of expressing himself. Depending, of course, on the situation, it may simply be more effective for the general agent to pound his fist on the desk and say, "Get out of this office and go to work!" rather than to hint gently that the underwriter might do a better job if he were to make a few more calls each week.

[5] Stuart Chase has written an interesting book on the impact of words called *Power of Words* (New York: Harcourt, Brace & World, Inc., 1954).

We happen to live in a culture where it is not always acceptable to be completely accurate in our communications. One school of thought on how to get along with other people says that we must avoid at all costs being offensive or disturbing to the other person. We are taught that it is polite and even right to tell a "white lie" in order to spare someone's feelings. With this kind of cultural pressure affecting us all, is it any wonder that we have great difficulty in our simple efforts to communicate with each other?

Slippery words. The same words mean different things to different individuals and the same words can have different meanings at different times. The meaning of words can vary according to the group that we find ourselves in and according to the individual to whom we are speaking. On the back of a bakery truck, there is the slogan, "Good Pies Like Mother Used To Make." How does each of us interpret this slogan? It is likely that the mothers of some of us have made excellent pies while other mothers have made pies not fit for consumption. Because of our individual personal experience with pies made by mother, we are going to have individual and personal interpretations of this slogan. As a matter of fact, the word "good" which appears in that slogan is itself quite a slippery word. What does that word mean to each of us? If your boss tells you that you did a good job, he may mean that he has never seen a job done in quite as excellent a fashion as you have done it. On the other hand, you may feel that since he did not say that you did an *excellent* job, he is really not rating you very high.

Words like "good," "pretty," "valuable," and "intelligent" are words that are not only difficult to measure and define adequately, but that vary in meaning depending on our personal experiences, our level of education, and the way these words are placed in a sentence. When we speak, we can give different shades of meaning to a certain word by the way we say it, by our inflections, by a slightly lifted eyebrow, etc. When the word is written, the author cannot control the meaning of a word—he cannot use a tone of voice or a facial gesture to shade the meaning.

Some words which are especially slippery in meaning, in the sense that they can mean so many different things at different times for different people in different situations, are such words as "they," "we," and "that." As the life underwriter makes a statement about a certain insurance need of the prospect, the prospect may say, "I don't agree with that." It is very likely that the prospect will mean one thing when he refers to "that" while the life underwriter may interpret his statement as referring to something quite different. If the discussion continues long enough, this confusion may resolve itself. One or the other party in the conversation may suddenly get an insight and say, "Oh, I think you and I have been talking about two different things." What is just as likely, however, is that if there is a difference of meaning attached to the word "that," the discussion may not continue long enough for the uncertainty to be cleared up. It is imperative in any attempt to communicate that such vague words be pinned down to a more specific expression. We are fond of saying, "they tell me that . . ." when we are attempting to advance our own argument. The life underwriter may avoid some of this difficulty if he will only try to restate what he thinks the prospect is saying by using words that can be less easily misunderstood.

The word is not the thing. Many of the words that we use we have learned by hearing the word and seeing the object to which the word refers. When the infant first sees a chair, for example, it does not know what the object is or what it is for. It learns about the chair only by sitting on it, by falling off it, by bumping into it, by chewing on it, etc. As the infant experiences the chair and at the same time hears the word "chair" he acquires the ability to use the word "chair" as a symbol for the actual thing.

The word "chair" is not the actual object itself. The word is only a sign or symbol which stands for the object. This may seem obvious, but quite often we do confuse the word or label with the actual object. This simple confusion of words and objects causes a great deal of trouble in our attempts to communicate. We make this point about words and things for two reasons. One is that *no word ever completely describes or tells everything about the object to which it refers.* The language we use always contains a great amount of built-in inaccuracy. The second reason for emphasizing the nonidentity of words and objects is that, while we may all agree that certainly the word "chair" is not the actual chair itself, *there are many times when we act as if the word were the object.* Many individuals need only to hear the word "cancer" and they react with fear and apprehension. We react to the word as we might react to cancer itself. Too often, an individual avoids using the word "cancer" or even thinking about it, for fear that somehow talking about it might even make it happen. Because of this reaction towards the word, countless thousands of individuals avoid periodic physical examinations and even avoid consultation with a physician when some of the well-known danger signals make their appearance.

If this kind of thinking seems strange to you, just remember all the times that you have said, "I've had good luck so far—I'd better knock on wood." Well, consciously we might deny that we believe such a superstition to be true, but there is plenty of evidence to show us that unconsciously we react as if the superstition were true. Many a man hesitates to talk about the fact that his business is profitable for fear that something might happen to this profitability. Not only does this kind of false identification of the word with the object cause difficulty in communication, but it also causes great difficulty in our efforts to maintain a reasonable level of mental health. Many of the residents of mental hospitals are there precisely because they have confused various words with the objects and have had to avoid the words as well as the objects. We blush and are embarrassed at the mention of sexual objects and especially the four-letter sex terms in much the same way that we might if we were actually exposed to the objects or acts themselves.

We need to elaborate on the idea that a word or a phrase never completely describes the object or situation to which it refers. We can never say *all* that there is to say about an object such as a chair. This is probably because we can never know all that there is to know about any one object. Because we cannot completely describe reality with words, and because any attempt to do so is too time consuming, we take a short cut. We *abstract* what we think is probably the most important or prominent characteristic of an object or aspect of a situation and this is what we put into words. In other words, we are making only *partial statements* about any object or situation.

Words are abstractions. As abstractions words describe only parts of what it is we are talking about. Because there is almost always more that can be said about any given subject, experts working in

the field of *general semantics* suggest that we might remind ourselves of the incompleteness of our language by frequent use of the
words *et cetera*. If we say that the chair upon which we are sitting
is made of wood, is upholstered, is green, is made of oak, is comfortable, is handmade, we can indicate that more can be said by
simply adding the word et cetera, or etc. The real danger to good
communication comes when we use a certain word and then forget
that more could be said while assuming that we have, therefore,
said everything there is to say. If we say that a life underwriter is
not productive because he is "lazy" we are in trouble if we think
that we have completely described the situation. Much more can
and needs to be said in order to communicate fully about the
problem.

The frame of reference. Quite often in our attempts to communicate with other people, we jump to the conclusion that everyone else feels or thinks about a certain thing in the same way that
we do, i.e. we project our feeling into another person or situation.
When we attempt to motivate a person to do what we want him
to do, we normally use those devices which would be effective with
ourselves. If we expect to communicate effectively with another
individual, we must become aware of the probable meaning he
attaches to the words that either he uses or that we use. We must
recognize that *our tendency is to see the world in terms of our own
personal frame of reference.* Our view may or may not be in agreement with reality.

It is natural that the things that we see and the language we use
should reflect our own feelings and past experiences. The difficulty
comes instead from our failure to be aware that we are projecting.[6]
We would be more accurate in our attempts to communicate if we
would only add the words, "it seems to me" to various statements
that we make. This would serve to remind us that the language that
we use, while it has a clear meaning to us, may not be quite so
clear to our listener. When we make statements about other people,
quite often the statements reflect our own personal standards or
our own lack of understanding of the individual.

---

[6] For an example of projection, see Chapter 5, p. 192.

Improving communication with words

Using operational definitions. Words are slippery things in the sense that their meaning can change according to the person using the words, according to the time, the group, etc. The language that we use is exceedingly inexact. Not only are words quite inadequate to describe situations or to convey information accurately, but the way we use them contributes to this inexactness of language. Many words that we use to describe people are very general in nature, that is, they could apply to any one of a number of other people, but we often use them as if they were very specific and accurate descriptions of the particular individual we have in mind. When we use such terms as "lazy," "dominant," "money-motivated," to describe anyone else, we are in great danger of introducing gross errors in our communications. Because the word "lazy" is such a general term, the mental picture that it creates in one person's mind can be far different from the mental picture in someone else's mind. Using this kind of term blocks clear thinking about the individual. We may either consciously or unconsciously say to ourselves, "That guy is lazy, he was born lazy, and he's always going to be lazy." The term "lazy" has a ring of finality about it and implies that there is no necessity to think further about that individual.

To clarify our communication and also *to remove blocks in our own thinking* about that individual, we would be much better off to substitute for the overgeneralized term "lazy" an operational definition of the individual's behavior. We might say of this individual, instead, that "he doesn't work hard enough." This comes closer to describing his actual behavior, but in addition to that sets the stage for some kind of action which we might take or which that individual might take to overcome the problem. But we need to go still further. If we are going to attempt more accuracy in our communications, we must *refine our operational definition.* We might then say, "That individual, according to my standard, is not making as many calls as I think he should, is not starting his work day early enough, and is not using his spare time in the evenings or on weekends to get more work done." In defining the term "lazy" in terms of the actual operations or behavior involved, not only have we done a better job of describing the individual's behavior, but we also have listed some possible causes and solutions to the problem involved. We decrease our understanding of people when we use broad labels to describe them. We increase our understanding of people when we strive to formulate operational definitions of their behavior.

The general agent or manager who maintains that he looks for a "dominant" individual, without formulating in his own mind what a dominant individual does, is in danger of never finding such an individual and consequently of making poor selection decisions. First of all, no individual is dominant in all situations. The general agent would be more accurate in communications, not only with his assistant but also with himself, if he were to state that he was looking for a man who had demonstrated an ability to control or strongly influence the behavior of others under certain very specific conditions. Unless the general agent does this, he is in danger of never going beyond a rather hazy or vague notion in his own mind as to what a dominant individual is. He is likely to make the mistake of hiring an agent who is rebellious and who speaks up and talks back, but who is not competent in actually swaying people's behavior in a situation such as the sale of life insurance.

The term money-motivated is another such general, loose term which is often used but rarely understood. We cannot tell that a prospective underwriter is money-motivated simply by listening to the man's statement that he wants to make a large amount of money. There is really no way that we can measure his inner motives in this regard. But we can come close to measuring whether or not he has made money in the past or whether he has gone out of his way to make more than a usual amount of money in the past. The prospective underwriter's *statement* as to his drives is less significant than his *demonstrated behavior*.

Thus, we will do the best job of communicating if we describe the actual behavior in which an individual is engaging. As we use operational definitions of events rather than loose, vague labels, we will find that we are communicating with each other with much more precision, and there will be much less chance of being misunderstood.

Using plurals. To make further attempts at greater precision in our language, we would do well to use *plurals* in describing human behavior whenever it is appropriate. For example, if we wish to know why a person lost his last job, the questioning should be in terms of the *reasons* why rather than the *reason* why. When the underwriter is trying to understand why he did not make a sale, if he searches for the cause, he is likely to be quite rigid in his thinking. Not only are there likely to be several causes for each lost sale, but perhaps different causes each time that a sale is lost. Every situation is likely to involve a new set or a new combination of reasons. If we get into the habit of looking for *multiple determinants of behavior,* we are more likely to avoid being blinded by one too-general and ill-fitting label of behavior.

Using qualifying terms. We can make still further advances in precision in our conversation and our communication by the use of *qualifying terms.* Rather than saying to ourselves, "Mr. Jones is certainly no prospect for insurance," we might be more realistic and eventually more successful in changing Mr. Jones' behavior if we think this way: "Mr. Jones, today, in his office, at lunch time, just before leaving on his out-of-town trip, in the presence of his secretary, *etc.,* does not appear to be a good prospect for insurance." We must recognize that Mr. Jones today is not the same as Mr. Jones yesterday or Mr. Jones tomorrow. Mr. Jones in his office is not the same as Mr. Jones in his home. Here again we see that language and the way we use it can have a considerable effect on our ability to change or motivate the behavior of other people.

4

Blocks and Aids
to Communication

It is a rare individual who does not feel that people in general do not understand him. We frequently feel that we are not appreciated. We often feel that we haven't been able to get our point across to someone else. What employee has not felt at one time or another that his boss didn't understand him or appreciate his efforts? Haven't you often tried to tell someone else how you would like a job done only to find that they did almost the opposite because they didn't understand you? The boss doesn't understand why his secretary gets so upset when she has to stay after five o'clock to finish a letter. The secretary, on the other hand, has difficulty understanding why the letter cannot be put in the mail tomorrow just as well. All of us, perhaps every day, find that there are many times when we are not being understood.

Just how do we get our ideas across to other people? How can we make sure that other people know what we mean? How can we get the other fellow to accept our ideas? How can we persuade the other person to do what we think is best for him? Because we live in a society that is built and maintained through communication by means of a language, we are almost constantly sending and receiving communications. We have seen how the message that leaves the sender is *not necessarily* the same message picked up by the receiver. There will always be a certain amount of distortion in the message picked up by the receiver.

In Chapter 3 we referred to the three elements of communication. There are also three general sources of communication distortion. A message can go astray because of distortion introduced by the *sender* of the message, distortion occurring during the *transmission* of the message, and distortion occurring within the *receiver* of the message. These distortions can be physical (mumbled speech, noise on the line, a hearing loss) or psychological and semantic (wrong use of words, "blind spots," inattention, overgeneralized meanings attached to the words used, etc.). This chapter will examine some of the psychological and semantic blocks and aids to communication which can occur, not only in conversations between two or more people, but in the thousands of mental conversations we have with ourselves every day.

Why Messages Go Astray

Self-centeredness

One of the chief problems which prevents effective and accurate communication is that we are all essentially self-centered. We are the center of our own universe. Our behavior is based on the way that we perceive things and our perceptions are based, in turn, on our own individual past experiences. Our perceptions are really our own personalized interpretations of reality. No two of us see the same events in exactly the same way. It is quite amazing that people can communicate and cooperate with each other as well as they do in view of the fact that (1) each of us perceives the world in our own personal way, (2) we have our own personal meanings for those symbols which we call words, and (3) each of us has slightly different goals for which we are striving.

Most of us would like to be considered unselfish, as we usually mean that term. The most unselfish of us, however, cannot "get outside ourselves" or be independent from our own fundamental and very personal desires. It is likely that our most unselfish tasks are largely motivated by very personal satisfactions which we hope to obtain. Because there is this broad and often unrecognized tendency to be self-centered, *we can improve the effectiveness and accuracy of our communications to others if we will begin by making a greater effort to understand the other person.*

We have not really communicated a message to another person until that person receives the message and takes some kind of physical or mental action as a result of it. If the message is received in a distorted form, we, as the sender of that message, must be the first to take the responsibility for any distortion which occurs. We should be ready to say, "I don't believe I've made myself clear" and then try again to send a clearer message. A natural but self-centered tendency is to assert that our listener is simply a "dodo" if he has failed to get our message. We assume that because the words we use are perfectly clear to us they should be clear also to the listener, and if they are not, it is the listener's fault. This kind of thinking is simply further evidence of our self-centeredness.

This preoccupation with ourselves blocks communication in still another way. Much of the talk in which we engage is really talk about ourselves. We talk about *our* point of view on foreign affairs, *our* opinion as to how someone else should be doing his work, *our* interpretation of how a job should be done, etc. We reveal a great deal about ourselves as persons simply by talking, but this is likely to keep us from listening to others, thus causing a block in communication. There is the occasional individual who is afraid not only to reveal himself but afraid to get too close to other people. He may resort to one of the most effective ways known of blocking communication both ways: he may avoid saying anything of value and avoid listening, by simply talking, talking, and talking some more. Such individuals seem to follow the dictum that "the best defense is a good offense," for they produce a veritable barrage of words inundating all those around them and producing a kind of numbness which paralyzes exchange of information. Just as one can be the most lonely while in the midst of a huge crowd, so can we avoid saying anything by the simple technique of producing a great volume of prattle.

While some individuals seems to use this method of noncommunication almost exclusively, we would make a mistake if we thought that we ourselves did not occasionally engage in such a maneuver. We have all had the experience of steering a conversation away from a subject which would be bothersome to us by the simple expedient of talking rapidly about some other subject. The life underwriter does this very thing during an insurance sale situation in an unconscious attempt to prevent the prospect from saying no. It is, of course, a self-defeating mechanism because it also prevents the prospect from saying yes.

Constructing verbal walls not only protects the individual who is unwilling to communicate with others, but also camouflages the weakness of an individual who simply lacks knowledge. We are likely to get the longest and the wordiest explanations from people in those areas of knowledge where they are the weakest. The classroom instructor will take much longer to explain a concept that he doesn't understand than he will in dealing with a very familiar subject. Abraham Lincoln is reported to have said that if he had more time he would write a shorter letter. We can use our language to express ideas precisely and succinctly, or we can use words as a cover up for a lack of knowledge and an effective ban to mutual enlightenment.

Judging rather than listening

It is natural that much of our attention every day is centered upon ourselves. It is just as natural that we tend to *evaluate* and *judge* what other people say in terms of how their statement may affect us or in terms of our own personal opinion about the statement. While this is a natural tendency, it becomes, at the same time, one of the major blocks to communication between people.

If one of our friends happens to say to us, "Boy, I could really go for a steak smothered with mushrooms," we might say, "Ugh, I can't stand mushrooms!" When we say, "I can't stand mushrooms," we are really talking about ourselves and our preferences rather than listening to and trying to understand our friend. We judge what our friend has said, not from his point of view, but from our own. What he has said stimulates in us a desire to *talk* rather than a desire to *listen further* and communicate with him more clearly. As another example, if a prospect for life insurance says, "I think I need this insurance coverage but it costs too much," the life underwriter might say, "Oh, no it doesn't." Here the underwriter expressed his own personal evaluation of the prospect's statement instead of trying to find out more of what the prospect really meant. It is quite possible that the life underwriter could win this argument, but equally possible that no sale would be made. When we approve or disapprove of what another individual says, we tend to be not really listening to him but instead are thinking about ourselves. The speaker senses this, either consciously or unconsciously, and is likely to react with displeasure and certainly with a feeling that he is not really being listened to.

Perhaps there is little that we can do about our natural tendency to be concerned about ourselves, and to see the world in terms of our own frame of reference. But there is something that we can do to overcome the block in communication caused by our tendency to reply to statements by other individuals with immediate and obvious approval or disapproval. Carl R. Rogers, world famous because of his professional contributions to methods of psychotherapy, suggests that many misunderstandings can be eliminated in conversations by following a very simple rule. After someone makes a statement to us, *we must withhold our comments or our viewpoint until we have restated accurately the ideas and feelings expressed by the speaker in such a way that the speaker is satisfied with our summary of his message.* What this means is that before we present our point of view we must truly and genuinely understand the *frame of reference* of the speaker and understand his message from *his point of view.*

Interestingly enough, when we attempt to use this technique of communication, we find that the speaker is so impressed by our sincere efforts to understand him accurately that he takes great pains to be more accurate and to use less exaggeration in his statements. Once in a while the life underwriter may bump into a prospect who has had some previous unfavorable experience with the company he represents. The prospect may very well say, "I wouldn't buy insurance from your company if it were the last company on earth." The life underwriter could respond to this by saying, "You are all wrong about our company, it's one of the finest and largest in the country." This would be the underwriter's own personal evaluation of the prospect's statement. Or the salesman could say, "Boy, something has really made you bitter about our company. Would you mind telling me about it?" In this case, the underwriter is avoiding a personal judgment and is instead trying to understand the statement from the prospect's point of view. This simple intention to listen and understand, rather than judge, will not only aid communication between the prospect and the life underwriter, but will in all likelihood force the prospect to modify what he is saying until he may even reach the point of convincing himself that his objection is not well-founded. As we shall see later in the chapter, listening is not at all a passive process, but is instead an *active, conscious, deliberate,* and *intelligent* process of facilitating verbal communication.

One reason why a life underwriter might not be able to use this method of aiding communication is that he fears having his own beliefs and opinions changed. Really understanding another person's point of view carries with it the risk that we ourselves might be changed from our own viewpoint. Change is difficult to accept, and so perhaps many of us will continue to keep our own prejudices intact by turning a deaf ear to other people.

Confusing levels of abstraction

As we have said before, the words that we use do not accurately describe the objects to which they refer. A map of a region does not accurately describe that region, although it does describe certain salient features of it. Words are something like maps.[1] Just how correct and accurate a map is depends on the amount of detailed information supplied and the purpose for which the map is to be used. A flight map of a state looks quite different from a road map. Both are maps of the same territory, but they describe different aspects of that territory. When we drive from one city to the next, we use a road map of the state. But when we enter a large city we find our way about by using a street map of the city itself. The

[1] The comparison of words and maps was suggested by Alfred Korzybski, *Science and Sanity* (Lakeview, Illinois: Institute of General Semantics, 1948).

words that we use in daily conversation are symbolic maps of a territory. No matter how detailed a map may be, it still does not describe the territory with complete accuracy. In the same way, words do not describe an object or a person with complete accuracy.

If the map that we use conflicts in some way with the territory that is supposedly described, then the map must be considered in error and not the territory. In the same way, a word that we use to describe a person may be in conflict with the person as he actually is. Here again, we must consider that the word is in error and not the person about whom the word is used. Because a man is *called* a thief doesn't mean that he *is* a thief. This seems obvious, but we do often accept the word which describes a person as being more true than the person himself. We may believe that a person is incompetent because we use the word or label foreigner to describe him (if foreigner is associated with incompetence in our mind) without bothering to check whether or not actual incompetence exists. Whenever confusion results from an attempt to communicate, the confusion can almost always be resolved if both parties are wise enough and patient enough to test their respective maps or beliefs with objective reality. Prejudices, biases, and unrecognized cultural influences keep us from checking our perceptions with reality.

When we use a word or a series of words to describe an external reality, we are engaged in the process of abstracting. We do not describe everything there is to say about the situation, but instead pick out what to us seems most important. *There are different levels of abstraction,* however, and it is important to recognize the effect on the accuracy of communication of confusing one level of abstraction with another. If, for example, we were to attempt to describe where a person is at the present time, we could begin at a low level of abstraction by saying that he is seated at his desk at the east end of the room that he calls his office. We could become more abstract, that is, we could move up a scale of abstraction by saying that he is located in a suite of offices on the seventh floor of an office building. We continue on up the level of abstraction by stating that he is generally located on Peachtree Street in the city of Atlanta located in Fulton County, in the state of Georgia in the United States of America, on the continent of North America located in the Western Hemisphere, etc. With each separate level of abstraction, we are describing his relative position in more and more general terms.

Using higher-level abstractions permits us to make generalizations, to form principles and to see over-all relationships. The higher we go in our abstracting process, or the more general we become in our description of a situation or object, the less accurate or precise we shall be in describing any *particular* object, situation, or individual. We lose accuracy because we leave out details in our description. Each level of abstraction has its own proper use in communication. *The danger comes when we confuse one level of abstraction with another.* If we wanted to locate the person whose position we were just describing, it would not be enough to learn that he is a resident of Georgia. We would need to know much more detail down to and including the specific room number of his office.

As we describe an individual with certain words or abstractions, we must be careful that we are not misled into thinking that we have accurately described that specific individual when we use a high-level term. The high-level abstraction "southerner" is a useful term as a generalization, but it says very, very little about a specific Mr. John Doe who happens to reside in the South. The term "southerner" as a term is an excellent one to describe a person who lives in the South. We dare not go beyond this level of meaning as we listen to or use the term southerner without being in great danger of vague, inaccurate, and dangerous communication. *We are confusing levels of astraction,* or jumping to a false conclusion if we think to ourselves that the term southerner describes personality characteristics, attitudes, biases, etc., of all people who live in the South. We are all individuals!

High-level abstractions are created partly in an attempt to help us understand and predict the behavior of other people. For example, one life underwriter may conclude after several years of experience that when a prospect immediately asks what the cash value of his policy may be in twenty years, this indicates a selfish motive in buying a life insurance policy. He might also conclude that if the prospect carefully inquired about the benefits of the policy for his family in the event of his death, this indicated his love and concern for his family. These are high-level abstractions which the underwriter has formed in his own mind and which he feels help him solve particular sales problems as they may arise. While *such high-level abstractions,* or generalizations, may apply in a majority of cases, *they do not necessarily apply in each particular instance.* If the life underwriter blindly assumes that any generalization is always true, then he is very likely to misperceive reality, or in other words, to misunderstand his client.

The underwriter must be aware of this tendency among his prospects to confuse higher-order abstractions with lower-order abstractions. One prospective client may say to himself that when he has listened to one life insurance salesman, he has listened to them all. He may, in addition, feel that one insurance policy is about the same as another. Unless the underwriter is aware that his prospect is making this false generalization, he will not be in a position to do anything about it.

We all form higher-level abstractions about people in many ways. Regardless of our own background, we are likely to have rather definite pictures which come to mind when we use the terms "management," "labor," "Catholic," "Irishman," or "truckdriver." We form our own high-level abstractions in an effort to understand better the similarities and differences among people or groups. *If our high-level abstractions suggest various possibilities or approaches to solving a problem, then they are very useful. If, however, we think that we are describing accurately a particular unique individual, then we are in difficulty.*

The tragedy of confusing levels of abstraction in our daily life is almost too enormous to be described. What talents are being wasted when we refuse to hire a person just because they happen to be a woman or a Jew or a Negro or Baptist! Nations fail to understand each other in the same way. Wars, persecutions, lynchings, and elaborate programs of mass extermination occur simply because of confusion between levels of abstraction. The important conclusion to be drawn here is that whenever it is at all possible, we should look at the reality of a situation to see whether or not the *facts* are what the label or words imply. We must examine each individual situation to see how it is unique or different and avoid over-generalization just because we notice *some* similarities to other situations.

Does the label describe the contents?

It is against the law to put a label on a can of peas or a tube of ointment which does not describe accurately what is inside. Unfortunately, we have no such laws which apply to the labels we use to describe people. The general agent or manager who describes all his agents as "selfish, ungrateful men" will probably do a poor job of managing or supervising them because he is failing to notice those various *important individual differences which make each man what he is*. Things which appear to be the same are never really the same and the actual differences may be more important than is realized. The father coming home from a business trip with toys for each of his children may think that the toys are exactly the same. It is likely that his children will point out to him just how wrong he is.

The general agent or manager may make serious errors in his selection decisions because of his tendency to apply inaccurate labels to the candidates whom he interviews. For example, the general agent may interview a candidate and discover that when he was thirteen years old he got his first job, started making his own money, and bought his own clothes. The high-level abstraction or label "worked hard at an early age" occurs to the agent and he thinks to himself that this candidate is an awful lot like Mike, the star producer of the agency. The general agent may get excited, say to himself: "I think this is going to be another Mike" and hire the candidate without much further evaluation. The candidate agent and "Mike" have certain similarities and because of this, the general agent forms a high-level abstraction in his effort to evaluate the candidate and solve his selection problem. Unfortunately, the label that the general agent has formed and has applied to his candidate may not necessarily conform to the actual facts.

This tendency to accept hastily formed labels as actual descriptions of the real object or person blocks effective communication in the selection interview, just as it does in the sale interview. No two candidates are exactly alike or even very much alike. No two insurance prospects are alike, either. As a life underwriter listens to an insurance prospect, he may notice that the prospect uses poor grammar. The life underwriter may then in his own mind apply the label not very bright to his prospect, and make an obvious attempt to talk down to his prospect. If by chance the prospect happens to use bad grammar but also happens to be quite intelligent, the prospect may resent the apparent patronizing attitude of the under-writer and may decide then and there never to buy insurance from him. The life underwriter has made the mistake of noticing one element of the man's behavior by forming a high-level abstraction or label of "not very bright" which, in this case, was a far from accurate description. A real block in communication is the result. We might add that in such a situation the life underwriter may be the last person to know that he has grievously misjudged his prospect.

The weight of authority

The fact that we accept the word as being more true than the thing itself is the reason for widespread prejudice among human beings and for the popularity of scapegoats. Why do we make such obvious mistakes in our thinking? Why is it that we accept the label for the thing as being more accurate than the thing itself? Perhaps it depends partially on the way we are taught as children. Are we not taught to accept the authority of our parents without question? Are we not taught to accept what the teacher says without question?

When we see something in print, we are very likely to believe that it is true without questioning the validity of the statements. When we hear a bit of gossip about another individual, the tendency is very strong for us to swallow, without even chewing, the morsel of information rather than to check it out for ourselves. We may even commit the atrocity of regurgitating this morsel of gossip in the presence of someone else, without knowing or caring whether we are speaking the truth.

Blind acceptance of labels describing people, and blind acceptance of statements by an "authority" can be a real block to our own personal growth and maturity and a block to communication. Would Einstein have achieved his brilliant results if he had not questioned the existing authority? Would any invention be made if someone did not challenge the "truth" of what was being said in the classroom or written in books?

Progress is made in our civilization precisely because someone has dared to question persons of authority rather than merely accept their pronouncements. Unless we can resist this tendency within ourselves to accept labels blindly, we shall continue to make gross errors in our observations of the world, and, of course, at the same time, make gross errors in our attempts to communicate. It is sometimes more pleasant to maintain a fiction than it is to discover reality or the truth. What child does not struggle to maintain his belief in Santa Claus? It takes real courage to be honest with ourselves and with other people. It may be convenient to maintain a belief in a label or high-level abstraction rather than to dig in to discover the facts. Maturity as an individual and collectively as a nation will not follow unless there is a concerted effort to examine one's beliefs (and thereby one's language) to see if they do, indeed, need to be modified.

Whenever we run into a snag in our efforts to communicate with each other, or even to live with each other, a common reaction is to shrug our shoulders and say, "Well, that's human nature." We sometimes carry this one step further and say, "Let's just rely on common sense and everything will turn out all right." But contemporary writers are telling us that we had better start changing human nature or human nature will eliminate itself in one more large-scale war. Someone has pointed out that years ago common sense told men that the world was flat. The way that we think has much to do with determining human nature and also the kind of behavior which we accept as common sense.

The either-or problem

Our present civilization (and therefore our language and system of communication) is based on a system of logic or reasoning formulated by the Greek philosopher Aristotle, who did what seems to us now to be a simple thing. He merely observed how men behaved and how they thought; then he formulated some laws to describe this behavior. Aristotle said, in effect, that men act as if a thing is what it is, that anything must be either a particular thing or it must not be that thing, and that something cannot both be a particular thing and also not be that particular thing.[2] In other words, a chair is a chair, any particular thing is either a chair or is not a chair, and something cannot at the same time be a chair and not be a chair. What Aristotle observed about men was, therefore, that they think in an "either-or" way about the world they live in. Either something is the truth or it is not the truth and something cannot at the same time be the truth and not be the truth. This was the beginning of our formal system of logic and to us today it simply sounds like "common sense."

Expressing things in an either-or way is known as *dichotomizing*. A dichotomy is a division of something into two parts. In logic it is a division of a class of things into two opposed subclasses as for example, real and unreal. There are many things which can be logically dichotomized. People are either male or female. A woman is either pregnant or she is not pregnant. A life insurance candidate either goes for his physical examination or he does not. But there are many things which we deal with every day which cannot be logically dichotomized. Because this is so, either-or thinking can become a real problem if it is applied to all things indiscriminantly.

Many things are not black or white, but instead are shades of gray. Much of nature consists of a series of gradations rather than of things which can be reduced to an either-or status. The difficulty in communication and in all human relationships comes when we attempt to apply either-or thinking to a many-sided or multidimensional situation. We might say, for example, that failure is the opposite of success. We may think that we have either achieved success or we have failed. We may also feel that we cannot succeed and fail with a particular project at the same time. There is probably nothing more potent than this kind of thinking in causing maladjustments among men. The tendency in our culture to see success and failure in either-or terms invariably gives rise to frustration and to gross feelings of inferiority.

What is success? Ask any one of your friends this question and

[2] For the interested reader, these three observations are known respectively as (1) the law of identity, (2) the law of the excluded middle, and (3) the law of non-contradiction. A discussion of Aristotelian logic and its implications can be found in Alfred Korzybski, *Science and Sanity.*

you are very likely to get an extremely vague and ill-defined answer. A man may not know exactly what success means to him, but will drive himself relentlessly for years in an effort to seek it. Success is, for some men, like the carrot dangled in front of the donkey. We know that there is something "out there" that we are trying to reach, but we may never feel completely sure that we have reached it. If, because we have never reached success, we must feel that we are, therefore, "failures," our life is likely to be a series of never-ending frustrations. It seems more realistic to measure success and failure, not in either-or terms, but as a succession of minor successes or minor victories all along the way. Success is relative rather than absolute. We can achieve partial success as well as partial failure. It is the inability to accept this simple fact of life that leads many people to serious mental and emotional maladjustments.

Making inappropriate either-or judgments about ourselves not only contributes to maladjustments and errors in communication, but this very kind of thinking keeps us from seeking help for our maladjustments. What individual likes to think of himself as mentally ill? The assumption that most of us hold is that either we are mentally ill or we are not. But this just doesn't make sense. If we will think for a moment in terms of physical illness, it will be easier to recognize that mental illness is a matter of gradation or degree. We can easily admit to ourselves and others that we can have minor physical aches or pains and that we are slightly ill. With afflictions of a more serious nature, we can be moderately or grossly ill even to the point of being almost completely incapacitated. In precisely the same way, we are all, at some time or another, slightly, moderately, grossly, or completely incapacitated by mental illness.

Either-or thinking about matters which are not black or white undermines our communication with each other (and especially with ourselves!) and makes it difficult for us to learn. Common words that can tip us off to the fact that we are thinking in either-or terms are the words always, never, all, none, completely, forever, etc. Our use of high-level abstractions, or labels, to describe people, is frequently dichotomous in nature. The general agent or manager who states that he wants to hire a dominant salesman is implying that such a person is always completely dominant in all situations and is never submissive or controlled by other people. If this is what the general agent or manager is searching for, he is very likely to be continually disappointed. If he were to look, instead, for a man who has the ability to control individuals more often than not in situations like those represented by life insurance sales, then he is more likely to find the individual he wants. If the general agent or manager thinks in an either-or fashion about dominance while he is interviewing a candidate life underwriter, and he discovers that his candidate has once behaved in a way which does not indicate dominance, the general agent or manager may jump to the conclusion that the candidate is not "dominant." It is more reasonable to attempt to determine under what circumstances and in what situations this particular candidate is able to control people, and to what degree. The difficulty with this kind of careful thinking is that it does not permit us the luxury of putting people into pigeonholes. But the fact remains that people do *not* fit neatly into pigeonholes.

The Listening Process

Communication is, after all, the transfer of knowledge *and* understanding from one person to another. It is obvious that if we attempt to communicate verbally with a deaf person, our message simply will not get across. But many of us with normal hearing ability turn a "deaf ear" to what other people are attempting to communicate to us. One of the most effective tools that the life underwriter has at his disposal to help him be successful in selling life insurance is his own effective listening ability. If, in listening to another person, we hear only the words that he uses but fail to understand what he is trying to say, then communication is not taking place (and we have lost a great deal of our ability to motivate behavior changes in other people.) Hearing is a simply physical activity, but real listening is an active attempt to understand someone else's viewpoint which may differ from our own.[3]

---

[3] For further reading on becoming more skilled as a listener, these texts are suggested: Dominick A. Barbara, *The Art of Listening* (Springfield, Illinois: Charles C. Thomas, Publisher, 1958); R. G. Nichols and L. A. Stevens, *Are You Listening?* (New York: McGraw-Hill Book Co., Inc., 1957).

Whom do we choose as our friends? We like those people who listen to us. Of course, this isn't the only reason for choosing friends, but it is an important one. Whom do we like to work with? Again, we enjoy most working with people who listen to us and apparently show interest in us. By whom are we most likely to be influenced? Aren't we usually more responsive to someone who has demonstrated his desire to listen to us and to consider carefully our feelings in various matters? Listening is one way of showing our real interest in and regard for other people. But how often do we really listen to someone else? We like to be listened to. We like to have other people show interest in us. We like to feel important and worthwhile and we hope that other people consider us to be important and worthwhile. But just how good a job do we ourselves do as listeners?

Listening is rare

We shall not make the mistake of overgeneralizing about life underwriters, but we can observe that a great many are poor listeners. Each of us as we go about our daily business has various worries and concerns with which we are *rather naturally* preoccupied. We worry about our production record, bank account, our marriage, or our children in school. Because of this preoccupation with ourselves, real listening to other people is relatively rare. We cannot listen too well if we are overly concerned with ourselves and our own problems.

It follows, then, that if we expect to become better listeners, we need to be less preoccupied with ourselves and more genuinely interested in other people. That is, of course, a tall order and not something that can be accomplished merely by resolving to do so. If the life underwriter is truly interested in being more effective in controlling his prospect's behavior, then it should become important to him to make gains in his own maturity and his ability to focus interest and attention on other people rather than mostly on himself. Real gains in listening ability will come only as one becomes mature enough to minimize his own selfish motives and find real satisfaction in contributing something to others.

Why is it that good listening is so rare? There are several other reasons. When many of us were children, we were often told, in effect, that "children should be seen and not heard." When parents apply undue pressure upon their children to mold them into obedient and attentive listeners to their parents, then the children in self-defense may actually learn to block out much of what is said to them. Demanding that the child listen may force the child to react by not "hearing." If the parent combines great pressure for the child to listen to him with a failure to listen sympathetically to the child, the child does the only thing that he can do: he doesn't listen. He resorts to the unconscious mechanism of "psychological deafness" to one degree or another. This means that the child can unconsciously block awareness of his sensory impressions; can be disobedient to his parents and at the same time avoid conscious feelings of guilt for his disobedience. In extreme cases this can result in a kind of deafness which is as impressive and as total as actual physiological deafness.

Probably nothing facilitates listening more than an atmosphere of sympathetic appreciation and acceptance on the part of the parent. Parents can do much to help their children grow in listening ability by making the child feel that his viewpoint is appreciated at least part of the time. The child who grows up without having sympathetic listeners around him is more likely to indulge in passive activities such as television, radio, or movies. Parents who force their children to listen may lead their children to face painful life situations by "turning off" their listening mechanism instead of by listening for ways to solve problems.

Another reason for our lack of effective listening ability has to do with the way we are taught in school. Much of the emphasis, at first, is on learning how to read and on acquiring reading skill. New words to be learned are written on the board or are presented on flash cards. Even instructions from the teacher are written out on the board again with emphasis placed on learning to read the instructions rather than on listening to instructions. In addition to this, verbal instructions in a classroom in the first few grades of school are almost always repeated many times by the teacher. This repetition of instruction makes it less necessary for the child himself to take the responsibility for really listening and understanding the spoken instructions the first time. This may cause the child to develop the habit of not really listening to what is said because the child knows that if it is important it will be repeated. This kind of instruction probably teaches the child how *not* to listen.

After the school years, as we enter into business activities, we find that pressure is applied on men to write memos rather than to rely on the spoken word. While there are very good reasons for writing down important information, dependence on writing rather than speaking or listening certainly gives us little real practice in learning better how to listen.

Blocks to listening

It is hard for us to listen because to listen attentively to another person's ideas or opinions means that we ourselves become vulnerable to the possibility that our own thinking may need changing. Change is uncomfortable. We may indeed live in a time of constant change, but this apparently does not make it any easier for most of us to accept change. We reach a kind of personal equilibrium where we have learned how to act and behave so as to avoid punishment and to gain praise. Once having achieved that delicate equilibrium, we are loathe to change it.

Real listening to another person, then, is an acknowledgment that he may have something to tell us that we don't already know. This brings up the often feared possibility that we must make a new adjustment based partly on the new information that we have just received. If someone says something to us with which we disagree, we are most likely to say, "You are wrong." It takes real courage to admit to ourselves that possibly we are wrong.

Many people do not really want to understand others or to be understood completely. We hide many of our true feelings from other people. Perhaps most of us are engaged in daily self-deception as well as the deception of other people. This very human tendency is a further obstacle to acquiring real skill as a listener. Because of our reluctance to reveal ourselves to other people, we tend to be satisfied too quickly with the external details of things and the external characteristics of other people.

There is often a fear of deep personal involvement with other people. In most of our conversations we like to talk and listen only if the conversation does not go too deep or does not become too intimate. We keep ourselves, then, at an *emotional arm's length* from other people. Effective listening cannot take place between two people holding each other off at arm's length. The poor or ineffectual listener is likely to be on the defensive while he is "listening," that is, he is likely to be waiting until the speaker stops so that he can express his rebuttal or somehow attack the speaker. The life underwriter will often be presenting his sales talk to prospects who may be very poor listeners themselves. This obstacle to communication and to the sale of life insurance is compounded if the life underwriter himself also happens to be a poor listener. In a conversation involving *two poor listeners,* we can expect that very little behavior change will occur.

Empty listening

Much of what passes for listening is instead an empty compulsive effort to maintain self-esteem. How often have you laughed at a joke which you really did not understand? Were you not trying to hide the fact that you did not understand in order to avoid the implication that you weren't very intelligent? *Much of our communication is rendered ineffective because of our unwillingness to ask questions or somehow indicate that we have not understood the conversation.* This kind of *empty communication* is what keeps nations worlds apart. For some reason or another, we rarely permit ourselves to become emotionally involved with other people or with the world around us. Perhaps we are afraid of being hurt, of losing our self-esteem, or losing our status, but whatever the reason, this fear will keep us from really listening to other people.

Listening is an active skill

There is nothing passive about effective listening. Listening can be quite an aggressive tool for the underwriter to use in his sales effort. If the underwriter believes that the ability to communicate to his prospect is necessary to modify the behavior of that prospect, then it follows that listening is one of the most important skills that the underwriter can develop.

Like most skills, listening can be improved with intelligent practice. Note that we say "intelligent" practice. We are used to hearing and believing that "practice makes perfect," but this, of course, is not true if we practice the wrong thing. Listening does improve with practice, but only if the practice is intelligently planned. That is, the practice must involve some way to measure its effectiveness and some plan for systematic improvement. It is not enough merely to be silent as someone else speaks. This is not necessarily listening.

The good listener listens "between the lines." One of the reasons that we listen so poorly is that we think at a more rapid pace than we hear. When someone is speaking to us, we have a lot of spare time for other thoughts to creep into our minds and provide competition for what the speaker is saying. *Effective listening is hard work!* The easiest thing to do is to listen to only part of what the speaker is saying, listen only to those things that we want to hear, or in some way distort, modify, and censor what the speaker is saying. To be listening actively means that we must be constantly applying all of our spare thinking time to what is being said. This constant active awareness that is demanded in effective listening infers an awareness that not only what is said is important, but also what is *not* said. Sometimes silence can speak more eloquently than words. A word omitted or an idea not mentioned can be as significant as something said. If the underwriter compliments his wife on each of the separate items she has prepared for dinner but says nothing about the biscuits (which are rock hard), she is more than likely to hear clearly the omitted words.

If one hopes to be a skillful listener, it is important to be actively *analyzing* and *weighing* what the speaker is saying. Our evaluation of what is said, however, can also be one of the greatest obstacles to effective listening. When we listen to a statement made by someone else, our first reaction is likely to be whether we agree or disagree with it. At that moment we probably are not listening simply because we are busy preparing our own rebuttal or argument against the speaker if we happen to disagree with him. *Good listening is something of a scientific procedure.* The scientist carefully observes and records the data which he receives, but he is careful that he does not record only that data which is favorable to his hypothesis while failing to record that data which is unfavorable.

The scientist does not "listen" only to the data that he wants to hear because he is interested in ascertaining the truth. The good listener must adopt this same attitude.

Learning to listen

The power of real listening is tremendous. Good, effective listening is so rare that when it does occur the speaker is likely to feel extremely warm and friendly and cooperative toward such a listener. Salesmen are given much training in how to present ideas and how to overcome sales resistance or objections. Experienced salesmen have discovered that sensitive and intelligent listening can be the very device which will encourage a customer to talk himself into making a purchase. *Great pressure* can be placed on the prospect either *to overcome his own objections* or *to come to a decision to buy* simply through the device of listening. The salesman can probably bring more pressure to bear on the prospect through sheer silence on his part than he ever can through a barrage of sales arguments.

How can we improve our listening ability? How can we control the behavior of other people by listening? How can we be sure we will get our points across if we spend more time listening? We can improve our listening ability only through hard conscientious work, but there are some specific techniques which can be of some help.

When we are listening to what someone else is saying, it is useful to try to restate in our own words what we think the speaker has just said. This technique does two things: first, it forces us, as the listener, to greater awareness of what the speaker is saying and second, it indicates to the speaker that we have really been listening. The life underwriter's ability to *catch the meaning* behind what his prospect is saying is of utmost importance in his efforts to guide that prospect toward the sale. Experienced and successful life underwriters will often use the prospect's own statements about his needs to convince him to buy insurance.

If we are to improve in our listening ability, we must listen longer, listen more often, listen with respect, listen with feedback, listen without premature evaluation, and listen critically. This may sound like a lot of work, but the life underwriter has not attained his present status without a good deal of hard work, and if a little additional effort helps him to use his ability more effectively, it will be well worth it.

Listen longer. Most of the time as we begin to listen to someone, we are searching for the answer to a problem. We examine the first few words which the speaker says, trying to see if our answer is contained in them. If we get something that approximates the answer we are expecting to hear, our usual reaction is to stop listening. We may stop listening by simply refusing to listen any longer, by interrupting the speaker, or by allowing ourselves to be distracted in any number of ways. The first rule in learning to be a better listener, then, is simply to give yourself more time to listen. There are plenty of things that the listener can be doing while he is listening longer. For example, the listener can put himself in the speaker's shoes and try to feel what the speaker must be feeling. The listener may be wondering about the speaker's background and trying to interpret what the speaker is saying in light of what is known about him.

The salesman who listens longer, who allows his prospect to voice his objections, raise questions, and discuss his own situation more fully, may actually be allowing his prospect to help close the sale himself. It is difficult for most people to express themselves adequately. Quite often the first several statements that a person makes about any given subject do not contain all of the thoughts and feelings that the speaker wishes to communicate. If the listener will simply listen longer, he will give the speaker an opportunity not only to express himself more fully but also to listen to himself and thereby to modify his thoughts and feelings and eventually express himself in a much more accurate and reliable fashion. A speaker may begin to express a point of view knowing full well that he wants to add qualifying phrases later on. If the listener breaks in before the speaker has had a chance to amplify his statements, the speaker is likely to feel offended and also misunderstood. Listening longer is certain to pay valuable dividends to the life underwriter.

Listen more often. It takes practice to learn how to listen just as it takes practice to learn any other skill. The underwriter who wishes to become an accomplished listener will take every opportunity at his disposal to practice listening. He will attempt to listen more often. There are many times when we can practice listening. If we are concerned about the growth of our children, we can practice listening to them at least sometime during each day. If this seems like time wasted, we might well consider the eventual price that we may have to pay if our child becomes the one out of ten who eventually needs professional help for a serious mental illness. Really listening to our own children can be of immense help to them in their efforts to grow.

The life underwriter who is married may find that his wife is a valuable asset to him not only personally but in his business. His wife is almost certain to be more enthusiastic about searching for prospects and leads if she feels that her husband is consistently making an effort to understand and appreciate her by simply listening to her. Here is another opportunity for the life underwriter to practice listening. A problem that many general agents or managers have with their agents is in getting them to listen during training or field activities. The life underwriter may feel that he can establish his independence only by doing things his own way, rather than by following the advice of his manager or general agent. Someone has printed a humorous sign for the office wall which states, "When all else fails, try doing it the way the boss says." Is it possible that the life underwriter may be losing valuable advice or insight by not listening more often to his boss as well as to his colleagues?

Listen with respect. The life underwriter learns that he is in a vocation that has as one of its aims that of providing a service to people by helping them plan toward financial security. The C. L. U. program is dedicated to the idea that men in life insurance should strive toward greater professionalism. One way of defining what is meant by the professional approach is that the interests of the client become paramount. The life underwriter who sells insurance solely for his own financial gain has lost or perhaps has never found the concept of providing in a professional way the insurance program which best suits his prospect. Such an underwriter may find it difficult to listen to his client with respect.

Much of what man achieves depends upon his ability to understand others, and this in turn depends upon his ability to verbalize his thoughts and feelings. *Real understanding* between people comes when there is an *implicit agreement that each individual recognizes the basic right of another individual to his own integrity and worth.* Effective listening, therefore, depends on our ability to see others as unique personalities with beliefs, thoughts, and values of their own. Listening and understanding are based on the *interest* of the listener in recognizing the integrity of others. Without a deep and genuine regard and respect for the other person, listening will be shallow and ineffective.

Some of us have learned to *pretend* that we are listening. We have coached ourselves to sit with bright eyes and a rapt expression apparently taking in every word that a speaker utters. This, of course, is false listening, that is, listening without a genuine motive of wanting to understand. It is very likely that the only person who is fooled to any extent is the pseudo-listener himself. In addition to being unable to listen, such a person adds insult to injury because he seems to say by his behavior that the person to whom he is apparently listening has so little intelligence that he cannot see through this sham. It is a rare individual who does not recognize this kind of contempt on the part of a fake listener.

Listen with feedback. Anyone who has ever learned to throw a ball knows that you gain skill in throwing with accuracy only by being able to see how far off target the throw is each time. If we were to practice throwing while we were blindfolded, probably no learning would take place. The learning of anything requires that we have an adequate system of receiving feed-back information to provide for necessary changes in our behavior. In learning to listen, there are really two kinds of feedback. One occurs *within* the listener or speaker and the other occurs *between* two or more people. When we listen, and when we speak, we can be reflective about what we are saying or hearing. When we listen to a speaker we can be forming hypotheses in the same way that a scientist does and these hypotheses can be tested continuously. When we do this, we can say to ourselves, "In the light of what he has just said, he must feel this way. Let me check on that possibility by listening to him some more."

In the insurance sales situation, when the prospect is speaking, he must have some kind of feedback or some response from the underwriter in order to feel that the underwriter is really listening

to him. Some life underwriters have learned to sit through a conversation with another person with an almost immovable poker
face. Apparently, it is important to this person that he not reveal
anything of his own personal reactions during the conversation.
This can be extremely unsettling to anyone speaking to him. Such
a life underwriter may indeed sit in silence and give the prospect
plenty of time to express himself, but if the underwriter does not
give some indication to his prospect of how he is responding to
what the prospect says, this kind of listening can disrupt communication. If the listener will occasionally respond to the speaker with
an "uh-huh" or "oh, yes, I see," he will do much to encourage the
speaker to express himself more eloquently.

Listen without premature evaluation. Nothing blocks communication, and especially listening, more effectively than prejudices or
premature evaluation of the person to whom we are listening. There
is a natural tendency for us to listen to and remember those things
which tend to support our own biases and prejudices. We may feel
that a new acquaintance is a pretty fine fellow when we discover
that he is a former member of our old college fraternity, or voted
for the same presidential candidate. We listen to him differently
now that he is "one of us." The life underwriter who forms conclusions about a speaker that are based on prejudices and on premature evaluations of the speaker is likely to be about as effective in
his listening as the batter who swings before the ball is pitched.

Listen critically. We need to be critical in our listening behavior,
not in the sense of finding fault with the speaker, but in the sense
of making a careful analysis of the speaker, his cultural background,
the message he is apparently trying to transmit, our own personal
prejudices and blind spots, etc. Much meaning is lost in translating
an idea from one language to another. We understand and expect
this when dealing with a foreign language. What is not as obvious
is the meaning that is lost in translation every time a speaker trans-
mits a message to a listener in their common language. Only in the
broadest sense do all of us in this country "speak the same language." The disturbances in communication which are the most
difficult and perplexing to handle are those which occur when we
assume that a certain word or phrase has a common meaning to
each of us, when in reality we each have our own personal mean-

ing. Slight differences in interpretation are more difficult to detect than gross differences and are therefore actually more disruptive to communication.

The enormous consequences of confusion in communication are dramatized by an incident that occurred at the end of World War II.[4] Near the end of the war, the allies sent to Japan an ultimatum demanding that Japan surrender or be destroyed. It is reported that the Japanese cabinet was ready to agree to the ultimatum but wanted some time to consider the proposal. In the reply from Japan the word "mokusatsu" was used to carry the meaning "to withhold comment temporarily." But this same Japanese word can also mean "to ignore." Because of the mix-up in translation, the allies received the Japanese message that their Cabinet was ignoring the demand to surrender. No one can say for sure, but if this one word had not been misinterpreted, perhaps it would not have been necessary to drop an atomic bomb on Japan and destroy literally thousands of lives.

To Sum Up

If it is important for us to think before we speak, it is no less important for us to think while we listen. We have, in language, a tool which can promote the continued rise of our civilization or destroy it. The life underwriter has at his disposal this same tool with which he can make either more or less use of his innate and learned capacities. The proper use of language and of listening can give the life underwriter greater control over his own behavior and that of other people, or it can become a sticky web of confusion which limits his effectiveness and shuts him away from growth experiences.

[4] William J. Coughlin, "The Great Mokusatsu Mistake," *Harpers Magazine,* March, 1958, p. 31.

PART THREE

MAN
IN MOTIVATION

The life underwriter is well aware of the fact that people have to be motivated to buy life insurance. What may not be so obvious is the complexity of motivational patterns. Motives do not operate in a simple mechanical fashion. Rarely does a single motive exist as a "hot button" which the underwriter can push to prompt a prospect to buy. We do things for *many* reasons. We are moved, or motivated, by needs and desires which may be conscious or unconscious, positive or negative, rational or irrational, and learned or inherited. Furthermore, it is characteristic of man that he often wants things which are themselves in conflict. The way in which he handles these conflicts is some measure of the mental and emotional maturity he has attained.

In the sales interview the life underwriter is trying to motivate the prospect and at the same time the prospect is trying to motivate the life underwriter. How this "battle of the motives" works out is a fascinating drama that is only partly understood by the participants. The life underwriter will win this contest more often if he will learn how motives are formed and what he, personally, can do to persuade his prospect to change his attitudes and behavior.

To be effective the life underwriter has the double job of achieving a better understanding of his own motives as well as those of his prospect. For the student who is highly motivated to become an excellent, professional life insurance practitioner, the material in this section also can be used as a guide for *his own growth and development.*

5

The Fundamentals of Motivation

Every day we spend most of our time either trying to get other people to do things or trying to do or avoid doing what someone else wants us to do. Part of the time we are satisfied with our efforts but often we are frustrated. People don't always do what we want them to do. Sometimes we know why, but often we don't know. The behavior of people is baffling. Just about the time we think we have someone figured out, he does something that is unexpected and seems somehow inexplicable, and we must make a fresh attempt to try to understand him. Regardless of what we are doing, whether we are selling life insurance, managing agents, working professionally as an actuary, etc., we are concerned about getting other people to do things to our satisfaction. We are interested in motivating others to change their behavior.

A successful life underwriter has discovered that he is often able to get people to do what he wants them to do, but he may be unable to tell others how he accomplishes this. He may, in truth, be an expert in human motivation, but he is often inarticulate when it comes to explaining his ability. While there are some who seem naturally to be excellent motivators of people, probably most of us have to work pretty hard to become effective in changing the behavior of others. We can acquire skill as a motivator by learning many specific facts and principles of motivation and then by attempting to combine these separate elements into broad techniques which are successful in obtaining the desired results. Everything that has been discussed so far has a direct bearing on the outcome of each human relationship wherein one person is attempting to control the behavior of another person. The level of *intelligence,* the *emotional maturity,* the *unconscious feelings and thoughts,* the *social background* of each and the *words* that are used, all have some influence on the final outcome of any effort to motivate.

A Definition of Motivation

What does motivation mean and what are motives? The word *motivation* refers to the inner control of human behavior as it is affected by bodily conditions, learned interests, values, mental attitudes, and recognized or unrecognized goals or aspirations. Note that in defining the word motivation, reference is made to *inner control.* This recognizes the fact that, except for physical force or restraint, human behavior is the result of the way the individual inwardly perceives his world and is affected by it. The old saying "you can lead a horse to water but you can't make him drink" helps us remember that we can control the behavior of another person only by our ability to influence what that person perceives.

To the extent that we can control what a person perceives, we may be able to influence his behavior. This is the basic idea underlying all aspects of the motivation of human behavior. It is fundamental that we recognize that, at best, we can merely control some conditions which then either directly or indirectly affect the actual behavior of others. Strictly speaking, then, we cannot change other people. We can only attempt to control things that other people need or want, and hope that this control influences them to move in the direction we desire.

In discussing an individual *motive* we will be referring to some impulse or urge of the human being to reach for or try to attain some goal or objective. A motive has behind it, then, some kind of drive, energy, or force which impels one toward a given kind of goal or attainment which is related to the drive. A motive is not a state of being or an idea but is instead a *process* involving human energy, a *direction* for that energy, and an *end* to be obtained.

Motives may contradict each other; they may be positive or negative, may be based on biological needs or social desires, may be conscious or unconscious, may vary in strength from person to person and from culture to culture, and may change within any one person from time to time. Again, we emphasize that motivation is an extremely complex process and a very careful analysis is essential in understanding how human behavior is influenced.

Because motives involve goals, we could do a fair job of understanding what motivates a person if we could observe undetected everything that an individual did or said or accomplished during a period of time such as a week in the life of that individual. The life underwriter, of course, couldn't afford to do this with his prospects even if it were actually possible. The life underwriter who can "see" the most in the behavior of each prospect during the few minutes that he does have to observe will be in the best position to know how to appeal most directly and most effectively to the prospect's actual motives. Just as an artist can see more color in a landscape than a layman because he has been trained to do so, so can the life underwriter see more in the behavior of other people if he will train himself through a broader awareness of human behavior.[1]

General Principles of Motivation

Motivation is complex

It's a hot summer day. In the yard next door, the neighbor is pulling on the starter rope of his power mower trying to get it started. He's not having much luck, and he's getting madder by the minute.

---

[1] The broad field of motivation and related research methods are being constantly examined and changed by psychologists. Two texts examining the history of motivational theory and the validity of current thinking are: Dalbir Bindra, *Motivation: A Systematic Reinterpretation* (New York: The Ronald Press Co., 1959); R. S. Peters, *The Concept of Motivation* (New York: Humanities Press, Inc., 1958).

As we watch, we see him give the mower a vicious kick and storm into the house. Inside, through the open curtains, we can see him now stretched out in front of the TV set with a cold beer in his hand. This is just an isolated incident of human behavior like millions of other episodes occurring every day. But, it illustrates a point.

The man next door is merely trying to get a machine to work for him. He doesn't know much about the machine, but he has successfully started it before by simply pulling on the starter rope. Today, however, this doesn't work. Since our friend doesn't know very much about how or why the mower works, he is at a loss to know how to proceed. He is frustrated and reacts to this with considerable aggression and solves the problem by retreating. Doesn't this same kind of thing happen to all of us quite often? The life underwriter, basically, spends his professional life trying to get people to do things. He is interested in the motivation of people. He has to know how to get people to move. If he is reasonably successful, the life underwriter has found a way of "pulling the starting rope" of his prospects so that he can get them started purchasing life insurance.

As we consider the plight of the suburbanite temporarily overwhelmed by a machine we see that he is trying to move (or "motivate" if we may use the term) his power mower by pulling on the starter rope. This is a simple mechanical action which *seems* to lead to direct results. But much more than the pulling of the starter is necessary before the machine will run. Other conditions must be satisfied. There must be air and gasoline supplied in just the right mixture. There must be a spark to ignite the mixture. And there must be proper timing in bringing all these elements together. A small amount of rust on a tiny piece of the machine may be enough to keep it from moving. A drop or two of water in a certain place can nullify every other condition which may be perfect. A slight break in the insulation of a wire in the ignition system may keep the mower from fulfilling its function. Why does the power mower work? It works not just for one reason, or because one approach is used, but for a whole combination of reasons. The sparkplug may be dirty, but the mower may still run. The clogged air filter may restrict the passage of air, but the mower may still run. The gasoline may have too much oil in it, but the mower may still run. But two or more of these conditions existing at the same time may make it inoperative. To understand how a relatively simple machine like a power lawnmower works so that we can more effectively make it go becomes a more complex matter than it first seemed. By comparison, *the human machine is infinitely more complicated and complex.* Our task as students of human motivation is enormous if we hope to achieve even a rudimentary understanding and a moderate competence in motivation.

Human motivation is not a push-button operation

We cannot hope to learn separate rules to apply to separate problems in motivation. Literally thousands of books have been written as guides to the salesman on how to influence other people. Quite often these sales guides are descriptions of various rules on how to persuade people to buy. Many salesmen have discovered that even though they attempt to apply these rules, they do not achieve satisfying results. The approaches which seem to be so successful for the author do not seem to work at all for the reader. The probable explanation for this is that the field of motivation is so complex and the behavior of people is so unpredictable that *an attempt to apply generalized rules of human behavior in a mechanical fashion simply does not work.* In this section we will be discussing separate motives which influence human behavior, but it must be emphasized that such motives are isolated for discussion purposes only and that in practice human behavior is never the result of one single motive or motivational technique.

Human behavior is determined by multiple motives

To see how human behavior is the result of many *influences,* let us consider the following analogy. Watch a leaf as it begins to fall from a tree. We expect that it will fall to the ground because we know about the force of attraction known as gravity (one influence). But as we watch, we see that the leaf is abruptly stopped by coming to rest on a lower limb (another influence). As we continue to watch, we see that the leaf is again set in motion by what we guess to be a gust of wind (another influence). Because we have seen it happen before, we are not especially surprised to see the leaf now being carried upward and away from the ground. At this very moment, the leaf still is influenced by the pull of gravity, but now is moving in the opposite direction by a force which at the moment is counter to and stronger than the gravitational pull (opposing or conflicting influences). Now we see the leaf begin its gradual descent to the ground, but at the last moment it is plucked out of the air by a small boy who happens to be passing by (another influence). He holds, twists, and twirls it and begins to crumple it up in his hand until it is a compact ball (an influence that changes the characteristics of the object). As he gives the leaf a fling into the air, we notice that now it falls very quickly to the ground. But no, it is still in motion. It has fallen into a small stream of water along the curb and is now being carried quickly out of sight (continuing but hidden influences). Who knows where this leaf will finally come to rest?

In the same way, *human behavior is moved* in various and sometimes conflicting directions *by forces which we can only infer* (such as gravity and wind), *by forces which we can observe* (like the hand of the small boy), and *by forces which we will never know about* (like the stream, still moving the leaf, now out of sight).

We are often under the influence of pressures which are themselves opposed to each other. Our behavior, at any one time, is the result of many, many forces and pressures which impinge upon us from many different directions. In the field of physics, the movement of a body is often described as the resultant of vectors of force. Two forces pulling at right angles to each other on a single body move the body not in the direction of either one of the forces but in a third direction which is the resultant of the amount and the direction of the two forces. Human behavior is also the complex resultant of multiple forces acting in different directions.

Motivation is more than common sense

The obvious reasons for a man to buy life insurance are not necessarily the "real" reasons for his buying. The interest in discovering what motivates people to buy particular articles has stimulated great effort in the field of motivational research. Motivational research has as its goal the discovery of the underlying reasons that make a person buy one object rather than another, that is, why a person buys a Chevrolet rather than a Plymouth, a convertible rather than a sedan, etc. Those in the field of motivational research have made substantial progress because they have studied the process of human motivation scientifically.[2] They have not been willing to accept the stated or common sense reasons that people give for buying but instead have attempted to discover the underlying motives which influence the purchasing decisions that are made. The important point here is that the approach of motivational research is *objective* and *realistic* in solving problems of human motivation. It is important for the life underwriter to adopt this same attitude toward his own efforts to motivate his prospects. It takes more than common sense to understand the complex and dynamic nature of human motivation. A more complete understanding of this complex process will allow the creative life underwriter to make better use of his own resources and will allow him to put his technical training to more effective use.

Motivated behavior is goal-directed and persistent

Wherever motivation is involved, a goal for achievement is also involved. This does not mean that we always know what the goal is toward which we are motivated, for much motivation is on an unconscious level. This goal may be anything from food, shelter, or sexual activity to wealth, prestige, or power. Closely allied to this is the further principle that the human being shows persistence in moving or searching for goals. Some goals such as obtaining food do not seem to be learned, although the specific method of obtaining food may be learned, but many more of our conscious and unconscious goals are learned. We learn to seek certain goals because of the culture in which we were reared. We learn to want certain

[2] The interested reader is referred to this text for more information on motivational research: Ernest Dicter, *The Strategy of Desire* (Garden City, New York: Doubleday & Co., Inc., 1960).

goals because of the particular pattern of reward or punishment which has accompanied various past experiences in our life. We learn to seek goals because of the obvious exposure to situations in which the achievement of these goals is possible.

Our knowledge about human motivation is largely inferential

We can directly observe human behavior. But we can only infer the presence of the motives which may give rise to that behavior. As we watch the leaf being lifted higher and higher, we can only infer the presence of an upward draft of air. We cannot see the air movement, but can only see whatever is being carried by the air. We cannot see man's motive to obtain food, but can only observe that he does indeed search for food. We do not know that the life underwriter is money-motivated; we can only observe that he does indeed do many things which result in his making money.

Motivation and perception are intertwined

Learning to motivate other people is difficult (1) because people are *complex*, (2) because human behavior is *not very predictable*, but especially (3) because we can never escape the ever-present and largely *unmeasurable influence of our own motives*. Our efforts to motivate other people always involve ourselves and the needs and wants and goals for which we are striving. We cannot perceive any event or any example of human behavior without distorting, through personal interpretation, what reaches our senses. We are prisoners of our own frames of reference often without realizing it. The fact that our own past experiences, attitudes, and blind spots are so intimately involved in our efforts to observe other people means that we tend to lose the objectivity which we must have if we are to observe accurately and have a sound basis for later motivational efforts. The more we know about how motivation works, within ourselves as well as within those we are trying to change, the more influence we can have over other people. The life underwriter cannot assume that his prospect feels the same way about his family as the underwriter does about his own. We must understand that the prospect will have *his own reasons* based on *his own needs* and *his own desires* and *his own goals* for purchasing life insurance.[3]

When an individual wants to see only good things in another person or another activity, we commonly say that he has on rose-colored glasses. In the same way, all of us can have many pairs of glasses which we wear at different times, each pair of glasses reflecting our own experiences, values, attitudes, etc. If we have on "money-colored glasses" we will tend to see people in terms of their being motivated by a desire for money and of being frustrated and unhappy if they do not obtain large amounts of money. But if we are not aware that we are seeing things through "money-colored glasses," we are in danger of misinterpreting statements made by a prospect if he, for example, has little or no interest in money matters. In other words, we might make the mistake of oversimplifying the problem of motivating the prospect by thinking that he is motivated by just the one motive of money. The prospect may buy insurance for prestige reasons or for any one of a number of other reasons. The life underwriter must make every effort to minimize the distortion in perception which is caused by his own motives, his own experiences, values, and attitudes. It is essential to "see" the prospect's goal and objectives accurately if the life underwriter wishes to be successful in influencing the behavior of his prospect.

Biological Needs and Motivation

What is behind a motive? What is it that impels us toward a goal? What gives us the drive or the incentive or the urge to buy or to sell or to engage in any kind of human activity? The answer is, of course, that there are a great many things which impel us to behave the way we do. One of the easiest types of motivation to understand is that which results from physical or bodily conditions.

---

[3] The interrelationships between personality factors and motivation may be explored further in A. H. Maslow, *Motivation and Personality* (New York: Harper & Row, Publishers, 1954); Carl I. Hovland and Irving L. Janis, eds., *Personality and Persuasibility* (New Haven, Connecticut: Yale University Press, 1959).

Biological needs and need reduction

What is a need? A need is some requirement for man's adjustment to his environment. Basically, man "needs" to survive. Stemming from this broad need are such needs as water, food, air, protection from danger, and so forth. We can classify these as biological needs. Biological needs appear to be innate or inherited. In other words, we do not seem to have to learn that we have these needs. The infant, shortly after birth, has a biological need for food. He requires food to survive. A need then can be thought of as a lack of something which the person must have in order to sustain life.

How do needs motivate? In response to a need or requirement, the human being experiences a tension or drive to satisfy this need. Obtaining the goal or object which satisfies a biological need tends to reduce the strength of the tension or drive. When we are thirsty, we will start looking around for water and will continue some general activity in that direction until we find it. As soon as we have a drink, we have less interest or desire to search for more water. The longer we go without water, however, the greater is this biological need and the stronger is the tension. If we are without water for an abnormally long time, we become frantic in our efforts to find it and may think of little else until we are successful in our search. This relationship between biological *need, tension* or *drive,* and *reaching a goal* illustrates one kind of motivational process. We emphasize that this is only one kind of motivation, for human behavior appears to be a composite of many forces besides a simple response to a need, as we shall see.

Other bodily needs that we human beings have include a need for sleep, for food, for sexual activity, and for avoiding pain or discomfort. These needs are a part of life itself. Apparently we do not learn to need these things, but are born with these requirements.

Sometimes we continue to desire an object which ordinarily would satisfy a biological need, even though this need does not exist or is not very strong at the moment. After eating a heavy meal and feeling full, i.e., having reduced the drive to seek food in order to satisfy that basic need of hunger, we may still desire a piece of pie or cake for dessert. We desire the dessert not because of a biological need, but because of a social or *learned* need. The couple who orders *crepe suzettes* for dessert in a fine restaurant are probably motivated not by hunger but by curiosity, fascination at watching the flames, or delight in seeing the admiring glances from the people sitting around them.

While bodily needs result in tension or a drive toward a goal-object, sometimes the individual may not move towards the object which he requires to satisfy even this innate bodily need. A person suffering a severe depression, for example, may need food in order to survive, but instead may refuse to eat. Unless he is force fed, this patient may expire from malnutrition. Thus, while the body's periodic needs for nourishment, rest, etc. impel the human being in certain directions, they do not operate in a simple mechanical way. The various bodily needs influence each other, and social or learned needs also influence this biological motivational process.

Another characteristic of these basic bodily needs is their *wave-like functioning*. As the human being goes for longer and longer periods without food, the need for nourishment increases and the tension or drive resulting from this physical lack also increases until the need is satisfied. As nourishment is obtained, the tension decreases, but not for long, because soon the tension will begin increasing until it is again temporarily satisfied.

Learning to satisfy needs

A major step in the motivational process is the establishment of an assortment of learned responses which can act to satisfy the biological needs. The physical need itself impels the individual to activity, but it is through a learning process that the individual discovers the most efficient ways of satisfying the needs or reducing the tension which derives from them. If we are discussing the need to satisfy hunger, for example, we can see that food may be obtained by growing it, by exchanging money for it, or by stealing it. There are a number of ways, then, that we might go about satisfying our need for food or other biological needs. The motivational process also entails the location of a goal-object and the decision as to which of a number of possible activities might be used to reach the goal. Because these physical needs reoccur at periodic intervals, the repetition of need-reducing activities results in these activities becoming stamped in or *learned* as a habit. The strength of any habit will ordinarily be greater as the strength of the need and the frequency with which it must be dealt are increased.

It is important to remember that many biological drives operate together to motivate the human being. Thus the drives to satisfy such needs as hunger, thirst, sleep, and sexual activity are operating at the same time, although at different degrees of intensity. Often these needs conflict with each other. When this happens, usually the strongest drive will determine the pattern of behavior which results. When survival is being threatened, the unsatisfied need which constitutes the most serious threat to survival will usually be satisfied first. We have to say will *usually* be satisfied first because the human animal occasionally makes the decision to put survival second to achieving honor or saving face.

Biological needs and perceptual distortion

We have seen that physical needs are involved in inducing human behavior. Such needs also have a tendency to influence, or distort, our perceptual processes. When we are hungry, we tend to notice more signs of food or places where food can be obtained than when we are not hungry. We may even "see" a restaurant where none exists; that is, we might momentarily mistake a service station sign for a drive-in sign while driving down the highway just before dinnertime. If we have gone for a long time without food, we may find it almost impossible to think or talk about anything but food. It would follow from this that if a prospect for life insurance had gone for a long time without eating, he might be so interested in food that he would not be willing to listen to the underwriter's proposal. The same thing would happen if the prospect were excessively fatigued or were grossly uncomfortable either from too much heat or cold.

In most instances, however, the level of tension which we experience in daily life from an unsatisfied biological need (food, water, rest) remains so low that it rarely operates to the extent described above. Most of the time the life underwriter will be dealing with individuals who have not gone more than three or four hours without food. While these physical or bodily needs are important in understanding the motivation of the human being, they are usually so well satisfied that the other emotional and social motives outweigh them in importance in the underwriter's attempts to influence a prospect's behavior.[4]

Maintaining equilibrium

Much, but not all, human behavior stems from the existence of basic physiological or bodily needs. Our motives for providing ourselves with food, rest, shelter, and sexual activities have the function of maintaining an internal balance or equilibrium. The specific way in which we satisfy these bodily needs is determined by our culture. The cyclic or wave-like rise of tension and the satisfaction from a decrease in tension which characterizes these basic needs act as almost automatic motivational processes. This mechanism of maintaining a balance is called *homeostasis*. This means, literally, maintaining things as they are. The temperature of our blood, for example, maintains itself within a few tenths of a degree most of the time. When the internal body temperature begins to go up, we automatically begin perspiring and the evaporation of the perspiration tends to cool off the body. When the internal body temperature goes down, we automatically begin shivering and shaking and the heat generated from this muscle activity moves the body temperature back up where it should be.

As the intensity of the need increases, our general activity increases and usually stays at a high level until something happens to satisfy the need. Just as the wall thermostat controls the operation of the furnace according to the temperature in the room, so do we have literally thousands of "thermostats" in our body which help to regulate needs and drives. These are feed-back mechanisms which operate very much the way a heat thermostat works. As the furnace warms the room, the heat activates the wall thermostat which sends an electrical message to the furnace telling the furnace

---

[4] A technical but readable and comprehensive work on the many variables involved in motivations at all levels is J. S. Brown, *The Motivation of Behavior* (New York: McGraw-Hill Book Co., Inc., 1961).

to turn off. The gradual cooling of the room again activates the thermostat which again feeds information to the furnace, this time telling the furnace to turn on and supply heat. As long as there is fuel and a source of electricity, this cycle of action and reaction will constantly strive to maintain the equilibrium in temperature which is also constantly being unbalanced.

Acquiring the skill of riding a bicycle illustrates how we can learn to make the adjustments necessary to maintain our equilibrium or balance. When we first begin to ride, we find that we fall either to one side or to the other and are very clumsy in our efforts. With a little practice we learn to turn the wheel to the right if we start to fall to the right and make a turn to the left if we start to fall to the left. At this level of learning, our course down the highway is likely to be quite jerky and erratic. Although we are maintaining a kind of balance in that we are no longer falling off the bicycle, our balance is not being smoothly maintained. With more practice and greater skill, however, we become more sensitive to our tendency to fall in one direction or the other and make very minute, but rapid, turns of the front wheel to compensate for this. Our adjustment to the inherent tendency of the bicycle to fall over becomes so sensitive and rapid that we can steer an apparently straight path without any perceptible loss of equilibrium.

The examples of maintaining an equilibrium given so far are very crude compared to the mechanisms involved in maintaining a balance in our psychological or social lives. The theoretical law of supply and demand is an example of how a number of sociological and psychological forces tend to balance each other and achieve a relative stability or equilibrium. We immediately recognize that this economic principle is infinitely more complex and complicated than the operation of a wall thermostat. Levels of production and consumption do directly affect each other. The interaction is far from being perfect in maintaining any certain socioeconomic stability. We recognize a tendency, however, for the price of a desired object to go down as the object becomes more readily available. If the object is very scarce and many people desire it, then the price or the value that people place on the article is likely to increase. Occasionally we see examples of a demand increasing because the price has been arbitrarily increased. This is only one example of (and a possible reason for) the imperfection of those generalized statements about human behavior which we like to refer to as laws.

Emotional Motivation

Definitions of emotion

To understand how emotions can act as motives, we need to be sure we know just exactly what emotions really are. One is likely to have at least two reactions to the question of defining an emotion. The first is likely to be "Why, of course, I know what an emotion is! An emotion is the feeling of fear, anger, love or disgust." A second reaction to the question is "Defining an emotion by saying that it is fear, anger, love, etc. is really only giving it another name. It is really not a definition at all." Certainly this second reaction is more likely to lead us towards the kind of questioning about emotions that will allow us to understand and even predict the role that emotions play in the motivation of human beings.

In the heading of this section, we refer to the *definitions of emotion*. This implies right from the start that there is more than one definition of emotion. It suggests that we may be dealing with a kind of human behavior which is so broad and all-encompassing that a single definition would not begin to tell us all that we need to know in order to understand the concept of emotion. In Chapter 1, referring to the growth and development of emotions, we stated that an emotion was something that we felt and were often very much aware of. We saw that emotions somehow interfered with the normal, rational way of behaving. We saw also that while we were experiencing emotions, there seemed to be various external and internal reactions of the body, such as blushing, "butterflies in the stomach," pounding heart, and the like. But what, really, *is* an emotion?

Emotions are generally thought of as rather destructive, undesirable displays which must be somehow controlled or concealed. We may tell an excited friend, "Don't get so emotional—cool off and keep your head." Emotion in this sense is thought of as a general disorganization which occurs within an individual and makes it difficult for him to relate to another individual in a predictable and acceptable manner. Emotions can be defined as ". . . complex disturbances that are commonly recognized, distinguished, and named, in terms of the stimulus situation that induces them and the adjustments that an individual makes to this situation." [5] We are familiar with the predicament of the small boy who has memorized perfectly his part in the school play only to become completely speechless when he is pushed out onto the stage on the night of the performance. Something that he is experiencing, which we call emotion, has somehow interfered with his otherwise adequate abilities. Our definition of emotion, then, must surely include the concept of disruption or disorganization. But love is also an emotion and we cannot feel entirely satisfied in describing the emotion of love as a disorganizing and disruptive influence. Certainly love includes a desire to care for and to appreciate another individual as he or she is. This emotion of love is responsible for some of the most deeply satisfying and uplifting human experiences that we can ever know. Emotions, then, are states of psychological being which act also to facilitate or enrich human interactions.

Emotion can also be thought of as an awareness of pleasantness or unpleasantness. This definition of emotion refers to mental activity within a person without regard to his external behavior or the effect of this mental activity on his behavior. Our awareness of pleasure or displeasure, of course, depends upon our own past experiences. Emotion used in this sense becomes our conscious awareness of the evaluation we place upon a perception of events which may be taking place. Used in this sense, the word emotion means an interpretation of present experiences based on past experiences.

A further definition of an emotion is that it is a pattern of human reaction which involves definite changes in the body as a whole and especially in the internal organs, such as the heart, the stomach, and the sweat glands. During a state of so-called emotion, it has

[5] A new technical work in this area is: Paul Thomas Young, *Motivation and Emotion* (New York: John Wiley & Sons, Inc., 1961).

been determined that a certain portion of the brain sends signals to the internal organs of the body activating them and causing the individual to be aware of changes, in either increased comfort or discomfort, in his body. The portion of the brain referred to here is the thalamus and hypothalamus which activate the internal organs by means of the autonomic nervous system. One theory of emotion is that as we perceive a potentially dangerous or threatening situation, our interpretation of this sends a signal through the hypothalamus along the autonomic nervous system to the internal organ preparing us for fight or flight; that is, the perception of danger causes the heart rate to increase which is a preparatory step to enable us better to cope with the dangerous situation. It is further theorized that our awareness of these internal bodily changes is what we are conscious of as emotion.

Our definition of emotion, then, needs to include these several concepts of conscious experience of pleasure or displeasure, the existence of disruptive or adaptive influences, the presence of often profound internal and external bodily reactions, and our awareness of these reactions. An emotion, then, is a group of experiences which constitutes largely learned reactions to externally perceived situations. The whole person seems to be involved in emotional reactivity and the influence on his behavior is dramatic and extensive. We are probably safe in saying that in every motivating situation there is always the existence of some emotion, this emotion adding to or detracting from the consciously felt aims of the individuals or, in any event, influencing or coloring all of human behavior.

Emotions motivate behavior

Emotions motivate behavior in some of the same ways as do biological or physical needs. The presence of an emotion tends to give rise to a tension or drive toward an object, situation or person and obtaining this objective satisfies that emotion and helps restore a balance. Just as biological drives move the individual toward activities which assist in his survival, so do emotions aid in the survival of the human being. The emotion of fear, for example, helps keep the individual out of potentially threatening or fatal situations. The emotion of anger serves to direct our activities and mobilize additional strength to help us in overcoming a difficulty or obstacle. Emotions, like physical needs, act as drives to motivate the individual toward action. If one kind of activity does not lessen the tension, the force of the emotion acts to motivate the human being to try other methods of reducing the tension.

Emotions vs. biological drives as motives

Although they are interrelated, there are important differences between the way biological drives and emotions operate in the process of motivation. While biological drives are related to internal bodily changes, *emotions generally are stimulated by situations external to the individual.* In contrast to biological drives, which are pretty well fixed by heredity, *emotions are largely learned reactions.* Also, reaching the goal-object involved in emotional motives does not necessarily reduce the tension aroused by the emotions. Dodging one car fortunately does not reduce our helpful fear of other automobiles as we cross a busy street.

The primary emotions of anger, fear, love, hate, pleasure, disgust, etc., do, however, seem to be related to early experiences of satisfaction or frustration of the more basic biological drives. For example, the infant quickly learns that being fed is related to a feeling of pleasure and being deprived of food is related to anger. In the adult, not only can deprivation of food cause the emotion of fear and anxiety, but the mere anticipation of being deprived can result in anxiety. In times of national emergency when food rationing is threatened, many people experience a kind of panic which motivates them to buy and hoard surplus food supplies. Biological drives are increased or satisfied by the actual presence of the satisfying object, while emotional drives are increased or decreased largely by signs or symbols which stand for or remind us of biological needs. Emotions are often difficult to understand as motives precisely because they are symbolic and the actual biological need and its symbolic expression may be quite remote in time and distance. For instance, a man may still experience the emotion of anxiety in the presence of a school teacher who symbolically represents his own cruel and tyrannical father.

Emotions are intensely motivating

We know that emotions can lead to intensely motivating experiences. It is common knowledge that at times of stress, i.e., of intense fear or anger, we are capable of physical acts of strength and endurance which would be impossible under normal conditions. Emotions motivate human behavior in general much more than we realize. Almost everything that we do is colored by, or accompanied by, some feeling or emotion. We experience a deep sense of pleasure and satisfaction after having made a successful sale. We feel a disappointment or a dismay when we fail in some way. Emotion adds color and excitement to our daily activities. But emotions can also *affect our judgment, distort our perception* of other people and situations, and can even *make us physically ill.*

The emotions, especially the emotion of fear, are of tremendous interest to the life underwriter because of the role these play, not only in the motivation of the underwriter himself, but also in the underwriter's efforts to motivate or change the behavior of the prospect. Fear is an emotion which makes us ready to act. In situations of extreme threat to our survival, it is our fear of the situation which causes chemical and physiological changes in our body that give us temporary surges of the strength needed to fight or to flee. An underwriter may deliberately "back up the hearse to the prospect's door" in an effort to use the emotion of fear to motivate the prospect to buy fear-reducing life insurance.

Emotions are both useful and harmful

As we have seen, the emotion of fear is extremely useful in its function of helping us to survive. Fear is what keeps us from running across a heavily traveled road without looking. Fear is what makes us stand in long lines to receive life-saving inoculations at the time of a serious epidemic. But fear, or any emotion, can also be quite destructive and harmful to the individual. While fear can help us run faster if we are trying to escape a bull in a field, fear may also operate to paralyze an individual temporarily. We can become petrified with fright and thus be unable to cope with a threat. Fear can motivate an underwriter to make enough calls and attempt enough closes to provide the money to meet his family budget. But fear can also keep this same underwriter from making calls or attempting closes if his fear of being rejected by the prospect is greater than his economic need.

Emotions can also be classified as realistic and unrealistic. When a child is hurt by falling from a chair, he develops a realistic fear of high places. When such an emotion becomes so strong that it is unusual, unpredictable, or inappropriate, we use the term phobia to describe it. A person who has a phobia of height is unrealistically afraid and this emotion can become quite destructive. A phobia of heights may keep an individual from driving his automobile if it is necessary for him to cross a bridge anywhere along his route. But a phobia can sometimes be useful because it can help maintain an equilibrium or even prevent death. A person with a phobia involving high places may have an unconscious desire to commit suicide by throwing himself from a building. At least his phobia keeps him from going where he might be tempted to do this.

Emotions regulate behavior

Emotions have a regulatory influence on human behavior. As we move close to danger, the fear aroused may make us hesitate or retreat from the danger. The small child must be closely supervised because he has not yet developed fear. The learning of fear can help regulate behavior so as to maintain security, preserve life, and so forth. In this sense, then, emotions can operate as a feedback mechanism to maintain a status quo or equilibrium for the individual.

An example of how an emotion can help maintain equilibrium and preserve life can be seen in the case of a forty-five-year-old man who had suffered a heart attack. The heart attack was a fairly mild one, but the man was badly frightened by it. After his period of recovery, he was quite careful to avoid undue exertion or any kind of strain on the heart. Occasionally he would temporarily forget about the need for moderation in activity and would rapidly climb a flight of stairs in his hurry to make an appointment. Noticing his pounding heart, he would again be quite afraid and thereafter take pains to avoid stressful situations. Whenever the man was slow and deliberate in his movements, he had relatively little cause to be afraid. When he increased his activity and was in actual danger of straining his damaged heart, a resulting fear which was aroused regulated his behavior in a healthful and probably life-saving way.

Without this mechanism of fear, a heart attack victim may well contribute to his own death. In this particular case, that is exactly what happened. While he was not a heavy drinker, this man occasionally drank enough to become quite unsteady. On one occasion after such a drinking bout, with his judgment dulled and, more important, with his fear artificially allayed, he volunteered to help a friend push his automobile down a slight grade so that it could coast to a service station. Because his protective fear had been temporarily reduced by the alcohol, he did not avoid the dangerous overexertion. This effort resulted in a second and fatal heart attack.

Emotions can act as a feed-back mechanism in another way. We are familiar with the squeals which we sometimes hear from a public address system when the sound from a loudspeaker enters the microphone and in turn is amplified, fed out over the loud-speakers, and enters the microphone again only to be amplified even more. This is an example of feedback. A small impulse in such a system can rather quickly generate a large response. Emotions act in this way to become life-saving mechanisms for us. The almost imperceptible sound of a rattlesnake's warning is enough to mobilize us into the action of quickly jumping to one side to avoid being struck. In such cases a very small amount of sensation triggers a large and violent reaction which aids in the survival of the individual.

How emotions become motives

The way emotions become motives for behavior helps explain how these motives operate in the adult life underwriter. We learn to be afraid of things. We are not born with the emotion of fear, but instead acquire this emotion (and other emotions) through a series of learning situations. For instance, we can learn to be afraid of something because it becomes associated with something else which seems to threaten our survival or which threatens the satis-faction of one of our biological needs. The young infant, for ex-ample, does not seem to be afraid of snakes, mice, or other objects which may be feared by adults. The child later learns to be afraid of these things because the perception of them becomes associated with pain or displeasure or some kind of threat to him.

The child's emotion of fear has developed as a result of condi-tioning (see Chapter 1, page 28). The emotion thus learned be-comes a motive for behavior and can become generalized to many other situations which may occur in the future.

Emotions can become generalized

One important fact about the learning of emotions and the development of emotions as motivating forces is that an emotion can become generalized from one situation to another. An individ-ual has learned to be afraid of many things by the time he is old enough to sell life insurance. If he has had a particularly bad ex-perience with a dentist as a child, the underwriter may always feel uncomfortable whenever he is in the dentist's chair, or even when he is attempting to sell insurance to a dentist.

As we saw earlier, the child experiences many frustrations and, of course, many punishments in the process of growing up. In response to these frustrations and punishments, he may experience the emotions of anger and fear. To the child, a parent is seen as a source of authority. As the child grows, he meets other adults who are also authority-figures. These might include his teacher, the policeman on the corner, his sergeant or superior in the Army, and even his general agent or manager. The anger or fear first experienced with the parental authority-figures can become gen-eralized to other authority-figures. The life underwriter may have the same emotional reactions to an older fatherly-looking prospect that he originally had to his father. The life underwriter may thus be afraid of calling on anyone in a position of real authority. This could be a president of a company, a judge, a city or state official, or even a school teacher. Perhaps all of us experience a certain amount of discomfort when we are in the presence of a high-ranking official such as the mayor or governor or the President of the United States. It is probable that some of the discomfort we feel is an earlier learned fear which has generalized from our parent-child relationship.

Another example of the way emotions can become generalized from one situation to another can be seen in again discussing our reactions to authority-figures. In the literally hundreds of learning experiences that we go through as children, we receive punishment or praise from our elders. Most of these experiences take place while we are with our parents and are literally looking up to a person who appears to us to be a giant in terms of size. We thus associate correction or punishment or fear with the presence of something above us. Later on in life, whenever an individual is physically above us, we may tend to react to him as to an authority-figure and experience the earlier learned emotional reactions of fear, anger, or respect. A speaker stands on an elevated platform. The judge in the court room sits high above the defendant. The physical relationship, especially the vertical distance between the two people, may have much to do with the creation of fear and respect. In the sales situation, even such an apparently superficial thing as the height of the chairs may affect the outcome of the sale. The person sitting in the lower chair may feel somewhat subordinate, although usually on an unconscious level. The underwriter who rises from his chair to lean over the desk of his prospect while making a point may gain some authority in the eyes of his prospect and may motivate his prospect more than if he were to remain seated. Unfortunately, the prospect may also feel intimidated by this and have a negative reaction to the underwriter. Most of the time, these physical relationships with their emotion-rousing effects operate unconsciously on both persons involved.

One does not have to experience pain in a situation to acquire the emotion of fear or apprehension. Fear itself becomes something to be feared. If we are with another person who shows fear or anxiety, quite often we begin to feel afraid ourselves. We do not have to be bitten by a poisonous snake to be startled when we suddenly see one. Having been told about snakes or having seen the fear of another person startled by a snake is enough to make this fear reaction become generalized. The significance of this kind of generalization of emotional response in the sales situation should be obvious.

The general agent or manager who himself experiences *call reluctance* may unknowingly transfer some fear of making calls to his underwriters when they are making joint calls. The underwriter may "learn" from his supervisor to be afraid when otherwise he might not have known fear. This works the other way, too. The general agent or manager who is not afraid or reluctant to make calls may also transfer a feeling of confidence to the underwriter he is supervising.

Similarly, the life underwriter who is afraid as he enters a prospect's office may very well cause the prospect to feel uneasy, uncomfortable, and even afraid. We show our fear in many ways, that is, in our facial expressions, our bodily posture, and in a slight, almost unnoticeable, tremor in our voice. Thus, the fear that an underwriter may feel becomes a self-defeating mechanism. This perhaps explains why some underwriters are able to give a fine sales presentation but find it difficult to motivate the prospect to buy. The prospect may unconsciously feel the underwriter's apprehension or fear without realizing that he does so. The prospect is not likely to say, "I don't want to buy insurance from you because you make me feel uncomfortable." He is instead likely to say something like, "I want to think about it," or "I prefer to buy the policy from someone else," and the underwriter may never be the wiser.

The role of emotions is often overlooked

We live in a culture where grown men are supposed to act in a reasonable, logical way and avoid giving signs of feeling or emotions. It is almost unthinkable for a grown man to cry or even show signs of distress when he experiences a disappointment or frustration. We feel that emotional behavior, while it may be appropriate for a woman, is inappropriate for a man. Because of the way our society looks upon emotions and the expression of feeling, it is likely that we tend to overlook the role that this very important source of energy plays in our daily behavior. It is becoming increasingly recognized that many of our decisions, especially our decisions to buy, are made for emotional reasons rather than for rational or logical ones.

A life underwriter may find that he is organizing his time well, has a good list of prospects, makes many calls each week, but somehow fails to sell much life insurance. He has done everything that he reasonably can in a logical, rational way to try to make more sales, but has ignored one or two *emotional motives* within himself which may have been keeping him from being effective in the sales interview. The underwriter who fails to recognize that he experiences an unusual amount of fear when calling on prospects cannot do much to change his situation. Recognizing a fear is one of the first things we must do if we are to modify or overcome it.

The life underwriter who cannot allow himself to express genuine feeling or behave in an emotional way with a prospect may deny himself a most potent way of influencing his prospect's behavior. Many a prospect has bought an insurance policy while at the height of an emotional reaction stimulated by seeing his life underwriter express sincere concern for him or his family.

A seasoned underwriter telling a favorite insurance story of hardship may let tears come to his eyes, thus creating a great motivational impact on his prospect. Obviously this can also be overdone. We cannot go around giving unrestrained vent to our feelings, of course, but if we try too hard to cover up our feelings, we lose effectiveness as a persuader. We are less likely to be able to establish a motivating atmosphere with the prospect, less likely to be able to use the force of an emotional motive, less likely to be in tune with the prospect, and less likely to be able to sense the emotional motives of the prospect if we avoid any emotional expression.

We need to find a balance between being too emotional on the one hand and too suppressed or neutral on the other. An underwriter, especially if he is a younger man, will often mistakenly think that he will look older, more mature, and more sophisticated if he maintains a poker face and an air of studied indifference when calling on prospects. It is more likely that he will be seen as the artificial person he is. Rarely do we fool other people when we try to behave in ways we don't feel. We may think we fool others, but we usually don't.

Some men find that they are successful salesmen when they are selling a tangible product, but fail to succeed in selling life insurance. While there may be many reasons for this, at least one of the reasons probably has to do with the fact that life insurance selling involves more emotional situations. The life underwriter induces his prospect to think seriously about his own life and death, about his family and his obligations as a father and husband. These are highly emotionally-charged subjects. The life underwriter who becomes upset and disturbed in such emotional situations may be unable to deal effectively with an emotionally motivated prospect. If we are in a group and someone else brings up a subject which embarrasses us or makes us uncomfortable, we are very likely to try to change the subject. If, in the sales situation, a prospect brings up an objection based on an emotional motive, and this emotion is disturbing to the life underwriter, he may ignore the question and attempt to change the subject or otherwise escape a threatening situation. The prospect is likely to feel misunderstood and confused, and the chances of the sale are diminished.

Generalized emotions help explain complex behavior

Realizing how we learn emotional reactions and how these various emotions generalize to include new and often inappropriate situations helps explain why human behavior is so complex and often so baffling to us. It does not really "make sense" that a grown adult life underwriter should feel afraid when he is sitting in the office of the president of the company, but the fear is often there just the same. An underwriter may not see the connection between an earlier learning experience and his present emotional reaction. While it is not a simple process, the overcoming of a fear reaction to a present situation usually depends on the individual's ability to understand how he *learned* the fear reaction and how it has *generalized* to include present situations.

Just as emotional motives are learned early in life, so can they be unlearned or modified by later learning situations. If the life underwriter initially experiences fear when calling on authority-figures but subsequently achieves success or pleasure from this activity (or does not experience pain or punishment), then the emotional motive of fear is usually reduced. The success of the underwriter's attempt to overcome the crippling effect of a fear motive will depend largely on his gaining competence through good education and training, and on the ability of his general agent or manager to assist him in gaining new confidence in himself. There are many, many ways of doing this, such as systematically pointing out to the underwriter the things that he is doing well in selling situations and thereby turning a former situation of fear into one of pleasure. Relearning or modifying emotional responses often results from changes in our perspective or the way things look to us.

Empathy and understanding

Before leaving the subject of emotional motives, we should discuss the reaction of empathy, briefly mentioned in Chapter 1. We tend to respond favorably toward those people who we feel understand us. A genuine understanding of other people usually requires that we be able to feel the same feelings that they are experiencing. If one of our close friends has recently lost his mother or father, we will come much closer to understanding how he feels if we ourselves have had the same experience. We can feel empathetic with another person if we are able to *identify* with him or his situation, enter into his world, so to speak, and see it through his eyes. Empathy, then, is an emotional understanding of another person.

A good many objections to buying life insurance which a prospect may raise are based on emotional motives rather than rational reasons. The underwriter who is "in tune" with his prospect and is able to sense the operation of an emotional motive is in a good position to overcome an objection based on such a motive. All too often the underwriter is so self-centered and interested in his own situation (that is, in making the sale) that he is quite unable to be empathetic with his prospect and, therefore, to understand what the prospect is saying emotionally.

There is, of course, the danger that the life underwriter can become too closely identified with his prospect and accept an objection uncritically. Empathy can be a valuable sales tool for the underwriter, but it must be controlled. Since empathy is the placing of one's self emotionally into another person's situation, this can facilitate an emotional communication, but it may also lead to a distortion of perception. If we too closely identify with another person, *without proper discrimination,* we are likely to see things which are not there. We may "project" into another person our own reaction to his situation and erroneously assume that his reaction would be the same as ours.

An unrealistic projection of a feeling is illustrated by this story. A man was on his way to his next door neighbor's house to borrow a lawn mower when he began to think: "I hope my neighbor will let me borrow the lawn mower. The last time I borrowed it I did not return it for a long time and he got pretty mad. It might be that he will remind me of this and refuse to give me the lawn mower. It seems to me that he should give me another chance. But maybe he won't. It wouldn't be very neighborly of him to refuse to lend me the lawn mower just because I was late in bringing it back. In fact, it makes me mad to think he might turn me down I always suspected he didn't like me anyway." By this time our borrower has reached the neighbor's door, has knocked, and is now confronting his neighbor. Before the neighbor has a chance to say anything, our friend blurts out, "Well, you can just keep your darned lawn mower," and with that, he walks away. This is an example of how an individual has recognized, unconsciously, how he himself would react in a certain situation and has projected this feeling into his neighbor. This, of course, is not empathy or understanding. When we feel hostile and mean toward people in general, our natural reaction is to think that everyone else is hostile and mean too. We must avoid projecting our feelings if we want to see the world and other people as they really are.

One way to practice understanding a prospect and his emotional motives is to do what has been called "role-playing." In role-playing a life underwriter takes the part of a prospect for insurance and allows another underwriter to attempt to sell insurance to him. As the underwriter tries to imagine how the prospect may be reacting to a sales approach, he may get some valuable insight into the sales situation which he can then in turn use to modify his sales approach. Role-playing helps us become more sympathetic and understanding of other people on an emotional level.

Emotional motives are with us all day and every day. We cannot engage in a single activity either by ourselves or with other people without having some emotional motives in operation that affect our behavior. The more we know about how emotions affect our behavior and how they affect the behavior of other people, the more we can see how certain emotional reactions may not be appropriate for a given situation. We can then engage in new learning experiences and enjoy the *constructive benefits* of emotional motives rather than suffer the destructive consequences of them. Again we see that the life underwriter who has the broadest possible knowledge of human behavior (including his own) and is the most sensitive to the reactions of other people will be in a better position to influence their behavior.

Social Needs and Motivation

As we have seen, the operation of physical needs and the drive-reducing activities which result from them act in a *relatively mechanical way*. Persuading people to behave in certain ways because of what we say to them is a much more complex and less easily controlled activity. Social motives, as the term implies, have to do with the normal desires of the human being to associate with other people. The human being cannot be isolated from his society, and much of what he does as an individual is related to this apparent need to be an acceptable member of his society. We *learn* that it is important to get along with other people and that many of our satisfactions can come only from other people. It is true that we could live as an isolated individual by becoming a hermit, but most individuals choose to live in a group and sacrifice some personal freedom for the immense gain that comes from group activity. Man is a conforming animal. Man also has purely personal impulses and desires. With each individual there must be a *fusion* between his individual and personal needs and the needs of the group or groups of which he is a member. Out of this conflict between the individual and his group(s) grow social motives.

For sheer survival we do not need a twelve-room house, a Cadillac, a boat, a TV set, a life insurance policy, etc. But *we learn to need these things.* It is obvious we are using the term need in a different sense than was the case in the previous sections. Before, we talked about a physical or bodily need as being a requirement for survival. As we talk about *social motives* being based on an individual's need for association with other people, we might better substitute for "need" the words *want* or *desire*. Often an individual feels that he needs something which an impartial observer can see that he only wants or desires. In other words, in our daily activities we do not generally make a distinction between what we need and what we want. We need a haircut, not for survival purposes, but because we have learned that being neatly trimmed makes us more acceptable to others and this is something most of us want very much.

By the time we have reached adulthood, we have learned to want or desire an almost infinite variety of things. As with any learning, we tend to learn first or best those things which seem to lead to reward. The basic principle of learning discussed in Chapter 1 called the law of effect states that behavior which *seems* to lead to reward tends to be repeated while behavior which *seems* not to lead to reward or seems to lead to punishment tends not to be repeated. We use the word "seems" here because we usually act on the basis of what we believe to be true and not necessarily what is objectively true. As we go through life, some things which we do result in approval and affection from those people around us and other things that we do result in punishment. *Learning what to want or desire is essentially a part of the process of assimilating the culture in which we live.*

Desire to be with people

The infant is totally dependent upon his mother or some other adult for survival. The infant goes through periodic cycles of experiencing hunger and discomfort which are relieved by something that the mother does for him. Being in close contact with another individual is thus pleasurably associated with the satisfaction of wants. It seems natural, then, that all of us very early in life learn to desire the company of other people. For the child, a punishment

worse than spanking is to be made to stand in the corner or somehow to be isolated from the rest of the family. The most unpleasant
punishment we have devised for prisoners, short of death, is soli-
tary confinement. One of the outstanding symptoms of mental illness is the tendency of the patient to isolate himself from other
people. A patient in a mental hospital will frequently be seen to
stand apart rather than to engage in some group activity. Thus,
the *social motive to be with people* is one of our first learned motives and probably continues to be the strongest motive influencing
our behavior throughout life.

Desire to be accepted

Closely related to this social motive of desiring the company of
other people is the social motive of wanting to be liked and to
be accepted and respected by others. This motive to be accepted
is, of course, operating within both the prospect and the life
underwriter in the sales situation. The strength of this motive will
vary according to the importance to us of the other person or
group of persons. We are concerned about being wanted and respected by those people who are *important* to us, in the sense that
they control things that we want, such as love, money, or status.
If the life underwriter can identify himself with a group of which
his prospect is also a member, the underwriter's reception is likely
to be much warmer. If it can be demonstrated that the prospect
and the underwriter have a common friend, the prospect is much
less likely to give the underwriter a brush-off, thereby risking rejection himself. The desire to be liked is so important that the life
underwriter will frequently work harder to gain the approval and
friendship of his general agent or manager than he will to earn his
living. The desire for companionship, approval, and acceptance
plays a very important part in all business activities.
    The life underwriter who feels that he is not liked or respected
may react to this by trying very hard to gain this approval from
those with whom he comes in contact in his work or social life.
Where this motive is very strong, it stimulates the underwriter to
find all sorts of ways of gaining the approval and affection of others.

Some writers have referred to this as a "wooing" instinct or a desire to seduce people and thereby either gain affection from them or control over them.

Desire for affection

This social motive or desire for affection from others is one of the chief pressures toward conformity in behavior. As children, we are frequently punished or corrected by our parents, who threaten to take away their affection for us unless we do as they say. When the child does something wrong, the average parent will usually say, "You are a bad boy" rather than saying, "You have done a bad thing." Parents show love and affection to their children when the children "behave themselves" and tend to show anger and rejection when the children do not behave. Thus, we grow up associating a fear of rejection or loss of affection with wrongdoing. When the manager pounds his desk and tells the life underwriter to "get out there and make more calls" the life underwriter may scramble to do just this not only to retain his job, but also keep from losing the good will of his manager.

Desire to help others

Another social motive is the desire to be affectionate toward other people and to take care of, or to help, others. It is socially acceptable to do things for the welfare of other people. We learn that it is a pleasurable thing to receive the kind of recognition which accompanies an apparently unselfish desire to care for others. The desire to help others or to be altruistic probably cannot be separated from a more selfish desire to help ourselves. We often do things for others because it makes us feel good. The fact that this is so only illustrates again that our behavior is motivated by more than one desire or need at a time. While we may discuss motives one at a time, we must not make the mistake of thinking that any one motive ever exists entirely by itself. The life underwriter who does not have this desire to help may be thought of as cold or hostile. Where this desire or social motive becomes too strong, however, the life underwriter may find himself spending so much time providing service to his policyholders that he does not do enough searching for new business.

Desire to make money

The desire to make money is a social motive that perhaps has more importance in our present American culture than it does anywhere else in the world. Our worth as men in this society is frequently measured by the size of the paycheck we bring home. The definition of success which most businessmen give is in terms of money or financial security. The desire for money may be stronger in a man who grew up in a family of little means. But a man from a well-to-do family may also have a strong desire for money in order to maintain his socioeconomic status. Money to many people becomes almost the equivalent of affection. Many a man who has been denied normal affection as a child or who has an unhappy marriage has attempted to compensate unconsciously for this by an unusual degree of striving for money.

Christmas giving provides us with another example of how money can be equated to affection. A tendency of many people is to purchase the most expensive gifts for those they like the most. The recipient is likely to interpret the gift's probable cost as an indication of the degree of friendship or affection the giver has for him.

Desire for money plays an important part in the motivation of both the life underwriter and his prospect. Much additional insurance has been sold not so much because the prospect thought he needed an extra amount as because another five or ten thousand would bring him coverage up to an even $100,000 or some other even amount. How much insurance a man carries, for example, is often considered a measure of his money-making ability as well as of his concern for his family. Some men have bought large policies of several hundred thousand dollars in face value because of the underwriter's statement that "this puts you in a very elite class."

Desire to be dominant

Another very important social motive is the desire to control or influence the behavior of other people, or in other words, to be dominant. We learn to desire dominance because we have found satisfaction in controlling the behavior of others. A strong desire to dominate may be established in a child when he discovers that he is much more likely to have his own desires satisfied when he is controlling the situation rather than being controlled by it.

The life underwriter is in the business of controlling the behavior of other people, even to the extent of encouraging them to take action which they may actively resist. The desire for dominance, like all social motives, varies greatly according to the individual. One with a strong need and desire to dominate will be much more effective in changing the opinions, attitudes, and behavior of others than someone with a minimum desire for dominance. Such individuals are often regarded as natural leaders and are looked up to by the majority of people. An individual with a strong desire to dominate who has learned techniques of controlling behavior of other people may often *compel others to action by his very bearing or manner.*

The control of other people is frequently achieved through physical size or strength. In our culture a tall person is generally given more respect than a short person. The size of the underwriter will affect (but does not completely determine) the degree to which he can be dominant. A man small in stature may work much harder (overcompensate) to overcome any disadvantage he may have or thinks he has because of his size.

Desire to submit

In addition to the motive of dominance, there is perhaps the equally common *motive of submission.* These two contradictory motives can, and probably do, exist to a certain degree in all of us. To cooperate in a society we must of necessity be submissive in certain situations, such as in obeying traffic regulations or tax laws. While we all must submit to the general rules and laws of our society, in some individuals the desire to submit is a quite predominant motive. Life can be seen as a series of never-ending struggles to survive and to accomplish. We are constantly confronted with change, and change is often uncomfortable. The life underwriter, when he calls on a prospect, is trying to induce his prospect to change. He may arouse in the prospect's mind some vital questions about which a decision must be made. There will be in many prospects a strong (although unconscious) desire to submit to the underwriter and have the underwriter make these decisions for him. The desire to submit will be stronger, of course, if the underwriter is respected and liked by his prospects. There is a certain amount of pleasure to be gained from giving in and being submissive to another individual. It eliminates the necessity for struggle and exertion in decision-making.

Military service was emotionally satisfying to many men because a great many of life's decisions were made for them. If the desire to submit is very strong on the part of the life underwriter, he is likely to be sold by his prospects more often than he, in turn, sells them. The strong general agent or manager can discourage the growth of strength and dominance in his agents if he exerts too much control over them himself. The manager who forces his agents to respect him and to follow the rules of the agency to the letter and without exception may be building an agency of relatively submissive men. Dominance and submission are learned reactions. We are not born as a dominant or a submissive individual. While it is not likely that an underwriter can change completely from being predominantly submissive to becoming predominantly dominant, it is possible for him to become more effective in controlling or influencing the behavior of his prospects.

Desire to compete and win

Closely related to this motive of dominance is a learned desire for healthy aggressiveness and rivalry. The desire to compete and win is frequently strong enough in some men to motivate them more highly than financial rewards might. The desire to "keep up with the Joneses" or perhaps to excel the Joneses is a common characteristic in our culture. The insurance sales situation is also a competitive situation in which the prospect and the life underwriter are attempting to sell each other. The prospect may be attempting to sell the life underwriter on the idea that he doesn't need insurance just as vigorously as the underwriter is trying to sell him insurance. The prospect is often trying to dominate and control the underwriter and may feel that he has won a kind of victory if he can get the underwriter out of his office without having signed an application blank.

Desire to protect our self-image

There are many other social motives, or desires, including the desire for status, power, security, achievement, acquisition, autonomy, order or structure, recognition, and others. One of the more important social motives, however, is the desire to protect our self-image, which we spoke about in Chapter 1. Whether or not we can verbalize what we see, each of us have a certain view of ourself. We think of ourselves as being generous, kind, honest, trustworthy, etc., and we tend to resist anything which disturbs this image. One of the most shattering personal experiences is to overhear two people talking about us. We may be made to realize that the image that other people have of us does not exactly correspond to our own self-image.

Maintaining emotional distance. We realize certain things about ourselves which we hope other people don't see. We may feel inadequate or inferior, and yet hope that others do not notice this. Our desire to maintain a favorable self-image may keep us from saying too much about ourselves or our feelings to another individual. If this fear of exposing ourselves is very strong, we may go to extreme lengths to maintain an emotional distance between ourselves and other people. We may feel that if our friends really knew what we were like, they wouldn't like us any more. Unfortunately, this desire to maintain our self-image may also keep us from learning valuable things about ourselves and others.

Rationalization by forgetting. Another way that we attempt to protect our self-image is to rationalize our behavior; i.e., to forget or to blame someone else. Rationalization is a device which we all use at one time or another to explain something that we have done so that it appears more acceptable than it would if the real reason were given.

An underwriter may join a civic club because he wants to contribute something to his community but perhaps more accurately because he hopes that it will give him a favorable entrée to some choice insurance prospects. An individual may rationalize that his infidelity is excusable because "my wife doesn't understand me." We resort to rationalization when we don't want to face our real motives. Rationalization does have the function of tending to reduce, at least temporarily, any anxiety we may have because of motives that we feel are unacceptable. We retain our image of ourselves as being reasonable, rational individuals of good judgment by *explaining away* those occasions when we are quite unreasonable, irrational, and show poor judgment. The easiest thing in the world is to forget something that is unpleasant to us. We can retain our self-image as a mature, sensible businessman if we are able to forget the one or two recent occasions when we made a fool of ourself.

Forgetting is often a very healthy mechanism. The individual who is *unable* to forget some traumatic event such as wartime combat experiences may be filled with anxiety almost beyond endurance. Like everything else, however, forgetting can be serious if it is overdone. We may forget an appointment we have made with our manager for the purpose of discussing why our production has been down, but missing this appointment may very well lead to further complications. While we may protect our self-image by conveniently forgetting things which conflict with our idealized image of ourself, it is much more mature and constructive to face the unpleasant memories or experiences and to attempt to achieve a more adequate adjustment.

Rationalization by blaming someone else. Another easy mechanism to use in our effort to preserve our favorable self-image is to blame someone else when things go wrong. We all know people who never make a mistake and are always right. We also know how hard it is to get along with them. But each of us probably tends to deny responsibility for many more of our failures than we are ready to admit. For example, an underwriter may kid himself by thinking that sales are down around Christmas time because people are too busy shopping, that the first of the year is bad because people are just getting over the holiday season, or that March and April is the time when everyone is concerned about income tax, etc. These are reasons some underwriters give for their failure to produce an adequate volume of life insurance. If the reader of this text finds it very easy to see reasons for not making a sale, and these reasons almost always involve *someone else,* it may be time for him to take stock and see if he is not really just fooling himself.

Motives Can Be Conscious or Unconscious

Most people buy life insurance to provide an emergency fund, a family income, a life income for the wife, education for the children, or retirement for old age. *Or do they?*

We have talked before about the existence of the unconscious part of our psychological being. In this decade of the sixties, the public in general has come to accept this rather mysterious notion that we do not always know what motivates us. But many have accepted this notion in much the same spirit that they accept the admonition to "be careful how you drive, the life you save may be your own." They accept it as a good idea—but for someone else.

Most well-educated people will agree that behavior is motivated by unconscious urgings, and yet will privately reject the notion that they themselves would be so foolish as to do something without actually knowing why. When it comes right down to it, we all want to feel as if we are making purely rational decisions when we buy the house we live in, the furniture, the new automobile, or a life insurance policy. How many people would readily admit that they buy a supercharged Thunderbolt automobile because it gives them a feeling of greater sexual virility? Who wants to admit that he smokes in order to feel more grown up, to reduce the uneasiness and anxiety he feels with others, or to continue the same enjoyable sucking activity he experienced as an infant? And yet research studies indicate that these and many more unconscious motives influence our buying decisions.

Refusal to face certain motives

History shows that men have always had some very noble impulses. But history also reveals that human beings have many impulses which are far from noble. As we saw in the section on protection of our self-image, we frequently hide certain motives even from ourselves. An anxious mother may vigorously deny that she has hostile feelings toward her own children. She may attempt to prove her point by bending over backward to show how concerned and protective she is with them. There is adequate clinical and scientific evidence to show that a certain amount of hostility on the part of parents toward their children is quite "normal" and that excessive hovering over children, protecting them from all conceivable sources of minor injuries or insults, is an attempt on the part of the parents to disguise their unconscious hostility from themselves.

In some ways it is easiest to run and hide from that which is unpleasant. It takes courage to face the truth. It takes maturity to recognize those things within ourselves which make us uncomfortable as well as to recognize those things of which we can be proud. Perhaps the maturity of a nation can be measured by the extent to which the mass of its people are lethargic or indifferent to a world crisis even when it threatens their very survival. It seems difficult for most people to acknowledge openly the existence of unconscious motives, especially when these motives may not be particularly flattering. And so it is that we go about living and behaving and buying life insurance for reasons only part of which we are willing to acknowledge and therefore to talk about.

Unconscious motives and reasonable explanations

The life underwriter must sell insurance by fighting a battle on two fronts. He must move his prospect to buy on the basis of unconscious, emotional motives, but at the same time he must supply the prospect with what looks like a rational, logical, mature reason for buying life insurance. Much selling goes on because the salesman is able to give the buyer a good-sounding reason for giving in to an emotional impulse to buy. Many a family has purchased an automobile far too expensive for their budget because the salesman has convinced them that "you deserve the very best."

What are some possible unconscious motives that people may have for buying life insurance? Strangely enough, it is often because of a man's hostility toward his family that he buys life insurance. Family life is not always completely satisfying to all men.

To some it represents restriction, hardship, and a good bit of pain and anguish because of the problems which inevitably arise from time to time. But to admit such feelings to anyone, even to ourselves, would make us look like scoundrels. One way to overcome the guilt that we may feel because of such unacceptable impulses is to buy things for the family. Much buying, especially at Christmas time, can be traced rather directly to an effort on a person's part to convince himself and the recipient that there is great affection existing between them, thus pacifying his own guilt feelings.

Without doubt the purchase of life insurance is often made because of the genuine love and regard that the man holds for his family. The policyholder may be proving his emotional maturity by this act of giving life insurance. A policyholder frequently experiences the greatest depth of feeling for his family at the moment he has assured himself that a sufficient estate has been guaranteed for their protection and benefit. We have seen how money and affection are related in our culture. A policyholder may very well feel that the larger amount of his insurance, the more love he has for his family.

In our culture, money is also related to power. Feelings of sexual inadequacy are quite common among American men, and the urge to earn a large income is sometimes an unconscious desire to demonstrate one's potency as a male. In such cases the purchase of a large life insurance policy is based on the motive, perhaps unconscious, of proving sexual adequacy.

There are probably few among us who are not frightened by the thought of our own death. While we cannot avoid death, we can symbolically postpone it. Part of the joy of having a family and rearing children is the thought that somehow we live on in our children. We may also receive some comfort in the thought that we can continue to provide for our families even after physical death. This is a very powerful human emotion and undoubtedly influences the sale of life insurance.

It was reported that a young college student purchased some flight insurance just before boarding a plane to go home for a week end visit with his girl. The student made the policy payable to her and the policy was, of course, mailed to her. The student summed up his reason for this by saying, "It's amazing what you can get for a quarter." What emotional and perhaps unconscious motives do you suppose he was feeling?

Another unconscious motive operating during a life insurance sale involves the wife of the prospect. Again we need to talk about unconscious hostile impulses. Many a wife feels that marriage has ruined her career. She feels that she has been unreasonably tied down with children and that somehow it is all her husband's fault. For these or any number of reasons, a wife frequently feels hostility towards her husband, but is unable to acknowledge this to herself. (Of course, some wives are well aware of the hostility they feel toward their husbands and may show it openly!) During the life insurance sale, the inevitability of the husband's death is, of course, part of the discussion. Sitting in on this conversation may be alarming to the wife partly because it threatens to make her unconscious hostile impulses come close to the surface of consciousness. This would be an anxiety-arousing experience for the wife. Because of her urge to terminate this uncomfortable conversation, the wife may present unreasonable and irrelevant objections to the purchase of the policy. She may even unconsciously seek a sense of reassurance from the life underwriter. The life underwriter who senses discomfort on the part of the wife and can help her feel more comfortable may be on his way toward making a sale.

If a prospect is hesitating to buy life insurance for emotional reasons, and if these emotional reasons are unconscious, a logical argument on the part of the life underwriter is of little value. The underwriter cannot become a psychologist and probe deeply into his prospect's unconscious to find the objections hidden there. But he can broaden his awareness of unconscious motivation in general and become more skilled in drawing out his prospect in conversation. The more free the prospect feels to discuss his hopes and fears with the underwriter, the more able the underwriter will be to fit an insurance plan to the prospect's needs correctly and professionally.

Discovering unconscious motives

If the prospect has unconscious motives which may keep him from buying life insurance, how can the life underwriter go about

206 MAN IN MOTIVATION

discovering these? We must say that the life underwriter can probably do very little toward discovering the *full* extent of unconscious and perhaps unacceptable emotional motives that are opposing the sale of life insurance. But on the other hand he may get some clues if he uses a certain amount of skill in his interview with the prospect.

Asking the prospect why he is not buying will probably not cause him to tell all of his objections. The more the underwriter can get the prospect to talk about himself, his life situation, the way he feels about life insurance in general, the way he feels about other kinds of investments, etc., the more likely he is to sense what some of the unspoken objections might be. This, at least, can give the underwriter some hypotheses to test, or assumptions to try out, in his attempt to persuade the prospect to sign the application. A professional interviewer is usually well equipped to understand rather quickly some of the unconscious emotions and motives which may be operating within a person. The professional interviewer does this by doing very little talking himself, but being very active in his listening.

As we saw in a previous chapter, listening is not simply a passive process but properly done is quite an active procedure. If the underwriter asks his prospect, "How do you feel about life insurance in general?" he may get a better idea of the prospect's hidden objections than he would if he were to ask the prospect, "How do you like the features of this policy I have here?" We can often get much more information by questioning a person indirectly than we can by using a sort of third-degree, grilling technique. The life underwriter can encourage his prospect to continue talking at length by merely saying, "That's interesting. Tell me more," or by saying, "I can understand how you feel about that—please go on."

Motives Can Be Positive or Negative

We can control the behavior of others through an appeal to their motives by promising *to satisfy* them if they will behave as we desire. We can also influence their behavior by threatening *to take away some satisfactions* which they may already have. Thus, we can move people in a positive way by giving satisfaction or we can move them in a negative way by threatening or decreasing satisfaction. The behavior of people is influenced by both reward and punishment. The chief effect of punishment seems to be to produce a greater variety of responses. If a person is punished for behaving in a certain way, he is likely to try a new way of behaving. Punishment may not by itself bring an individual to do a desired thing, but it does introduce some change in his behavior so that the desired response may occur and can then be rewarded.

A life underwriter can motivate a prospect to purchase insurance by frightening him, by threatening to reject him, by making him feel guilty, and so forth. By using such negative motives, the life underwriter can induce his prospect to avoid procrastinating and to follow the underwriter's suggestions. The use of negative motives is effective because they influence an individual to avoid something. While the underwriter may make his sale by using primarily negative motives, he may also induce his prospect to *avoid him* in the future! The use of positive motives, i.e., showing the prospect the rewards of signing the insurance application, has the advantage of strengthening the relationship between the prospect and the underwriter and also of being a more constructive influence on the prospect in terms of his own emotional growth and development.

It has been said that the sale of life insurance is a character-building occupation. The life underwriter builds character when he encourages his prospect to be concerned about things other than himself. There are probably fewer selfish reasons for buying life insurance than for most purchases. To reward a prospect for his more generous and responsible motives is certainly a healthier influence than to coerce behavior by threats, embarrassment, or humiliation.

Negative motivation is used frequently by management as well as in rearing children because in many ways it is easier and quicker to use than positive motivation. It takes less time to slap a child for misbehaving than it does to explain the more desirable behavior and find ways for making this rewarding. The general agent or manager may shame his underwriter into leaving the office and making calls, but it is doubtful that the additional calls the life underwriter makes will be very profitable. Where negative motivation is used predominantly, those who are so motivated may follow directions with greater obedience but at the same time they are less spontaneous and creative. The life underwriter who uses negative motivation to coerce his prospect to sign the application will probably find it more difficult to get good referred leads from his new client. This client may even give the underwriter some bad leads as a sort of revenge. It may also be that the client who purchased because of negative motivation is more apt to let his policy lapse than one who purchased through positive motivation.

Motives and Levels of Aspiration

This has been a discussion of some of the motives which influence our behavior. When we refer to these motives, we are talking about the presence of an impulse, a drive, or a tension which moves us toward a goal. It seems to be characteristic of the human being that he sets goals for himself and then tends to move toward reaching those goals. Some of these goals have been set for him, that is, the goal of attaining food and rest, and of preserving life. The individual strives for other goals, much more personal in nature because of the pleasure that he thinks he will receive.

If we are to be satisfied in our attempt to reach the goals that we set for ourselves, these goals have to be *obtainable*. We sometimes set goals for ourselves which cannot be obtained. It is a common American myth that anyone, if he tries hard enough and wants to badly enough, can be anything or do anything. While we can achieve more with more effort, some things that we may desire are essentially impossible. Everyone, for example, cannot be President of the United States. Everyone cannot run a mile in less than four minutes. Everyone cannot create something comparable to Einstein's theory of relativity. In fact, probably few of us can even understand such a theory.

The way an individual sets goals for himself has much to do with the over-all satisfaction which he achieves in life. If we habitually set goals for ourselves which are impossible to attain, we are likely to be frustrated much of the time. The level at which a person sets his goal is called the *level of aspiration*. If this level of aspiration is reasonably higher than the *level of present accomplishment*, most of us seem inspired to work harder to reach for a higher level of accomplishment. But if the level of aspiration is unrealistically high, extreme frustration or complete lack of effort can result. If we are attempting to improve our skill as a high jumper, for example, moving the bar an inch higher than our previous record may inspire us to make one tremendous leap. But if the bar is moved twelve inches higher, we will not even try to jump. The life underwriter who sets an unrealistically high goal of production for himself may not only experience frustration, but may react by eventually giving up and leaving the life insurance business.

The Motive of Self-Actualization

After the human being has satisfied his basic needs for survival and for protection from danger, he begins to respond to a higher level of motives. This second level of motivation includes the desire to achieve satisfaction and comfort from other people in the form of love, affection, and the pleasure of being part of a group. When this second level of motives is reasonably well satisfied, a still higher motive asserts itself. This third level of motivation is referred to as the motive of *self-actualization*.

Man seems to have a drive to make full use of the capacities or abilities he has. He apparently needs to grow, to develop, to improve himself, and to make the best use of the particular and unique talents which he has. Unlike the biological needs and the social motives, the motive for self-actualization seems only to increase in strength as it is satisfied. While we stop searching for food when we satisfy our hunger, and we relax somewhat in our search for affection when we become a loved and respected member of a group, we seem to want even more growth as we succeed in growing.

By growth we mean something more than normal physical and mental maturing. We mean the expanding ability of man to make use of those qualities which make him unique among animals. Growth or self-actualization is the creative, building urge in the human being to deal with his fellow creatures on a more mutually satisfactory level. Human growth involves becoming a responsible, self-directing, self-knowing person who moves toward becoming everything of which he is humanly capable.

Growth implies a direction. But what is that direction to be for each of us? If self-actualization means reaching the height of our capacity or achieving an ultimate purpose, what is that purpose? What are our goals in life? We refer once again to the question we asked at the beginning of Chapter 1, "Who am I?" Do we not need to achieve a better understanding of who we are in terms of our chief talents in order to move toward realizing the full use of those talents?

"What do I want from life?" may seem like a senseless question to some, and to others a terribly hard but necessary question to answer. But do we not need to come up with some kind of answer to this question in order to achieve a sense of direction in realizing our potential? These two questions are worth reflection and thought.

6

Motivation and Behavior Change

The life underwriter is in the business of persuasion. By the time he has been in this business for a year or more he has persuaded some and failed to persuade others to buy life insurance. To do this, some underwriters use the "hard sell," some use the "soft sell," while others may not be conscious of using any particular method. The desired result, however, is to influence the prospect's behavior in a direction which is favorable for the prospect and also favorable for the underwriter. The underwriter wants to persuade the prospect that it is in his best interests to buy more insurance.

In a strict sense, the life underwriter cannot directly change the behavior of his prospect, any more than he can learn how to swim for the one whom he is instructing. The swimming instructor may encourage, may cajole, may teach technique, and may even throw his pupil into the water, but he never can succeed in making his pupil learn how to swim. His pupil must do the learning himself. We can teach others but we cannot learn for them. In the same way, the life underwriter cannot directly control the behavior of his prospect. He can only control some of the variables which in turn may cause the prospect to alter his pattern of behavior. We

212 MAN IN MOTIVATION

stress this point to re-emphasize the inner-control aspect of motivation. The life underwriter causes a behavior change in the prospect not because of what he says but because of what the prospect hears, not because of what the underwriter wants but because of what the prospect wants, not because of the plan and the supporting figures presented by the underwriter but because the prospect sees a way to gain satisfaction or avoid discomfort.

The effectiveness of persuasion obviously depends upon the skill of the persuader, but the skillful persuader is one who sees or can find out the direction in which his prospect is already leaning so that the persuader can give a well-planned "push" toward buying life insurance. There are many paths that insurance prospects take toward buying life insurance. The effective persuader can see the path his prospect is already on and can make it easier for the prospect to find his way along this path. We deliberately "make" a plant grow taller not by directly pulling it up, but by providing the right atmosphere of water, soil, and light. In the same sense, we can have only an indirect, although powerful, influence on the behavior of another individual.

Acquiring skill as a persuader means gaining a greater measure of control over other people. To what extent and for what purposes this control is used by the student of human behavior are questions of great importance and concern. It leads us to consider the problem of ethics.

The Ethics of Persuasion

Man has always had an inclination to persuade or motivate the behavior of his fellow men. Until very recently in man's long history, this persuasion has been largely by actual physical force in the form of a stone, a club, torture chambers, imprisonment or the threat of imprisonment, wars, etc. As mankind has become more civilized, his methods of persuasion have tended to move from the purely physical to the more mental or psychological. Indeed man has discovered that in some instances "the pen is mightier than the sword." The development of language and man's increasing use of it have given him another tool to use in motivating the behavior of others. Of course, the increased use of psychological measures does not mean that the more basic forms of persuasion have been abandoned. But in the last hundred years, we have made relatively great strides in our psychological understanding of ourselves and have thereby achieved the possibility of a greater and greater control over others.

The rapid development of psychological knowledge and the wide-spread dissemination of this information to laymen in the present century presents us with the possibility of greatly increasing the potentialities of man, his dignity and his security, but it can become a tool of despots and dictators (in business as well as in government) to control the masses for the selfish gain of the few. This has been the problem of every great advance in knowledge such as the invention of gunpowder or atomic energy, the discovery of germs, or the achievement of rapid transportation and communication. *The more control* we achieve over the behavior of other people, *the more responsibility* we must take for the proper exercise of that control. The young child is quite limited in his ability to control his surroundings or to control machines. We first give the child a tricycle to ride which he can control and which requires no more responsibility than the child is able to assume. As the child grows into adulthood and acquires greater ability to control machines, he is allowed to operate a more complicated machine such as the automobile, control of which directly affects the lives of other people. We rightfully expect him to assume a much greater responsibility along with his increased control. The high accident rate on our highways makes us forcefully aware of what can happen when an individual with the ability to control an auto retains the sense of responsibility of a child.

The student of behavior is in effect accumulating a body of knowledge which is relatively as advanced and as complicated as the automobile. Armed with this new maneuverability, the student must also consider the responsibility that accompanies this increased control. *The student must consider the ethics of persuasion.*

Ethical behavior with an automobile is relatively easy to see and to control. When the driver of an automobile misuses his control by going counter to the established rules of conduct or by injuring someone, this is usually observed by someone else and appropriate steps are taken to correct his behavior. But in the case of using mental persuasion, great damage can sometimes be done without others being aware of it and without corrective action being possible. In mental persuasion, brainwashing, hypnotism, or threats are extreme forms which are less observable and against which defenses are not always possible. Still less observable is the skillful use of psychological principles in everyday human relations, principles which allow one person to manipulate the behavior of another in extremely subtle and "nonvisible" ways. Such persuasion is potentially more powerful and dangerous than the more obvious forms such as physical force or hypnotism.

We would all agree that the brainwashing techniques and psychological tortures developed by various governments to manipulate human behavior are clearly unethical in terms of our cultural standards of morals.[1] These subtle forms of mental persuasion are repugnant to us usually because they are associated with evil goals on the part of the manipulator. Business organizations, however, highly encourage the conscious and deliberate motivation of human behavior by the use of all the known techniques of emotional appeals, the pressures of shame, fear, affection, security, etc., as a way of increasing sales and obtaining cooperation from employees. When is the control of other human beings by psychological measures right and when is it wrong? What is the difference between the brainwashing that has taken place in prison camps which we reject and the techniques of advertising and salesmanship which we accept? Are the techniques ethical when the goals of the persuader are good and unethical when the goals of the persuader are bad? How should the student of human behavior use his knowledge of how the human being is motivated? Perhaps the whole question of the ethics of persuasion can be dismissed simply as one salesman did when he said, "After all, the customer doesn't ever buy my product unless he really wants it. We can't make him want it. We can only appeal to the motives that are already there." But we definitely *do* influence the behavior, and even the goals and values,

---

[1] A discussion of such manipulation and its demoralizing effects is found in Joost A. M. Meerloo, *The Rape of the Mind* (Cleveland, Ohio: World Publishing Co., 1956).

of other people. Our impact on other people is far greater than we realize.

In the various recognized professions there has evolved a body of rules, regulations, and standards of behavior which has become established as the ideal and which is called the code of ethics of that profession. The student of human behavior who studies methods and techniques for better motivating the behavior of his fellow man is not similarly restricted by a code of ethics (unless he happens to be a member of such a recognized professional group at the same time). The student of human motivation can use his knowledge in at least two ways: he can manipulate the behavior of other people with the sole aim of making more money for himself or gaining more power over them, or he can use his insight into human behavior in order to understand people and their real needs and to solve their problems better through his particular business knowledge or skill. There are no answers provided here as to how a person should behave or how he should use his specialized knowledge of the motivation of human behavior. This question must be answered by each individual within his own situation and according to his own conscience. It is vital, however, that the student of human behavior be made aware that as he increases his control over his fellow men, he must also assume more responsibility for the way his motivational efforts affect them.

The way each of us decides how we will use our knowledge of psychological methods of persuasion depends ultimately on our own system of value judgments. The life underwriter makes use of motivational principles in ways that depend on his values, and the insurance prospect responds to these motivational efforts in ways which depend on *his* system of values. A study of values and value systems is, therefore, a vital part of our understanding of the how and why of human behavior.

Value Systems

Everyone has an *involved* and *highly stable* system of judgments or evaluations which he makes about himself and everything which surrounds him. Man is an evaluating animal. He makes judgments of right or wrong, good or bad, important or unimportant. The consistent and particular way in which each of us makes these judgments is known as our *system of values.*

The importance of understanding value systems

All behavior is caused by something. Every action we take is the result of our reaction to various internal or external stimuli which impinge upon us and about which we make judgments, either consciously or unconsciously. We learn to prefer various patterns of behavior and our preferences are based on our judgment that the chosen behavior will bring us satisfaction rather than dissatisfaction. Behavior, then, is based on a system of values. What motivates one person does not necessarily motivate another. Each individual's system of values determines what motivating conditions will or will not influence his behavior.

The life underwriter who wishes to persuade others will do this more knowingly and with more control if he will make his appeal coincide, or appear to coincide, with the system of values held by the object of his persuasion. The underwriter's presentation may be well-prepared, logical, and well-expressed, but if it does not make the prospect feel that his values are being furthered, the sale is not likely to be made. This is not to say that the prospect is aware of his own values or even conscious that they are involved in the life insurance presentation, but the motivational power of these values will be involved just the same.

As an example, a basic *value* of a male prospect may be *male supremacy,* or the belief that this is a man's world and that women should not make decisions or have any control in financial matters. A further *attitude* held by the prospect based on this value may be that a woman should not be left a large sum of money upon the death of her husband. Let us suppose that this value and its accompanying attitudes are unconscious. The prospect may verbally agree that he has an obligation to provide an estate for his wife but feels unwilling to buy more life insurance than is needed to provide for his burial and other final costs. If the underwriter can encourage his prospect to talk freely about his family, he may discover that the prospect also highly values a good education for his children. An attitude related to this value would be that life insurance should be purchased to guarantee this value. The prospect may then be faced with a dilemma. He may want to provide money for his family for education, but not want his wife to have money which she might foolishly spend. The dilemma may be difficult to resolve especially if he cannot consciously admit to himself that he is reluctant for his widow to inherit money. A common reaction to conflict is to stay put, to put off a decision and maintain a status quo. The prospect may simply refuse to purchase the insurance and furthermore may not consciously know why he is refusing.

The underwriter will make a sale, in this case, only if he is astute enough to sense these conflicting values and can stress ideas in accord with the one value of education which may motivate the prospect to buy. Proper use of settlement options may also provide a way of resolving the conflict. Careful listening, a thorough knowledge of life insurance fundamentals, and a broad awareness of human motivation can serve the underwriter well.

Values of our American culture

There are many values which can be found consistently throughout all parts of the American culture. One of the basic values in the American culture is that of *personal freedom*. The child will see rather early in life that he has freedom to choose his own religion, his own political affiliation, and his vocation (his free choice is, of course, "determined" by many obvious and hidden influences).

Change and *improvement* for its own sake is another important value in America. Sociologists point out that this value most likely stems from the history of our country. In exploring the frontier of an undeveloped land, early Americans had almost nothing to start with, and any change that they could bring about represented progress. Most Americans value the latest model automobile because it is of the current year, rather than because it is a mechanical improvement over last year's model.

Americans also value the possibility of their *children rising higher* in status, education, and income than they themselves did. This value is, of course, held more strongly by some than by others. When it is a strongly held value, the life underwriter may well find the prospect responding with greatest interest when the insurance plans offer to provide a means of reaching this particular goal.

Americans value *hard work* and *material success*. This value is frequently extended to mean that through hard work one can earn the reward of the good life in the hereafter. It is probable that the value of hard work and the ceaseless activity to get ahead is changing somewhat in our culture. Men are frequently more concerned with job security than with the opportunity to advance. There is also greater emphasis on the value of obtaining security through private insurance plans as well as through governmental subsidy and support.

A strong value pervading our culture is the belief that a man should *work out his own solutions to problems*. The modern American is motivated to attempt to see his surroundings objectively and to discover how he may manipulate his environment to solve his problems. In other words, this is the value of rationalism or using the scientific method to solve our problems.

Other values of the American culture include the belief in *equality*, the belief in the *importance and dignity of the individual*, and *compassion for the unfortunate*. This last humanitarian value probably motivates some men to engage in the profession of life underwriting.

Some values contradict each other

The values we hold often contradict one another. Americans will state emphatically that they believe in the equality of man, but some in the next breath will indicate that certain races and religious groups are inferior to others. Others may believe that honesty is the best policy, and at the same time will do whatever they can to capture a certain market or make a profit in business.

Different parts of our society can hold values which are in conflict. These values can be in such conflict and be strong enough to cause a nation such as ours to engage in a civil war. Values in a society may be well accepted and held by most people, and yet be very difficult to achieve. For instance, in this country we value the opportunity of education for all. However, some may literally not be free to pursue higher education, perhaps because they must obtain employment in order to support a family.

Another value conflict of importance is that between the value of individual initiative and the value of conforming to an organization or, in other words, subordinating personal goals to those of the group. This kind of a conflict in values may be resolved not by abandoning one in favor of the other, but instead, by finding a healthy and workable balance between the two. The ability to establish a workable balance between such conflicting values is perhaps a fair definition of personal maturity.

The value of being humble or not making an ostentatious show of achievements or possessions can conflict with the value of proving financial success by displaying material possessions. Closely related to this is the value of being thrifty or saving and the conflicting value of supporting our national economy by being a conscientious consumer of goods. We may be told that it is wise to set aside some money for a rainy day but that we are also doing our duty to our country by buying now in order to stimulate a possible sagging economy.

Millions of Americans have entered the armed services holding to the value that taking human life is wrong, only to be told that in a war it becomes extremely important to kill. Official reports indicate that a high percentage of men carrying a rifle in a combat area did not pull the trigger even when their own lives were being threatened.[2] These men resolved their personal conflict over these opposing values by simply holding firmly to one and refusing to act in accordance with the other. Another common way of responding to double standards or conflicting values is to maintain the belief that the end justifies the means. A person may think to himself that whatever he has to do to get the job done is all right, since the goal he is working for seems good and right to him.

The life underwriter may not be productive simply because he has either a conflict in values or is not behaving in a manner con-

2 Bill Davidson, "Why Half Our Combat Soldiers Fail to Shoot," *Collier's*, November 8, 1952, p. 17.

sistent with his values. The life underwriter may value the concept of selling life insurance, but may also value even more highly the personal friendships and club memberships which he enjoys. He may find himself in so much demand to head committees and raise funds, etc., that he has little time left to sell insurance. In a situation like this, he may need to recognize that the values which motivate him the most are not being adequately satisfied by his chosen vocation. His decision may well be to leave the life insurance field and find a job which allows him to behave in ways more consistent with his *chief* values.

Values underlie attitudes

Values are broad judgments or evaluations made by the individual, while attitudes are more specific judgments or opinions. Values serve as broad guides to action while attitudes are more specific. Most of us would find it difficult to verbalize just what our main values are, but we find it easier to indicate our specific attitudes toward those things or individuals we deal with every day. An attitude is a predisposition to act or behave in a certain way.

Attitudes

Attitude change leads to behavior change

By the time we have reached adulthood we have formed literally thousands of attitudes which help determine what our behavior will be. We make many almost automatic decisions each day because of these various attitudes based on years of accumulated experiences. Human behavior is *predictable* because we are *relatively consistent* in the way we respond to the same kinds of problems day after day. Our behavior is relatively consistent because our network of attitudes is relatively consistent. Attitudes do change, but they tend to change rather slowly. Values tend to change even more slowly than specific attitudes. The life underwriter who is attempting to change the behavior of his prospect may often need to encourage his prospect to make changes in his attitudes before the prospect will direct his behavior toward buying life insurance.

Attitude change can be conscious or unconscious

In the earlier discussions of the unconscious we saw that much of our psychological being is beyond our awareness. In the same way, many of our attitudes or predispositions to behavior are beyond the level of our conscious awareness. These hidden attitudes that we carry around with us affect every conceivable phase of our life. In many cases life insurance is purchased because of attitudes which the purchaser does not realize he has. Of course, the prospect may also refuse to buy life insurance because of his hidden attitudes. Such hidden attitudes sometimes change, however, without the prospect's being aware that a change is taking place. The prospect who has hidden negative attitudes toward life insurance salesmen may consciously feel that he has no particular bias against them. He may simply refuse to grant the underwriter an appointment, thinking to himself, "I'm just not ready to buy yet." If he subsequently discovers that his former college friend has entered the life insurance business, his hidden negative attitude may be partially or wholly reversed. Attitudes are changed because *we receive new information* which bears on the object of the attitude or because *we have new experiences* which are counter to the expectancies we have had resulting from the old attitudes.

We frequently refer to hidden attitudes as blind spots. For all practical purposes, we are blind to certain perceptions in the area of our rigidly held attitudes or prejudices. People who know us can often see these blind spots that are invisible to ourselves. The life underwriter who refuses to allow his general agent or manager to accompany him during a sales interview, or who refuses to listen to comments or observations by others, may be missing a valuable learning opportunity which would help him become more effective as a persuader of others.

Death and our attitudes toward it

The concept of death and the values and attitudes which surround it represent one of the most difficult of all concepts for us to think about. Considering the possibility of our own death is a shock because it so vividly reminds us that we do not go on living forever. If we have come close to death through injury or illness, the upsetting nature of this experience frequently motivates us to take life more seriously and even to question and alter some of the values we hold. The thought of death, either our own or that of someone near to us, is a frightening thing partly because death is the symbol of being completely alone or isolated from other human beings. To the small child the death of a parent is certainly a great loss but often the child unconsciously feels a sense of rejection. In the child's mind, it is almost as if the deceased parent wanted to reject or abandon the child and this is, of course, an upsetting thought for him.

The death or even the thought of the death of a loved one can often cause severe guilt feelings. When an individual is unable to accept, within himself, the *normal* aggressive and hostile feelings which he has toward those close to him, he feels guilty about these impulses whenever the thought of death threatens to make these unacceptable impulses become conscious. Children are frequently unable to separate their thoughts from the external world of reality. Because a young child thinks or wishes something, he will often believe that the thing has actually happened or will happen soon. Remnants of this kind of thinking persist in the adult who, at the time of a colleague's death, may unconsciously feel that because he disliked his colleague when he was alive, he is somehow partly responsible for this man's death. The life underwriter will normally be arousing intense conscious and unconscious emotional reactions in his prospects as he discusses life insurance with them and, by implication, their eventual death.

Many underwriters attempt to sell life insurance by deliberately reminding their prospects of their eventual or perhaps imminent death. Some are adept at drawing vivid pictures of crippling illnesses and at causing panic in prospects by confronting them with the thought of actual or near death. Of course, as we grow older, it is more likely that our contemporaries, either friends and relatives, have experienced severe injuries, illness, or perhaps death and hence we are more easily moved by discussions of such events. It may often be the case, however, that when a life underwriter emphasizes death to a prospect, he finds the interview being quickly terminated because the prospect wants to rid himself of this source of annoyance and discomfort. The successful life underwriter who senses the prospect's need to avoid any discussion which might involve thoughts of his own death may decide to emphasize instead the saving aspects of purchasing life insurance.

Death and anxiety

Most of us feel considerable anxiety when we think of either our own approaching death or that of other people. Anxiety is characterized by a feeling of helplessness and confusion in a situation of danger. The anxious person frequently feels that there is nothing he can do to avoid or escape the danger. One *defense* against this anxiety that man has evolved concerning death is the *belief of a life after death*. This belief is an important part of most religions. Some people find great comfort in feeling that they live on in their descendants. Certainly it is true that the genes which we once carried within ourselves produce and repeat many of our own traits and characteristics in future generations. It is possible that a man may feel his continued existence through his children may be better guaranteed by providing for them through a life insurance program.

Just as the small child lives only for today, the immature adult lives only within the limitations of his own lifetime. The man who has reached a higher level of maturity normally possesses wider time perspectives, that is, he has succeeded in stepping out of his own individual life span and he sees himself as part of a long-term pattern. He sees his life partly as a connecting link between his parent's life and his children's life and the life of future generations. This leads many men to desire and shape a kind of life which will enhance the welfare of their children and of society after their lifetime. Buying life insurance is one expression of this kind of concern.

Attitudes are difficult to measure

In trying to learn something about a person's attitude toward any particular subject we cannot place too much reliance on that person's own report of what his attitude is. One reason for this is that an individual may not want to divulge his true attitude and may therefore express quite a different attitude from the one he holds. A second reason that a personally quoted attitude is unreliable is that the individual himself may not understand his own attitude.

A life underwriter asking a prospective client what his attitude is toward a particular policy may or may not get a true and valid answer. Ordinarily a person's *behavior* is a truer indication of his attitude than are his expressed statements. A general agent may interview a prospective life underwriter who maintains that he wants to earn a large amount of money. If it is discovered that the candidate has up to this time not demonstrated any excessive drive for money, that is, if he has devoted much of his time to play activities, civic activities, or just plain loafing, then it is more than likely that making money is not a strong value and his true attitude is that while money is desirable, other things, such as prestige, power, pleasure, etc. are actually of higher value to him. Actions speak louder than words!

Attitudes can be helpful and harmful

Many attitudes are useful. The fact that we hold certain attitudes toward diverse subjects gives a certain amount of order to our life. It gives that consistency to behavior that we refer to as personality. Because we have overcome certain problems in the past and have thereby acquired certain values and attitudes, we can frequently avoid some of the same mistakes by following these attitudes.

While it is advantageous to have predetermined ways of behaving, that is, to possess attitudes, it can also be a rather serious disadvantage. While the attitudes we have may allow us to move consistently toward certain goals, they may also blind us to certain new possibilities which are inherent in any given situation. Some attitudes, if they are rigidly held, may lead us to prejudge certain situations and thereby perceive them inaccurately. While attitudes may help us adapt to certain situations, they may also cause us to be nonadaptable. When rigidly held, attitudes are relied on too much and little attention is paid to objective reality. This we call *prejudice,* that is, acting in a certain predetermined way without proper regard for the present facts or situations.

Rigidly held attitudes may keep us from trying solutions to problems that may be rewarding. For example the life underwriter may learn from his general agent or manager that making cold calls is not the way to sell life insurance. This attitude may prevent the life underwriter from ever trying this type of prospecting when actually he may be a person who could do very well with that approach.

The life underwriter will deal every day with strongly prejudiced individuals. Without a doubt every reader of this material will himself be strongly prejudiced in certain directions. None of us is free from prejudice. Each of us is certainly free to form and maintain prejudice, but if an individual wishes to become as realistic as possible in his relationships with others, then it is important to attempt an honest appraisal of one's own prejudices so that allowances can be made for them.

Attitude Change and Persuasion

Role of the life underwriter

Life insurance is not easy to sell. Rarely does a customer approach a life insurance underwriter and ask to buy some life insurance. Many people throw up their hands when approached by a life underwriter, and say something like "Not another life insurance agent! I have more insurance now than I can pay for. I'm insurance poor," or "You're better off to buy term insurance and invest the difference," or "Why should I buy life insurance? I am in good health." Any life underwriter is able to add many similar statements that express firm attitudes on the part of the speakers. The life underwriter, as a persuader, has the task of changing the attitudes of his prospects concerning life insurance from negative to positive.

Persuasion techniques

Avoid arguments. In ordinary conversation when we meet anyone who expresses an attitude or opinion different from ours, and we wish to change it to correspond with our own thinking, our usual reaction is to begin arguing with him. If a Democrat and a Republican are discussing politics, their argument usually leads to such evaluative phrases as "You're crazy," or "You don't know what you're talking about." There probably is no more effective way to muff an opportunity to change an attitude than to begin a personal argument. And yet many salesmen react to an objection raised by a customer by immediately trying to argue the customer out of his objection. One principle of persuasion, then, is to avoid becoming involved in an argument with the prospect.

There is probably nothing more effective in taking the wind out of someone else's sails than to simply say, "Yes, you're right." After you have said this, you can always say, "But I wonder if you have ever thought of this . . ." If we force a prospect to defend his negative attitude toward life insurance, he may become more firm in his defense of his attitude. But if we can use a "Yes, but . . ." approach, he is more likely to think that we are an agreeable fellow and listen to our proposition.

When a prospect brings up a negative attitude concerning life insurance, the life underwriter might handle this effectively and set the stage for persuading the prospect to change his attitude by merely saying, "I can understand that you feel life insurance is too expensive. I'm interested in what you mean. Could you tell me more about it?" After the prospect has run the full course in describing his reasons for thinking that life insurance is too expensive, a life underwriter might then ask him to repeat several of the important points that he has made. By the time the prospect has had this much opportunity to verbalize his negative attitude or opinion he very frequently will tone it down so much that it hardly resembles his initial assertion. The life underwriter demonstrates his interest in the prospect by requesting a fuller explanation of the initial statement and this tends to be disarming to a prospect who has a negative attitude. The prospect in many cases will realize just how foolish his initial statement was—a benefit of good listening. He will have been "softened up" and be more ready to adopt a revised attitude.

Review and revise beliefs. Before attitudes and opinions can be changed there often needs to be a change in the person's beliefs or knowledge. A prospect may feel that the life insurance policy is not a good buy because, "All you do is pay money in and you never get anything out of it." The life underwriter can point out that it is really a form of investment under which cash values will accumulate. This new information may be enough to help the prospect see life insurance in a different light and perhaps change his initial attitude toward it.

Establish rapport. Most people are quite open to suggestion. When a person we like starts to wear a new style suit, we are likely to buy a suit of the same style, even though we may have felt a few days ago that it looked funny. The more highly the persuader is regarded by those whom he is attempting to influence, the more effective will be his efforts to change attitudes and opinions. The salesman who attempts to "sell himself first" is essentially raising his esteem in the eyes of his prospects. The underwriter is seen by the prospect as being more believable if they have established a rapport, i.e. a relationship which is close or sympathetic. Much insurance has been sold because of nothing more dramatic than a twinkle in the eye. When the prospect and the life underwriter can establish a common ground or perhaps can share a joke or an understanding, the underwriter is in a much more favorable position to change the attitudes and opinions of his prospect.

Establish credentials. The persuasiveness of the life underwriter will depend largely on how expert the prospect feels that he is. Even such a simple thing as the underwriter making a minor mistake in arithmetic in the presence of the prospect can raise doubt in the latter's mind about the expertness of the underwriter. On the positive side, the life underwriter can create in the mind of his prospect the impression of competence by rapidly and accurately grasping the full significance of the prospect's insurance problem. Somehow indicating to the prospect that the life underwriter has his C.L.U. degree, that he has handled other complicated insurance problems, that the underwriter's agency employs various specialists or experts in estate planning, pension plans, etc., will all help convey the impression to the prospect that the underwriter is both *willing* and *able* to be of help to him. Of course, this kind of information coming from a third party is more effective than if it comes from the life underwriter himself.

The third-party influence of a satisfied client can be of more help to the underwriter than is often realized. The new client who has just purchased insurance from the underwriter will perhaps never be more enthusiastic about the underwriter and his company than he is just then. This client is often more willing to give referred leads and even to "build up" the underwriter to these referrals than the latter may suspect. But the client may not know just what to say to the friend to whom he would refer the underwriter. If the underwriter can do a careful and appropriate job of "coaching" his client on what to say, the client will appreciate it and can in turn be of great help in establishing the underwriter's "credentials" with new insurance prospects. Obviously the client will not want words put in his mouth, but he may want to hear how other clients have introduced the underwriter to new insurance prospects.

Use of testimonials. The more important the prospect thinks the underwriter is, the more easily will the underwriter be able to persuade or change the opinions and attitudes of the prospect. The underwriter can increase his importance in the eyes of the prospect by the use of testimonials or by discreet name dropping. If the underwriter can establish that he has already sold insurance to someone who is highly regarded by his present prospect, the prospect is likely to be more easily swayed by the underwriter. One underwriter succeeds in getting a satisfied client to write letters to his friends introducing the underwriter and endorsing him as a helpful, qualified insurance expert.

Reveal your sincerity. The motive the prospect sees in the underwriter will make a difference in how effective the underwriter is in changing the prospect's attitude. If the prospect thinks the underwriter is making the sale only to make money, he will be more resistant to influence than if he thinks the underwriter is genuinely and strongly concerned about him as an individual.

An underwriter was having difficulty convincing a prospect that he should buy a fairly large policy now rather than wait a few months. The prospect was about to go on a long vacation trip. Just before the prospect left town, the underwriter visited his office and said, "John, I've been so concerned about your going on this long trip without this additional coverage that we talked about, that I have had my company issue a policy in your name and all we have to do is have you examined and it can be put into effect."

John was impressed, in this case, by what seemed to him to be a very worthy motive on the part of his underwriter, and he immediately wrote out a check for the insurance.

Establish similarities of interest. The more ways the underwriter can show that he holds many of the same views held by his prospect, the more effective will the underwriter be in changing some of the prospect's attitudes and opinions. It is important for the underwriter to find as many areas of agreement or similarity between himself and his prospect as possible. We are influenced more by someone whom we like or who we feel is sympathetic with us than we are by someone who is unsympathetic. In this regard, humor can be very effective. Enjoying a humorous experience or story together tends to establish a similarity of interest.

Use repetition. The more often a life underwriter states a point of view, the more likely he is to get his point across to the prospect. Radio and TV commercials recognize this principle and broadcast the same commercial thousands of times, with the net results that the consumer is "convinced." However, if the prospect is disturbed or upset by the statement the life underwriter is making, repetition will only increase the prospect's aggravation.

In the intimate personal relationship which the underwriter establishes with his prospect, repeating a point or an idea may be more effective if the life underwriter repeats his statements in slightly different ways, varying the wording while expressing the same idea. Simply repeating a memorized sentence may give the prospect the feeling that the life underwriter is somehow talking down to him or underestimating his intelligence.

Request more change than you expect to get. In influencing or changing the attitudes of others we are frequently effective in producing the desired change if we initially try to obtain a greater change in attitude than we actually expect. This technique is used effectively in negotiations between governments and in the give-and-take involved in bargaining or haggling over the price of an object.

Every teen-age boy knows that if he wants to "touch" his dad for five dollars for a date he is better off to ask for more than that. Generally, the greater the shift in attitude or opinion we ask of a person, the greater the change is likely to be. Frequently, simply asking a prospect, "Would you rather take the full $50,000 now or $25,000 now and put off the additional twenty-five until April?" will help persuade the prospect to decide to buy a $25,000 policy now when otherwise he might have been willing to purchase only $20,000 or $15,000.

Use group pressure. An individual is definitely swayed in the direction he thinks a group of which he is a member is moving. An assistant vice president of a bank is more likely to be influenced by the underwriter who can say, "More than 5,000 bankers have already purchased this policy." A person may also be swayed by the opinion of a group of which he is not a member but to which he would like to belong. Undoubtedly many people have bought an "executive policy" who were not themselves executives but who liked the idea of being associated with that group.

Remove mental blocks. Attitudes are changed when the mental block to change is removed or minimized. The prospect may refuse to accept a rated policy because it seems to him to be an admission of some personal inadequacy or inferiority. This mental block will have to be removed or at least recognized by the life underwriter before such a policy will be paid for by the prospect. Reassuring such a man that he is demonstrating his high regard for his family by buying the insurance may focus the prospect's attention on another goal that is important to him and help remove his concern about his inadequacy.

Simply because a prospect verbalizes a negative attitude toward life insurance doesn't mean that his attitude must necessarily be changed for him to purchase life insurance. The underwriter who can sympathize with the prospect's point of view may eventually be able to *move around* the negative point by emphasizing the more positive advantages to the owning of life insurance. "Accentuate the positive, eliminate the negative," may be effective in overcoming negative attitudes. The underwriter who insists on hammering away on the prospect's negative attitude without letup may "win the argument and lose the sale."

Perhaps the negative attitude expressed by the prospect as an objection is something the prospect is really indifferent about. The girl will often say no to her boy friend when perhaps she only means maybe.

Use physical contact. Physical contact between two people can be an element of persuasion. The very simple act of throwing our arm over another person's shoulder actually says a lot. Ordinarily we do not touch people unless we like them. Shaking hands is a custom and is done automatically. But other kinds of physical contact, such as placing a hand on the prospect's arm, taking the prospect's hand to place a fountain pen in it, or even putting slight pressure on his back in order to move him in the direction of a doctor's office for an examination have been useful techniques of persuasion when used with care and at an appropriate time.

Standing *too* close to the prospect, or touching him *too* soon, however, can be threatening and may disturb what has up to that time been a growing relationship of warmth and trust. The underwriter who knows his prospect well enough can, at the moment of the close, *gently guide* his prospect into the chair, hand him a pen and order, "John, sign that application!" To a friend this is not being offensively overbearing, but shows only genuine regard and an effort to help him overcome his indecision. Remember that a professional life underwriter should have a sincere conviction that the decision to buy is a correct and a wise one for his client before he uses a physical push or any other extreme effort to motivate.

Play hard to get. Another technique of persuasion that seems to work well in sales or in courtship is to "play hard to get." At a crucial time during the sales presentation, if the underwriter suggests that perhaps the prospect may not be able to qualify for the policy, this may become the biggest reason for this prospect to decide to go ahead with his insurance plan. If we place an obstacle in someone's path, his tendency is to exert more energy in order to overcome the obstacle. But this is true only if it looks as if the obstacle can be overcome. If the obstacle looms too large, then the reaction is likely to be a giving-up or a drastically reduced effort to succeed. At the right moment, the suggestion to a prospect that he probably can't afford to buy much insurance may be the key that will urge him to want more than he had originally planned to buy. This is sometimes referred to as the "negative sell."

Ego building. There is no one more important to the prospect than he himself. In most conversations we are looking for an opportunity to have our say, or are searching for something in what others are saying that affects us directly and personally. The human being seems to have much of his interest and attention focused on himself most of the time. If the life underwriter deliberately exercises certain techniques to enhance the feeling of self-importance in his prospect, he will be in a better position to apply persuasive influence.

One simple way of helping the prospect feel more important is the judicious use of his *name* during the sales interview. *We like to hear the sound of our own name.* It seems to add a personal touch if someone begins a statement to us by speaking our name first. The underwriter probably comes closer to touching his prospect's emotions if he refers to the prospect's children and wife by name also, rather than merely saying "your children" or "your wife."

Everyone has this very human desire to feel important. If the underwriter can spot things the prospect has done that really are important, a conscious effort to refer to them and to compliment the prospect sincerely on his accomplishments will do much to place the underwriter in a more powerfully persuasive position.

Assemble all possible objections to attitude change. In applying persuasion to another individual we are essentially answering objections that that individual is posing for us. Often it seems that as soon as we answer one objection, the other person always thinks of another one. One technique of persuasion which has been successfully used is to assemble all of the prospect's possible objections before answering any of them. It may even be desirable to stimulate the prospect to think of still more objections when it seems that he has nearly finished. When the prospect says that there are no more objections, the persuader can proceed to answer each objection in turn so that at last there is considerable pressure on the prospect to buy since he no longer has any more objections. Such a statement as, "If I successfully answer your last objection, will you buy?" puts the prospect in a kind of box from which it is difficult to escape. If the rest of the interview has been favorable, this kind of persuasive influence is likely to result in a change of behavior, if not in attitude.

In any situation of persuasion, anyone is more likely to give in or submit if he can win something for himself at the same time. The prospect who has successfully proved his point to the underwriter may be more inclined to accept a suggestion from the underwriter.

Avoid being too smooth. The more believable the persuader appears to be, the more effective his efforts will be in changing attitudes and opinions. TV announcers who use flawless English and rattle off a prepared pitch appear less effective than those who stumble a little bit as many of us do in a normal conversation. When we listen to a person who is too smooth in his presentation, we are likely to get the feeling that he has memorized what he is saying and that he is insincere or is not really talking to us personally. The skillful salesman will pause, appear to consider objections before answering them, and will avoid too quick or automatic an answer to the prospect's objection. Otherwise the prospect may feel that the underwriter is not considering his objections carefully enough.

Especially when we are unsure of ourselves, we may try to dazzle our listener by using big words or a technical vocabulary. But if we are to be persuasive with another person, we must avoid confusing or irritating him. The prospect will be uncomfortable if he does not understand a big word or if he has to ask us what a word means. He may not ask for clarification at all, and the underwriter will have lost some persuasive impact.

Motivation through Interviewing Techniques

The life underwriter is interested in changing the behavior of his prospect. He can do this most effectively if he can predict what the future behavior of his prospect is likely to be. We can predict a person's *future* behavior reasonably well by making a very careful analysis of the way he is behaving at the present time. Past and present behavior is one of the best indications of future behavior.

The sales interview

If the underwriter will make an effort to find out how his prospect is living now, that is, what his goals, his values, his attitudes, his habits, and his aversions are at the present time, he will be in a much better position to predict which of a number of emotional appeals might work best with this particular prospect.

People love to be listened to. Listening to someone demonstrates our interest and regard for him, and at the same time, enables us to learn a great deal about him as an individual. It is obvious that if a prospect talks a lot about his own college days, or is bemoaning the fact that he did not get to college but he hopes his children will, the building up of an educational fund for his children may be the thing which will sell life insurance to him. If the prospect shows in his general conversation that he is highly motivated to achieve prestige in his community, the life underwriter may point out subtly that only the most important men in town own large amounts of life insurance.

Perhaps the most the life underwriter can do in his efforts to learn more about his prospect is to make certain assumptions regarding him and then proceed to test these assumptions by what seems the best approach. The broader the knowledge of human behavior, *including his own*, that the life underwriter has the more likely he is to be able to make reasonably valid assumptions. Furthermore, and perhaps most important as the interview proceeds, this knowledge lets him make the *adjustments* in approach indicated by a *careful analysis* of the prospect's reactions and behavior. This is, again, an example of the feed-back process at work.

The purposes of the sales interview. Doing a good job of interviewing the prospect for life insurance can accomplish at least two things: (1) as a result of finding out something about the way the client lives and works and thinks, the life underwriter can tell something about what sales approach to use, and (2) the interview can also help the prospect crystallize within his own mind those things in his life which are really important to him. To accomplish these objectives it is essential that the life underwriter help the prospect feel at ease in talking to him. Usually we talk freely about our goals and our life dreams only when we feel reasonably comfortable with the person to whom we are talking.

Give and take. The sales interview that the life underwriter conducts is truly a give-and-take situation between the underwriter and his prospect. In a sense the prospect is interviewing the life underwriter just as much as the underwriter is interviewing the prospect. Much of the interaction between these two people is carried on by gestures, postures, facial expressions, and other physical behavior. Much of what we *are* and many of our own *motivations* are expressed by facial expressions and mannerisms. It is difficult to show interest in another person if we do not feel genuinely interested. The underwriter can, of course, try various techniques of indicating interest—sitting forward in his chair, leaning forward, putting a bright and eagerly expectant look on his face, etc.—but it is doubtful that such behavior, if artificial, will help put the prospect at ease.

If the underwriter is interested in knowing as much as possible about his prospect's life pattern, he will need to ask questions and in general let the prospect do most of the talking at first. If the underwriter proceeds by asking a number of rather direct questions which can be answered with a yes or no, he will get relatively little information, and will probably make the prospect feel as if he is being grilled or interrogated. More general questions should be used, like: "You seem to have a pretty nice business here. How did you get started?" or "You say you have a fifteen-year-old boy? What do you think he'll do when he leaves high school?" The underwriter will need to be constantly aware of the things which seem to generate real interest and excitement in the prospect. This is hard to do if the life underwriter is concerned mostly with his own problems and is not genuinely interested in helping his prospect. The self-centeredness of a salesman may be one reason that he competes and works hard for personal accomplishment, but self-centeredness can also make it difficult for a life underwriter to conduct a successful interview during which he must do a good deal of listening.

Interviewing principles

The sales interview, then, has several functions. It must be a way of *getting information;* it must be a time for *giving information;* and it must be effective in *changing behavior.* There are a number of principles of interviewing which may help the underwriter to be successful in achieving these several functions.

Build an atmosphere of freedom. First of all the underwriter must create an atmosphere of freedom in which the prospect finds it easy to talk about himself. Much has been written about the importance of the good personal appearance of the life underwriter and also about the necessity for being considerate and friendly. All of these things, of course, are important in *helping a prospect feel comfortable* while talking to someone who is in many cases a complete stranger. If the life underwriter is reasonably relaxed and comfortable, he is likely to create such an atmosphere when in the company of others. If instead he is anxious and tense, he is very likely to make his prospects feel uncomfortable. It may well be that the anxious, tense life underwriter needs to relocate himself in a vocation in which he can be more comfortable. But this is another problem.

Create the "you" interest. We have talked about the importance of the life underwriter's being *genuinely interested in his prospect*. It is perhaps unrealistic to suppose that he can be interested in all people. There will be some in whom we can more easily get interested than in others. The well-known sales technique of emphasizing the "you" interest has a bearing here. The more the life underwriter can use the words "you," "yours," "his," etc. in place of "I," "me," or "mine," the more he will be directing his interest toward the other person.

Many insurance sales are actually made at the outset of the interview. In the first few minutes both the prospect and the underwriter are sizing each other up and probably deciding whether they like each other or not. The rest of the sales interview may be more a matter of working out the details of an insurance plan, rather than selling a prospect the idea that he has a need.

Interview in a setting free from distractions. Establishing this atmosphere of freedom for the prospect to talk about himself takes into consideration certain mechanical features of the sales setting. The ideal sales interview should be in a *setting free from distractions.* There is, of course, some value in holding a sales interview during lunch or dinner, in that generally we are more relaxed while we are eating than while we are sitting at a desk. But mealtimes are full of distractions. The conversation must be interrupted to order the food, to look about the room, to pause while being served, etc. All such distractions will make it easy for the conversation to stray away from the important and main issues.

Another source of distraction in the sales interview is the *presence of a third person.* Some underwriters have found that they are extremely successful in selling insurance to both the prospect and his wife. The relationship between two people, however, is far different than the relationship between three people. There is a truism that "three is a crowd." As we talk with another individual, we are usually very watchful to see how he is reacting to what we say. This is valuable feedback for us so that we can alter what we are saying if it appears that our listener is not following us or is reacting unfavorably. This is more difficult to do with two other people than it is with one. Some businessmen have their office situated so that their secretary is within hearing range. If this is the case, the life underwriter would probably be wise to suggest that they get together in a different place or perhaps that they be able to close the office door. If the businessman is going to confide in the life underwriter regarding his personal life goals, he is less likely to do so if a third person is listening.

One of the most disrupting distractions for a sales interview can be telephone calls. It may be worthwhile for the life underwriter to ask the prospect if his secretary can take phone calls for a while until they finish their discussion. Most businessmen will recognize the value of such a suggestion. Rarely would a prospect feel that this suggestion indicated impertinence on the part of the underwriter.

Another source of distraction in the sales interview is the prospect's *future appointment* of which the underwriter is unaware. If the prospect is mentally thinking to himself that he is going to be late for his next appointment, he is not apt to listen very intently to the underwriter. This may be an especially annoying distraction if the life underwriter had agreed to take only fifteen minutes of the prospect's time and then proceeded to stay much longer.

Controlling the interview. While it is important for the life underwriter to practice listening and to be relatively silent while he is trying to get facts from his prospect or learn something about his prospect's life situation, it would be a mistake simply to encourage the prospect to start talking and not to maintain some control over the interview. The life underwriter can control the interview and still give his prospect plenty of freedom of expression. He maintains this control by the way he comments on what the prospect says. If the prospect mentions that he hopes to see his son grow up to be an engineer, the life underwriter may well emphasize this by saying, "One of your important goals in life, then, is to provide a good education for your son." If the underwriter shows genuine interest in this statement by the prospect, the prospect is likely to realize it and may focus more of his own attention on this specific point. By recognizing and stressing the prospect's statement the underwriter has encouraged him to stay on one subject.

Some individuals appear to be able to talk endlessly without saying anything. If the life underwriter does not step in and attempt to give the conversation some direction, he may spend an afternoon listening but not selling. The life underwriter might simply say, "What you are sayirg is very interesting and I hope we can talk some more about it sometime, but now let me ask you, about how much do you think you could save a month?" etc.

Avoid embarrassment. The prospect will talk more easily if the first few questions the underwriter asks are questions which can be answered relatively easily and without embarrassment. To some men their financial standing and information about their income, etc. are the most personal and private things they can imagine. To plunge directly into this area might be a serious blunder. Most often we enjoy talking about our work, but here again the life underwriter must be alert to signs that the prospect feels uncomfortable in talking about this subject, and perhaps he should avoid probing any deeper in the initial stages of the interview. Talking about a man's eventual death is indelicate enough as a subject, but to add insult to injury by probing too soon into a man's financial status (and, indirectly, his economic *adequacy*) may create so much discomfort that some prospects will wish to terminate the interview.

Stimulate talking. Occasionally the underwriter will have the problem of getting a prospect to be more talkative. If the prospect will not express himself, especially by stating the objections he has, the underwriter is almost powerless to attempt to meet those objections. So it becomes important to be able to encourage the prospect to talk freely and easily. Establishing the right atmosphere at the beginning is important, but other techniques may have to be used throughout the interview. Some underwriters do an excellent job of establishing a warm, permissive atmosphere at the beginning of the interview, but forget that this atmosphere needs to be maintained throughout. Tactless remarks, inappropriate jokes, or over-eagerness on the part of the underwriter during the interview may do much to disrupt a favorable atmosphere. Here *silence* can be an excellent technique to encourage the other person to continue talking. If we have asked a question and received an answer, but we do not begin talking again ourselves, the other person is very likely to continue talking. If we look as if we expect the prospect to amplify the answer he just gave us, he is very likely to do just that.

In closing the sale, if the prospect has agreed that he wants a certain monthly income, a certain amount for an educational fund, etc., and the policy under consideration satisfies these requirements, silence on the part of the underwriter will either put pressure on the prospect to do what he must do, that is, agree to purchase the policy, or the silence will urge him to raise an objection which can then be answered by the underwriter.

Silence can apply a great deal of pressure to an individual. It can be used effectively in the sales interview, but its use must not be abused. Allowing too much silence may turn a favorable setting into an awkward, embarrassing situation. It is a fact, however, that the life underwriter usually feels more awkward during a period of silence than his prospect does. If the underwriter breaks the silence while his prospect is still forming an answer or a question in his mind, he may well have spoiled a closing opportunity.

Use the prospect's language. In the sales interview it is important to use words which the prospect understands. Technical words should be avoided unless the underwriter can be sure the prospect knows their exact meaning. If the prospect does not understand something that the life underwriter has said, he may hesitate to say, "I don't understand what that word means." Instead, he may continue not understanding and may, therefore, simply not buy. The life underwriter can easily check on this by asking, "Tell me how you think this will work out in your case." By getting an expression of his prospect's understanding of the conversation so far, the underwriter will have an opportunity to restate any misunderstood ideas and so achieve a better understanding between them. It is important to take the trouble to use terms that they are easily understood by the prospect.

Demonstrate your understanding. The way the interview is conducted can either encourage or inhibit communication. To demonstrate that he really understands what the prospect is saying, the
underwriter may repeat what he thinks has just been said. The
underwriter might well say, "As I understand it, you would like to
have your family have a $5,000 emergency fund; and during the
critical years, when your children are growing up, you want your
family to have an income of $350 per month. Is that right?"

Rewarding or punishing the prospect. The life underwriter has
the ability to reward or punish his prospect during the sales interview. As the prospect makes certain statements which are favorable
to the insurance sale, the life underwriter can certainly nod his head,
smile, and say, "Yes, that's right," or simply "Uh-huh." In controlled
experiments on interviewing, where the interviewer systematically
"rewarded" certain statements made by the one being interviewed
by such a simple comment as "Uh-huh," that individual's behavior
changed in the desired direction without his even being aware of it.

The life underwriter has this same influence on his client during
his sales interview. One sales technique that has been used successfully is to ask the prospect a number of questions or state a
number of conclusions in such a way that the prospect is likely to
say "yes" to each of them until the very last question where the
life underwriter tries for a "close." The hope is that while the
prospect is in the frame of mind to agree with what the underwriter
says he will also agree to sign the application.

Make use of preliminary commitments. If during the interview
the prospect says something of vital importance that makes an
excellent point in favor of his buying insurance, the underwriter
may very well encourage him to repeat this point. There are at
least two reasons for doing this. First of all, we are much less likely
to change our opinion on anything once we have expressed it
publicly. If we have not told anyone how we stand on an issue, we
can change our opinion without "losing face," but if we committed
ourselves, and especially if we have committed ourselves strongly,
we are more likely to stick to our original assertion. The second
reason that it is important to emphasize such a significant statement by the prospect is that it can be used to help close the sale.
If the prospect has stated unequivocally that he must have a certain

amount of money for his family, and the life underwriter shows him that it is possible for him to achieve that by investing a certain amount of money each month, the underwriter can bring pressure to bear on the prospect by referring to the prospect's *own public commitment.*

Improving interviewing skills

Increased skill in interviewing techniques can be a great asset to the life underwriter. One way of improving our interviewing skill is to tape record an interview we have conducted, play it back and thus put ourselves in a better position to observe both the strengths and weaknesses of our performance. Tape recording an insurance sales interview might be difficult because of the distraction it would introduce to the prospect. It is assumed that the life underwriter would not record an interview without the prospect's knowledge and permission.

Having a sales supervisor accompany the underwriter is, of course, another way of learning something about our performance than we might not understand otherwise. Another way of attempting to improve our interviewing skill is simply to reflect within ourselves on how the interview is going. This, of course, requires that we be honest with ourselves and also that we be very perceptive of the reactions of the prospect and of ourselves.[3]

Obstacles to good interviews

There are several things that can keep an interview from fulfilling the several functions of getting information, giving information, and changing behavior.

The life underwriter. First of all, there is the personal bias of the life underwriter. The more the underwriter can see the prospect as he really is, the more likely he is to be able to predict and control the behavior of that prospect. The more prejudices, biases, or blind

---

[3] A discussion of interviewing, its techniques and dynamics, not written from the standpoint of selling but covering general principles of good interviewing is W. V. Bingham, B. V. Moore and J. W. Gustard, *How to Interview* (New York: Harper & Row, Publishers, 1959).

spots the life underwriter has the more likely he is to miss important points that the prospect may make during the interview. If he allows his own feelings to get involved during the interview, he is very likely to react subjectively rather than objectively. Complete objectivity is, of course, impossible for the life underwriter, or anyone, to maintain. After all, he does bring into the interview his own characteristics, his own life experiences, and his own personality. But while absolute objectivity may be an impossibility, it is important that he come as close to the ideal as possible.

All of us have had the experience of being introduced to someone and having an almost instant feeling of hostility. When it is possible to analyze such an experience carefully, it has been found that we unconsciously transfer feelings into the present situation that were originally felt in a previous situation. For example, one underwriter reported that as soon as he met his prospect, a small, wiry man wearing heavy, horn-rimmed glasses, he felt a negative reaction to him which was undoubtedly sensed by the prospect. Only after much self-reflection did the underwriter realize that his prospect greatly resembled an uncle with whom he had never been able to get along. Because the prospect reminded the underwriter of his disliked uncle, the resemblance triggered an unconscious impulse on the part of the underwriter. No life underwriter is going to be able to sell insurance to everyone he meets, but the more he can be aware of inappropriate feelings such as those just described, the more control he will have over each potential sales situation.

The prospect. Another source of disturbance in the sales interview is the prospect's unwillingness, prejudice, ignorance, or inability to express his thoughts clearly. If the underwriter happens to be of a faith or race toward which the prospect has a distinct prejudice, the best interviewing techniques in the world and the finest insurance policy may not result in a sale.

Glossing over individual differences between prospects. Neglecting to see the individuality of each prospect interferes with our ability to persuade him to change his attitudes and behavior. This seems obvious to us when we think about it, but is apparently very easily forgotten in practice. We have each had different learning experiences as we grew up, we each have different cultural backgrounds, and have formed our own unique way of responding to life. While we all have many motives in common, how we express those motives reflects our uniqueness as individuals whether we are underwriters or insurance prospects. Some people seem unable to postpone satisfaction and therefore place their current desires above any future desires or wants. Such individuals may find it hard to understand why they should be concerned about their family twenty years from now. One prospect stated, "I'm providing my family with a good living now, and after I'm gone my wife can always get another job like the one she had before we were married. I want to enjoy life now and the heck with the future." Such an individual might change his attitude if he were to realize the difficulty his forty-five-year-old wife might have in finding employment.

Other people deny themselves almost everything at the present time in order to be adequately prepared for the future. We run the greatest risk of ignoring this obvious fact of individual differences when we meet someone about whom we say, "He reminds me of another guy like this." When we deal with someone in a situation different from anything we have ever encountered, we are more likely to be especially observant and to approach the interview carefully, but when a situation looks similar to one that we have already experienced, we may overlook some of the differences that are really important. While we must use past experience and understanding to guide us in motivating human behavior, we must be careful to watch for significant, unique differences between behavior patterns.

The goal of the sales interview

The carefully conducted insurance sales interview will accomplish the goals of (1) helping the life underwriter to see the prospect's life situation, (2) helping the prospect to crystallize better what his own goals or his levels of aspiration are, and (3) helping the prospect see how having more life insurance can benefit him.

If the underwriter has done a careful job of helping his prospect verbalize his wants and desires in terms of financial planning, *the prospect will be in a better position to see the connection between his own desires and the financial plan outlined by the underwriter.*

The life underwriter's job, then, is one of somehow influencing or inducing the prospect to take a course of action that will result in satisfaction for *both* the prospect and the underwriter. Only if the outcome is mutually satisfactory to both will the purpose of the sales interview have been realized. The underwriter who is well prepared in insurance and in a knowledge of human behavior will experience the dual satisfaction of helping another person while succeeding in his own chosen profession.

PART FOUR

MAN
IN BALANCE

"Man doth not live by bread alone, but by every word that proceedeth out of the mouth of the Lord doth man live. (Deut. 8:3)

Man often does what he does because he wants either to gain pleasure or to avoid pain. His wants are many and they are frequently in conflict with each other. Man also does many things because he feels he ought to. This increases the probability of conflict. Everyone has at one time or another found himself in bitter and often irreconcilable conflict between what he *wants* to do and what he knows he *ought* to do.

In the first three parts of this book, we have seen how man develops from the dependent infant to the interdependent adult. We have seen how he learns from his group, how he makes an adjustment to it, and how the group adjusts itself to him. We have studied his developing language abilities and have seen how these abilities can either advance or destroy his civilization. And we have seen that man, as a social animal, is continuously involved in an effort to influence the behavior of his fellow man. From the earliest desperate struggle between two prehistoric men over a scrap of food to the complexities of modern society, man has been vitally concerned with increasing his ability to motivate or persuade others. Businessmen recognize that their success depends not only on their ability to accumulate capital and raw material but also on their ability to organize the efforts of other people and motivate them toward established objectives. The salesman's economic survival depends directly on his ability to understand and to apply the principles of motivation. While we have made important progress in our understanding of human behavior, we have noted that our understanding of why people behave the way they do and our ability to predict and control their behavior is still extremely limited.

We have seen that the pattern of human behavior is woven from tenuous threads of experience which reach back into our past. The human being is moved by many forces, past and present, some of which are antagonistic or in conflict. Man's effort to achieve a stability and a balance between these many opposing forces is the history of the development of individuals and civilizations.

The science of human behavior is not concerned with making moral judgments. The scientist makes no judgment as to the rightness or wrongness of what man does. He attempts only to observe, to understand, and to explain what man does. But in understanding human behavior, morality cannot be ignored. *Individual man places value on what he does.* He behaves sometimes not because he is obeying a biological urge or bending to group pressure, but because he is recognizing and responding to higher and transcending rules of the rightness and the wrongness of things. He is concerned with ethical behavior.

Part Four deals with some of the major conflicts which man faces, his efforts to resolve these conflicts and the role played by ethics in shaping man's behavior.

7

The Delicate
Equilibrium and Ethics

The Principle of Conflict and Balance

In the preceding sections we have pointed out that man is almost literally suspended between many forces and influences, all of which tend to move him in various directions. But the human being is not a static, passive thing that merely reacts to stimulation from his environment. He is, instead, in a constant state of dynamic interaction with his physical and social surroundings. Forces and influences in his environment do produce changes in his behavior, and the changes in an individual's behavior in turn influence to a certain extent his environment. Some psychologists believe that human motivation *is* the disequilibrium of the individual which leads him to take some kind of action in order to restore a proper equilibrium or balance. One broad generality that we can make about human behavior, then, is that *we are almost constantly seeking a healthy balance or equilibrium between the various pressures, forces, and influences impinging upon us as individuals.*

249

Conflict is pervasive

It is likely that the human being is never free from conflict as long as he is alive. Most of us can recognize that we are often confronted with two or more possible ways of acting at any given time and we are faced with the necessity of making a decision between these alternatives. Each of us is faced with many decisions which must be made every day. We must make major decisions like which girl to marry, which job to take, which political candidate to vote for, and many minor decisions such as what to have for breakfast, what to wear, what kind of automobile to buy. With almost every decision we make there are many reasons we could give for taking any one of several courses of action. We must make a choice. *Whenever a choice is necessary, there is always conflict.* In the case of many minor decisions, habit patterns tend to prevail and we hardly are aware of the choice-making process. But for some decisions, conflict, with its frustrations and difficulties, is a very real and conscious problem. This chapter will be devoted to a consideration of some of the major conflicts which we face and our resulting efforts to maintain a balance or equilibrium. We will also discuss the role that ethics plays in helping man make these countless decisions.

Some major conflicts

Let us look at some types of conflict situations which any of us are likely to face and in which we find ourselves suspended between opposing pressures. The life underwriter, for example, needs to read and understand a great deal about human behavior but not "too much." The individual needs to be creative and needs to try new things, but he must not deviate from the expected normal behavior "too much." The salesman needs to be a competitor and yet he must also cooperate with his manager, the company, and even fellow salesmen at times. We are taught to be honest; yet we are admonished to be "tactful" when expressing ourselves to another person.

The salesman must be aggressive; yet he should not become over-aggressive. We must maintain a certain level of fear as we move about in our daily activities so that we will keep ourselves out of dangerous situations, and yet we must not let this fear become too great or else we will be unable to lead productive lives. We must work hard to "make a name for ourselves" but we must not be so selfishly interested in our own progress that we forget or ignore our family, our fellow man, or society.

We are all suspended between apparently contradictory or antagonistic ideas, concepts, or ways of behaving. How is one to decide just where the happy medium is? How should we decide how far to go in one direction or in another? The answer to this problem is one of the most difficult ones mankind has ever tried to discover. The attempts we make to find this balance between opposing interests is essentially the story of human relationships.

Man disturbs his own equilibrium

It is important to note that the concept of man seeking a balance between opposing and conflicting pressures does not explain all of human behavior. Occasionally, we see man seeming to upset his own equilibrium deliberately in an effort to reach a new level of activity or adjustment. We think we reach a satisfactory level of adjustment or balance only to discover there may possibly be a still better way to adjust. Circumstances change and new adjustments and decisions become necessary. It is a continuous process.

Perhaps the philosopher Socrates was one of the first to question the way man thinks and behaves. While the people in his time were content with their simple, incomplete understanding of the world of material things and even of man himself, Socrates disturbed this pleasant equilibrium by asking, "How do we know these things are true? What do we mean when we use the words we use?" Such great thinkers as Copernicus, Galileo, Darwin, Freud, Einstein, and many others did not accept the standard answers and understanding with which most men were satisfied and comfortable. They even risked dishonor and death by moving against the tide of public opinion and belief in their search for truth. Without such men to disturb the blissful state of equilibrium in which most of us sleep, we would not achieve greater and greater mastery over our surroundings and ourselves.

Three Methods of Resolving Conflict

In resolving conflict man utilizes three general methods in making decisions which help him to maintain a satisfactory equilibrium. These three methods may be categorized briefly as (1) the automatic or emotional approach, (2) the rational, problem-solving approach, and (3) the ethical approach. It is important to note that these processes may be either conscious or unconscious and often all three are involved simultaneously.

We are influenced by automatic balancing mechanisms

Imagine yourself trying to walk a tightrope. You take a tentative step forward only to find that you are beginning to lean too far to one side. Your arms automatically move to help you restore your balance, but then, you have moved too far over to the other side and are about to fall in that direction. Again your arms and body seem to adjust themselves in an effort to regain your balance. As we walk down the street and are met by a gust of wind, we automatically lean in the direction of the wind to avoid being blown off our feet. In somewhat the same way we walk a tightrope throughout our lifetime. We maintain a balance between opposites or extremes. We have seemingly automatic and instantaneous emotional reactions to various pressures and forces around us. Our immediate, spontaneous, automatic reactions serve us well, for they help maintain our equilibrium, help us "keep our feet on the ground," and help us to resolve conflict situations.

Let us consider an example of how our constantly reacting and often unconscious emotional responses can help us move toward some kind of equilibrium. A general agent was interviewing a candidate life underwriter. In any selection interviewing situation, the general agent attempts to ascertain and evaluate both the good and bad points of the candidate. In making his decision to either hire or not to hire the candidate, the general agent must decide that the good points clearly outweigh the bad points. If he sees an equal number of good and bad points, he will be caught in a dilemma because the decision will be a difficult one to make. During this particular interview, the general agent was undecided about hiring the candidate until the candidate revealed that he belong to the general agent's college fraternity. Immediately the general agent was more favorably inclined to hire the candidate because they were fraternity brothers. An impartial observer of this interview could clearly see that from that point on the general agent did not really want to hear any more about the candidate's background because he might hear something negative. The general agent's emotional reaction to the candidate helped him resolve the conflict within his own mind simply by blinding himself to any other facts which might have tended to disturb the comfortable equilibrium he had now reached as he made the decision to hire the candidate. Psychologists describe this as psychological blindness. Perhaps all of us have "blind spots" in the sense that we fail to see what a more impartial observer would see. In our courting days when we are very anxious to be loved and in turn to love, we are very likely to see only those things which allow us to maintain our comfortable feeling that this is, indeed, true love. The idea that love is blind or even the concept of "rose colored glasses" are illustrations of the automatic emotional reactions to which human beings resort to avoid unpleasantness or to avoid disturbing the delicate equilibrium that has been established to reduce conflict.

The above discussion indicates that while automatic emotional reactions do help us to escape certain situations of conflict by reaching decisions and restoring a balance, these same reactions can also produce other difficulties and even greater conflict. Automatic responses which help us feel comfortable at any given time are usually effective only on a short term basis. The boy who tells a lie to escape punishment often finds it necessary to manufacture even larger fables later on.

We use a rational problem-solving approach

The first general method of maintaining our equilibrium acts in somewhat of a blind, automatic fashion. It is a child-like striving for pleasure and avoiding pain. Each of us is constantly ready to react to any conflict situation or any disequilibrium with an immediate and self-centered resistance to the pressure or force which is placing us in a state of disequilibrium. Partly because this general approach to conflict situations can very easily get us into further difficulty and partly because this method of adjusting to life does not lead to progress or advancement of our civilization, man turns to a more rational, thoughtful, problem-solving approach to conflict situations. He tries to reason through the several obstacles confronting him or the alternatives to action which are available to him.

Obviously we can solve problems, resolve conflicts, and restore equilibrium much more effectively if we use our intelligence in as objective a way as possible without being overly swayed by emotions. Solving problems in a rational, systematic way involves at least four major steps:

(1) We must define the problem as accurately as possible. Unless we know very clearly what our objective is, we will not be able to move toward and identify a solution.

(2) In problem solving we must assemble all the available information and establish the possible alternatives or solutions to the problem.

(3) We must analyze and evaluate each of the alternatives in order to see the major advantages and disadvantages of each.

(4) We must choose one of the alternatives and test it to see whether or not it does solve the problem.

If a general agent, for example, needs another life underwriter in his agency, he may recruit candidates through newspaper advertising, referral sources, his present agents, etc. He then interviews the candidates as objectively as possible and evaluates all the available information concerning each of the several candidates who come to his office, trying to weigh their relative chances of success. He then makes a decision and picks the candidate who he feels will do the best job. He then tests the man in actual field work to satisfy himself that he did, indeed, find a solution to his problem. If the man he selects does not succeed, he is again faced with the original problem and must try the process again.

Much of business is conducted in this rational, straightforward, problem-solving way. Business enterprises experience a constant stream of crises and conflicts which must be resolved. If the inventory of a certain product is running low, we reorder to bring the inventory up to the desired level. If the insurance prospect asks a technical question for which the underwriter has no answer, he tries to obtain the desired information to convey to the prospect in the hope that this will encourage the prospect to buy. Recognizing the problem and finding the most reasonable solution to it will more than likely lead to more predictable and satisfactory efforts to maintain proper equilibrium in business activities. But even this rational problem-solving approach can lead to further problems. The life underwriter who attempts to overcome the objections of the prospect may use his best reasoning facilities to find things to say to satisfy the prospect. The underwriter may also distort the truth or misrepresent the product or say something incorrect to overcome the prospect's objection. Making untrue statements to the prospect in order to solve the problem and make a sale cannot be criticized if we are thinking only in terms of resolving the conflict which is posed by lack of sales. This approach may well solve the problem for the salesman and remove him from a conflict situation, but it immediately raises the question of the "rightness" or the "wrongness" of what he is doing. Such actions may temporarily solve the problem for the salesman, but they may not necessarily solve the problem for the prospect. Because man has not been entirely satisfied with the results which are obtained when he conducts himself solely with the aim of doing what is necessary in order to solve problems or get the job done, he has felt it necessary to consider kinds of activities which *ought* to be done. Whenever we consider what *ought* to be done or what our personal *obligations* are to each other, we are considering the question of ethics.

We move toward an equilibrium through an awareness of ethics

When we face a dilemma, that is, when we are in conflict between several possible ways of reacting to a human situation, we very likely ask ourselves, "What should I do?" If one believes in a code of ethics and can relate it to a conflict situation in which he may find himself, then he may easily resolve his conflict and thereby re-establish an equilibrium by doing what is the right thing to do. If an employee is late for work and is in a state of conflict because he does not know what is the best excuse to give his boss, one way of resolving this conflict is to do what he knows is right to do and answer the boss truthfully.

We have discussed briefly three general methods which man uses, either consciously or unconsciously, in making those decisions which help him maintain a satisfactory equilibrium. Again, we need to stress that at any one given moment an individual will probably use all three of these methods simultaneously. In each of us there is a constant on-going, emotional, automatic mechanism which makes us lean toward maintaining or re-establishing an equilibrium at the same time that we are doing our conscious level best to engage in effective problem solving so that we can do the morally right thing. It is characteristic of man to make value judgments and to be aware of the concepts of right and wrong. It is equally true that man often does that which he knows to be wrong. Because of its importance in influencing human behavior, it is appropriate to examine further the general concept of ethics.

The Role of Ethics

What is ethics?

Ethics is concerned with the rightness or wrongness of human behavior. Ethics is a study of the standards that men live by. In studying ethics we are interested in what man feels he *ought* to do and how he makes decisions about what he ought to do. From the time that mankind has recorded his history, we see evidence that he has guided, or attempted to guide, his behavior by following a code of what is the right thing to do. It is, of course, equally true that man has often behaved in ways contrary to what he would agree was the right way for him to behave.

If we settle for the definition of ethics as being concerned with what men ought to do, we must immediately raise the question: According to whose opinion or whose authority do we judge what a person ought to do? It is obvious that two people or two nations can have two different notions as to what man ought to do. If we say that both individuals or groups can be right, then we are saying that ethics is purely relative and depends on one's point of view. This, obviously, cannot be true or else the concept of ethics will have no meaning as a general standard or guide for man's behavior.

The universality of ethics

Are there universal laws of ethics which tell us what we ought to do? Certainly, human beings from diverse cultures in different parts of the world all behave as if there were some common rules of behavior which should govern all people.[1] Even hardened criminals who flout civil laws still react and conduct themselves as if they believed in a higher code of morality or decency of behavior. One gang member may make a promise to another member, and both will feel that the promise is binding. If the one breaks his promise, both men recognize that a standard has been violated. In everything we do, we behave as if there is a universal law of nature which defines good or decent behavior. What one person regards as fairness in interpersonal relationships, another person may not feel is fair; but both would acknowledge that fairness is desirable. There is a remarkable agreement among human beings all over the world that certain ways of behaving are good while others are bad.

In order to study ethics and to understand its role in helping man decide what he should do, we must examine one general assumption which is made by the thinkers and writers in this field: *Man has a purpose for being and he ought to behave in order to realize that purpose.* The assumption continues with the idea that to the extent that man behaves in order to move toward reaching that purpose, he is behaving in a "good" way. To the extent that he behaves in a way which does not advance him toward that general purpose or end, he is behaving in a "bad" way. Most people would agree that

[1] C. S. Lewis presents a good argument for this thesis in his book *Mere Christianity* (New York: The Macmillan Company, 1953).

there is a purpose to human life, but there is much less agreement on exactly what that purpose is.

A search for a purpose

Even the man who declares that there is no purpose to life and sets about trying to convince people of this fact is himself acting with a purpose. In all cultures and in all ages of recorded history we see evidence that men experience an overpowering need to understand where they fit into the scheme of things. Even in the most primitive societies we find that the savage feels it important to invent stories and fables to explain the situation in which he finds himself. In more civilized cultures, man's effort to find meaning and purpose in life expresses itself in organized philosophies and religions. The great growth of science has given us increased knowledge about the world and what it *is*, but does not tell us what it *means*. Man is exceedingly lonely and because of this loneliness experiences great anxiety. The search for a purpose to life is really his attempt to find a relationship between himself and a larger, more encompassing totality. For many, this larger totally embracing something is given the name God. For some, the purpose of life can be summed up in the belief that man's primary aim is to become "one" with God. For others, the word or concept "God" is much too vague in meaning for them to be sure that they can believe in this existence as an end for man. They are disturbed by the man-like conception of a personal creator who lives in the sky and administers judgment from above. While they may have a great desire to relate to such an all-powerful, all-present being, they are likely to repress this desire because it doesn't make sense to them.

Especially as one reaches middle age (although also sometimes in youth) and one finds that he is halfway through his normal life expectancy, these questions are often raised: "What is the point of it all? Why are we working as hard as we are? Where are we going? Have we done the things that we should have done?" This moment of questioning is an anxious moment for most of us and may lead us to search more vigorously for the truth. If we can discover for ourselves and can believe in any one of the various systems of belief which are available, then we feel some sense of relief from the anxiety aroused by the question "What is the purpose of life?"

The psychological value of an unshakable belief in a religion is almost beyond measure. The individual who has rejected an organized religion and has not replaced it with firm belief in some other organized system of values is likely to feel profound despair.

The importance of belief

From a psychological, theological, and ethical point of view, *man needs to believe.* The child finds security in full and unquestioned belief in his parents. His early conception of God is likely to be as a kind of glorified father. The child thinks of God in terms of his parents which points to the great responsibility that parents have for the shaping of their children's minds. The child gains security by feeling the firm hand of authority of his parents. The child himself often wants and needs to be punished. That is, the child needs to feel the security which comes when people care enough for him to be concerned about what he does. It is an exceedingly disturbing thing for a child to find that his parents have lied to him or even that they are wrong in the information they have given him. The child is disturbed because his faith and his belief in his God-parents is disturbed. In exactly the same way, the adult finds security in relating to a higher authority in which he can believe. And, too, like the child the adult is profoundly disturbed when his belief is shaken. It is the normal, stable individual who has a well-organized system of belief. The neurotic or disturbed individual is often incapable of constructing a satisfactory philosophy of life.

Man needs to have faith in what he is doing, in his daily activities. Having faith in something means that we believe that it is worthwhile or good. If a businessman cannot believe in the goodness of building his company or of selling his product, an irreconcilable conflict is established. It is a common observation to see that a newly hired salesman for a firm does extremely well in selling the product for the first month or two but then apparently becomes "burned out." What often happens is that the salesman accepts with faith the statements about the product given to him by the managers of the business, but when he begin to find out some undesirable things about the product or he begins to believe what his customers say in a negative way about the product, the salesman then loses his faith. It is extremely difficult for us to be convincing in selling a product or an idea to another person unless we genuinely believe what we are saying. The businessman or salesman who finds himself operating at a low level of productivity often believes that "if I could only get better organized, I'd be more productive." We will often come closer to finding the real answer to lack of productivity if we will examine our system of beliefs in what we are doing.

Conscious yardsticks for determining moral behavior

The human being consciously uses different, rather definite standards to help him to decide what he should do at any given moment. One of the standards that most of us use in our early years is to do what our *parents* tell us to do. But doing what our parents tell us to do is not necessarily doing the ethically right thing. To take an extreme case, the pickpocket who teaches his young son to aid him in this activity is teaching his son the way he should behave in order to get a job done. But inevitably he also must teach his son that this is not the thing that *should* be done morally. No matter what this pickpocket says, he is forced to indicate to his child that they are not *really* doing the right thing because he must explain that they must be careful not to get caught, thereby acknowledging to himself and to his son that they are breaking a fundamental rule. We could find many an example to show us that different parents instruct their children in different ways as to what is the right and wrong thing to do. We cannot assume that parental authority is, therefore, the best or only basis for making moral decisions.

Some may argue that individual parents can be wrong about important moral issues, but that the great mass of people will invariably agree on the rightness or wrongness of ideas or activities. A person with this point of view would hold that what the majority of people agree on would be the morally right thing to do. People who do the customary thing usually feel that they are in the right. After all, they might argue, when we go against the things our society believes in, are we not either ridiculed, ostracized, or confined? But the same argument for not accepting parental authority as the basis for making moral decisions can also be used in opposing the idea of using *public opinion or custom* as the basis for moral decisions. Public opinion on what is right and wrong, after all, varies from one country to another, from one state to another, and even from one city to another. In addition to this, customary ways of thinking and behaving change with time. If we grant that custom or public opinion should be used as the standard for making moral decisions, then we must also grant that what is morally right and wrong itself changes from place to place or from time to time.

Public opinion is, of course, a powerful influence on how people behave and on what they believe. Many people go through life behaving in ways which encourage other people to grant them approval and acceptance. Their moral decisions are made not on the basis of what may be right in an absolute sense, but, instead, on the basis of what other people might feel is right at the time. The businessman who engages in questionable or misleading practices because "it is good business" and because "if I don't do it, my competitor will" is following the dictates of what he believes to be the customs of the business society. However, other groups of people in the same society are likely to say that these same standards are not right.

Can we assume that if we always obey the law in the strictest sense that we will always be doing the morally right thing? Here again, we must conclude that even the "law of the land" cannot be used as the basis for moral living. Laws, too, change from place to place and from time to time. We cannot assume that what is morally right also changes from time to time or from place to place. In addition, there are many things which can be thought of as being unethical which are not covered by laws. For example, if we break a promise to a friend, we find that this event is not covered by law. We frequently hear of cases where an individual violates the spirit but not the letter of the law.

Many of us sincerely feel that if we do what our *conscience* tells us to do, that we will be morally correct in our behavior. Here again, we can easily recognize that what one person's conscience may say very often differs from what another person's conscience dictates. It is true that we often behave the way we do because of the prompting of our conscience, but this is not to say that our conscience always dictates the absolutely right or wrong thing to do. The conscience of one person may move him to do his utmost to enforce racial segregation, while the conscience of another equally intelligent and mature individual may tell him that racial segregation is indefensible and must not be supported.

For most Christians and Jews The Ten Commandments are thought to be absolute, unquestionable laws of moral behavior revealed to man by God. To agree that the basis for moral decisions should be this Judaeo-Christian heritage with the recognized beliefs and commands contained in the Old Testament is a beginning, but it is only a beginning in our efforts to understand ethical behavior and to understand how to apply our beliefs to current life problems which present themselves to us every day. All of us must still translate these rather general principles and commands into the specific business or personal problems which we encounter. The more one understands the principles of ethics which he is following, the easier it is for him to behave in a way which we would call ethical.

Ethical Obligations of the Life Underwriter

There can be no doubt in anyone's mind that the individual assumes certain obligations when he enters the field of life underwriting. He has an obligation to his clients to provide the best possible advice and insurance coverage to satisfy their needs. He has an obligation to his company to sell a sufficient volume of life insurance to those prospects who are most likely to be good risks and who are likely to continue their premium payments. He has an obligation to his family to provide them with economic and psychological security. And he has an obligation to himself to do those things which allow him to make the best possible use of his talents. Obligations have to do with those things which *ought* to be done and thus we are concerned with ethical behavior. The sheer volume of books and articles published recently on the subject of business ethics and the ethics of selling attests to the fact that the business and consumer public is becoming more and more aware of the ethical obligations *and* problems which can and do arise in the normal course of business enterprise. It is natural that the life underwriter also should be concerned about the ethical problems which arise in selling life insurance.

It is widely held that the life underwriter assumes obligations of a professional nature in that the interests of his clients are paramount. A large body of knowledge must be acquired in order to reach a high level of competence, and high ethical standards of conduct are involved.[2] As in other professions, the life underwriter is in a position to offer advice in a very important area of life to clients, the great majority of whom are not able to judge adequately for themselves the quality of advice thus received. It should be obvious that the position of trust and confidence in which the underwriter allows himself to be placed carries with it an inescapable obligation to render the best possible advice for the good of the client.

But there are two additional obligations which must be discussed as we conclude this volume on the relationship of human behavior principles to life underwriting. The first of these is the twofold obligation to understand the client's family or business problem as it relates to life insurance matters and to be understood in turn as the solution is presented and explained to the client. In other words, the life underwriter is obliged to be an effective communicator, sensing and overcoming obstacles to clear understanding in order to fulfill his mission in a professional way. The second obligation stems from the fact that many prospective clients do not understand that they have a problem which life insurance, and only life insurance, can solve effectively. The life underwriter, therefore, must understand the principles of motivation as they may apply to each unique prospect so that he can motivate him to take action in solving some of his fundamental social and economic problems.

The study of human behavior is, therefore, not just desirable, it is necessary if the life underwriter is to discharge properly his obligations to his clients, to his company, to his family, and to himself.

---

[2] S. S. Huebner, *The Professional Concept in Life Underwriting* (Bryn Mawr, Pennsylvania: The American College of Life Underwriters, 1956). Expresses with great clarity the view that " 'Life underwriting' and 'profession' are compatible terms."

Bibliography

Anderson, H. H., *Creativity and Its Cultviation*. New York: Harper & Row, Publishers, 1959.

Asch, Solomon E., *Social Psychology*. Englewood Cliffs, New Jersey: Prentice-Hall, Inc., 1952.

Ashley Montagu, M. F., *Anthropology and Human Nature*. Boston: Porter Sargent Publishers, 1957.

Atkinson, John W., *Motives in Fantasy, Action and Society: A Method of Assessment and Study*. Princeton, New Jersey: D. Van Nostrand Co., Inc., 1958.

Barbara, Dominick A., *The Art of Listening*. Springfield, Illinois: Charles C. Thomas, Publisher, 1958.

Becker, Howard, *Man in Reciprocity*. New York: Frederick A. Praeger, Inc., 1956.

Benedict, Ruth, *Patterns of Culture*. Boston: Houghton Mifflin Co., 1934.

Bindra, Dalbir, *Motivation: A Systematic Reinterpretation*. New York: The Ronald Press Co., 1959.

Bingham, W. V., B. V. Moore and J. W. Gustard, *How to Interview*. New York: Harper & Row, Publishers, 1959.

Brameld, Theodore A., *Cultural Foundations of Education*. New York: Harper & Row, Publishers, 1957.

Brown, J. S., *The Motivation of Behavior*. New York: McGraw-Hill Book Co., Inc., 1961.

Burke, Kenneth, *A Grammar of Motives*. New York: George Braziller, Inc., 1955.

Chase, Stuart, *Power of Words*. New York: Harcourt, Brace & World, Inc., 1954.

Cheskin, L., *Why People Buy: Motivation Research and Its Successful Application*. New York: Liveright Publishing Corp., 1959.

Chesser, Eustace, *An Outline of Human Relationships*. New York: Hawthorn Books, Inc., 1960.

Cowell, F. R., *Culture in Private and Public Life*. New York: Frederick A. Praeger, Inc., 1959.

Dichter, Ernest, *The Strategy of Desire*. Garden City, New York: Doubleday & Co., Inc., 1960.

Douglas, W. O., *America Challenged*. Princeton, New Jersey: Princeton University Press, 1960.

Ford Foundation Report, Behavioral Sciences Division (Published by the Foundation, 1953.)

Fromm, Erich, *Escape from Freedom*. New York: Holt, Rinehart and Winston, Inc., 1941.

George, F. H., *Automation, Cybernetics and Society*. Piqua, Ohio: Leonard V. Hill, 1959.

Graham, Saxon, *American Culture*. New York: Harper & Row, Publishers, 1957.

Guilbaud, G. T., *What Is Cybernetics?* New York: Criterion Books, Inc., 1959.

Hall, Edward T., *The Silent Language*. Garden City, New York: Doubleday & Co., 1959.

Hayakawa, S. I., *Language in Action*. New York: Harcourt, Brace & World, 1941.

Hilgard, Ernest R., *Theories of Learning*. New York: Appleton-Century-Crofts, Inc., 1948.

Hoffsommer, Harold, *The Sociology of American Life*. Englewood Cliffs, New Jersey: Prentice-Hall, Inc., 1958.

Hovland, Carl I. and Irving L. Janis, eds., *Personality and Persuasibility*. New Haven, Connecticut: Yale University Press, 1959.

Huebner, S. S., *The Professional Concept in Life Underwriting*. Bryn Mawr, Pennsylvania: The American College of Life Underwriters, 1956.

Husband, R. W., *Applied Psychology*. New York: Harper & Row, Publishers, 1934.

Ingram, Karl C., *Talk That Gets Results*. New York: McGraw-Hill Book Co., Inc., 1957.

Johnson, Wendell, *People in Quandaries: The Semantics of Personal Adjustment*. New York: Harper & Row, Publishers, 1946.

Johnson, Wendell, *Your Most Enchanted Listener*. New York: Harper & Row, Publishers, 1956.

Kallen, Horace M., et al., *Cultural Pluralism and the American Idea*. Philadelphia: University of Pennsylvania Press, 1956.

Kluckhohn, Clyde, *Mirror for Men*. New York: McGraw-Hill Book Co., Inc., 1949.

———— *Personality in Nature, Society, and Culture*. New York: Alfred A. Knopf, Inc., 1953.

Korzybski, Alfred, *Science and Sanity*. Lakeview, Illinois: Institute of General Semantics, 1948.

Lee, Dorothy D., *Freedom and Culture*. Englewood Cliffs, New Jersey: Prentice-Hall, Inc., 1959.

Leeper, R. W. and Peter Madison, *Toward Understanding Human Personalities*. New York: Appleton-Century-Crofts, Inc., 1959.

Lewis, C. S., *Mere Christianity*. New York: The Macmillan Company, 1953.

Lindner, Robert, *Must You Conform?* New York: Holt, Rinehart and Winston, Inc., 1956.

Linton, Ralph, *The Study of Man*. New York: Appleton-Century-Crofts, Inc., 1936.

Logan, Frank A., *et al.*, *Behavior Theory and Social Science*. New Haven, Connecticut: Yale University Press, 1955.

Magee, John, *The General Semantics of Wall Street*. (Published by the author, 1958.)

Maltz, Maxwell, *Psycho-Cybernetics*. Englewood Cliffs, New Jersey: Prentice-Hall, Inc., 1960.

Maslow, A. H., *Motivation and Personality*. New York: Harper & Row, Publishers, 1954.

May, Rollo, *The Meaning of Anxiety*. New York: The Ronald Press Co., 1950.

Mead, Margaret, *Male and Female*. New York: William Morrow and Co., Inc., 1950.

Meadows, Paul, *The Culture of Industrial Man*. Lincoln, Nebraska: University of Nebraska Press, 1950.

Meerloo, Joost A. M., *The Rape of the Mind*. Cleveland, Ohio: World Publishing Co., 1956.

Mercer, B., *The Study of Society*. New York: Harcourt, Brace & World, Inc., 1958.

Mowrer, H. O., *Learning Theory and Personality Dynamics*. New York: The Ronald Press Co., 1950.

Mussen, Paul H. and John J. Conger, *Child Development and Personality*. New York: Harper & Row, Publishers, 1956.

Nebraska Symposium on Motivation, Vols. I-VIII, ed. Marshall R. Jones. Lincoln, Nebraska: University of Nebraska Press, 1954-1959.

Nichols, R. G. and L. A. Stevens, *Are You Listening?* New York: McGraw-Hill Book Co., Inc., 1957.

Olds, James, *The Growth and Structure of Motives*. New York: The Free Press of Glencoe, Illinois, 1956.

Peters, R. S., *The Concept of Motivation*. New York: Humanities Press, Inc., 1958.

Piaget, Jean, *The Language and Thought of the Child*. New York: Humanities Press, Inc., 1959.

Pressey, S. L. and R. G. Kuhlen, *Psychological Development through the Life Span*. New York: Harper & Row, Publishers, 1957.

Riesman, David, *et al.*, *The Lonely Crowd*. New Haven, Connecticut: Yale University Press, 1950.

Rogers, C. R., *On Becoming a Person*. Boston: Houghton Mifflin Co., 1961.

Russell, David H., *Children's Thinking*. Boston: Ginn and Co., 1956.

Samstag, Nicholas, *Persuasion for Profit*. Norman, Oklahoma: University of Oklahoma Press, 1958.

Solomon, Joseph C., *A Synthesis of Human Behavior*. Brattleboro, Vermont: Stephen Greene Press, 1954.

Sondel, Bess, *Humanity of Words: A Primer of Semantics*. Cleveland, Ohio: World Publishing Company, 1958.

Stone, L. Joseph and Joseph Church, *Childhood and Adolescence*. New York: Random House, Inc., 1957.

Symonds, Percival M., *Dynamic Psychology*. New York: Appleton-Century-Crofts, Inc., 1949.

Wallas, G., *The Art of Thought* (New York: Harcourt, Brace & World, Inc., 1926).

Wechsler, David, *The Measurement of Adult Intelligence*, 3rd ed. Baltimore: The Williams and Wilkins Company, 1944.

Whyte, W. Foote, *Man and Organization*. Homewood, Illinois: Richard D. Irwin, Inc., 1959.

Wiener, Norbert, *The Human Use of Human Beings: Cybernetics and Society*. Garden City, New York: Doubleday & Co., 1954.

Witkin, H. A., *Personality through Perception*. New York: Harper & Row, Publishers, 1954.

Wolfe, D. M., *The Image of Man in America*. Dallas, Texas: Southern Methodist University Press, 1957.

Young, P. T., *Motivation and Emotion*. New York: John Wiley & Sons, Inc., 1961.